Brooklyn Is America

Brooklyn Is America

by RALPH FOSTER WELD

COLUMBIA UNIVERSITY PRESS

NEW YORK · 1950

To

R.W.W.

Foreword

IN 1948 I CONTRIBUTED to the Brooklyn *Eagle* a series of feature articles on the various peoples of Brooklyn, from the Dutch pioneers of the mid-seventeenth century to the Puerto Ricans of the mid-twentieth. This book is a revision and expansion of those articles. If the *Eagle* had not seen fit to print—and pay for—the articles, the book would never have seen the light. This is only one of the *Eagle*'s many contributions to local history. Few newspapers can point to a comparable record. I wish here to pay my respects to that great newspaper for its unusual service to the community in this and other respects, and to express my appreciation for the courteous assistance extended to me by its staff, especially by the Executive Editor, Edwin B. Wilson.

The present work owes much to D. Irving Mead, because of Mr. Mead's active assistance and generous encouragement years ago, when I began my Brooklyn researches. I also remember with pleasure and gratitude the aid given me by the Honorable James G. McDonald, now Ambassador to Israel. Many other persons have sacrificed time and convenience to help me. I wish to thank the following for aid which I deeply appreciate: Colonel Benjamin T. Anuskewicz, Dr. Walter N. Beekman, Mrs. Arnold Cassuto, Mrs. Sophie Cello, the Reverend Dr. Phillips P. Elliott, Mrs. Eleanor Wibecan Foster, Charles E. Hirsimaki, Miss Edna Huntington, Harold R. Johnson, Frank A. Jurek, James A. Kelly, County Historian of Kings

County, Oscar A. Lewis, Rabbi Israel H. Levinthal, Herbert Miller, Peter Nowak, the Reverend Ivar F. Pearson, Dr. Lawrence D. Reddick, Rabbi Eugene Sack, Dr. Viola H. Spongberg, Mrs. Glenna Swenson, and Ruth Whiting Weld. I wish also to thank Karsten Roedder, Assistant Editor of *Nordisk Tidende,* for making available valuable articles published in that paper in 1948, written by Dr. A. N. Rygg; the staff of the Bureau of Applied Social Research, Columbia University, for aid in connection with my use of *The Puerto Rican Journey;* the staff of the Schomberg Collection; Miss Ida M. Lynn, for her skill and patience in editing the manuscript; and Miss Evelyn Merrin, for numberless courtesies that have made my work easier.

Finally, a special word of heartfelt thanks to Dr. William Bridgwater, the Editor of the Columbia University Press, for wise counsel so generously given in many pleasant conferences, for constructive criticism, and for something else besides—that intangible thing which we struggle to express when we use such inadequate words as "encouragement," "sympathy," and "inspiration."

R. F. W.

December, 1949

Contents

Twenty-six illustrations follow page 14.

Brooklyn's Particular Blend   3

The Dutch Pioneers   15

Yankee Enterprise   30

Irish Sons and Daughters   48

Yankee Heyday   62

Partial Eclipse of the Yankees   76

German Builders and Householders   86

A Jewish Community Takes Root   100

The Irish Take Over   115

The Versatile Italians   135

Three Centuries of Colored Brooklyn   153

The World's Biggest Jewish Community   174

Brooklyn's Northland   190

Eastern Europe Moves In   207

The Smaller Groups   222

E Pluribus Unum   233

Bibliography   249

Index   255

Brooklyn Is America

Brooklyn's Particular Blend

Brooklyn sprawls across the western tip of Long Island, huge and breathing. Between it and the little island of Manhattan there is the East River, which is, of course, not a river at all, but the end of Long Island Sound. Across the narrow run of the tide, Brooklyn is clearly visible from the skyscrapers and the streets of lower Manhattan. Yet certain Manhattanites and others are afflicted with a strange myopia. They can vision Long Island beyond Brooklyn; Port Washington, Oyster Bay, and Southampton are familiar to them. Brooklyn is, on the other hand, as remote as the fastnesses of Tibet, a vague and unreal land, possibly nonexistent. Thus, Lewis Mumford could once blandly say that Manhattan "needed a bridge connection with Long Island," therefore Brooklyn Bridge, inspiration of poets and artists, came into being.

Now Brooklyn Bridge is a fact in history. The truth is that although New York did need a bridge connection with the region beyond East River (with Brooklyn, to be precise), Manhattan at first did nothing about it. The bridge was not built by fiat from that fabulous island. Instead, Brooklyn flung the pathway over the water as the crowning act of a century of almost unparalleled growth and expansion. The vision, the plan, and the organization were Brooklyn's and Brooklyn paid the heavier part of the costs. New York finally co-operated, but in a complementary and secondary role. The bridge was erected to benefit two great cities, but perhaps chiefly to link Brooklyn with the continent. The genius of the Roeblings was used in a great act of creation which was Brooklyn's glory and, in a sense, Brooklyn's doom. The city was committing corporate suicide, for shortly afterward came political union with Manhattan. The other East River bridges were built later, and the initiative in such matters had passed across the river. No philosophical critic or brooding poet praises them. They merely carry traffic.

The bridge and extension of the subways and union with Manhattan brought change to Brooklyn, as floods of immigrants poured from the East Side's crowded tenements to swell the growth of Brooklyn with the poor of many countries. They were accepted and amalgamated into the borough, which is now the largest of New York's five by a million souls. The process of amalgamation was typical of the place, for from the very beginning racial and linguistic complexities have marked Brooklyn.

Its history from 1636 to 1950 is the story of the coming of various peoples: the Dutch, the English, the Irish, Germans, Negroes, Jews, Italians, Scandinavians, and lesser groups. Yet never was the progression simple. Among the early "Dutch" farmer-settlers were French-speaking Walloons from the southern Netherlands, and Lady Deborah Moody brought an English colony to Gravesend in 1643. Early in the colony's history Negroes appeared in the region. English rule began in 1664. More than a century later, after the Revolution, came the invasion of New England Yankees, of Yorkers and Jerseyites, and others of British blood from remoter regions. The Irish, coming first in numbers during the decade following the War of 1812, crowded in a generation later, when the German tide was beginning.

The threads of race and culture were woven in and out, and a new fabric emerged, while the city grew physically. There were separate country villages at first, villages that were gradually drawn together. When the first Brooklyn city charter was granted, in 1834, it covered only the old township of Brooklyn. Then settlement extended from Wallabout to Gowanus Bay, and the proud little city included the Navy Yard and Fort Greene Park districts, present downtown Brooklyn, South Brooklyn, and little else. Outside—and even for large spaces inside—there was the open country.

Beyond and separate lay villages and farm neighborhoods that now are part of the litany of Brooklyn place-names: Flatbush, Williamsburg, Greenpoint, Bushwick, New Utrecht. Then they were remote from Brooklyn. Flatbush was comfortably, securely, and determinedly Dutch. Williamsburg's chequered career brought it, along with Greenpoint and Bushwick, into Brooklyn in 1855. Many years later, in 1886, sparsely settled New Lots was absorbed, and another wave of annexation occurred in 1894. Flatbush then lost its jealously guarded independence, and the townships of New Utrecht and Gravesend also succumbed. With the acquisition of Flatlands two years later, the city of Brooklyn for the first time comprised all Kings County. Its own independence was to go two years later, in 1898, when Brooklyn, itself, much against the will of a large and vociferous part of its people, was absorbed into "Greater New York."

All these little settlements and all these peoples and more went to make up the Brooklyn that can be seen today from Manhattan's towers and can be known in the striped and varied streets. It is not well known, though paradoxically the name Brooklyn is familiar across the world, in the various corners of the United States, in South Africa and India, and in the Far North. Among all the scattered peoples of the world there are many who recognize the name and react to it.

Partly, perhaps, because the jokesmiths of the ubiquitous

radio have discovered the comic possibility of the "Brooklyn accent" and have found that they can raise a guffaw by merely reciting the name Brooklyn with a certain stress. Partly, perhaps, because a remarkably efficient, yet colorful, baseball team has won the hearts of sports-lovers. Partly, of a certainty, because in the last war nearly a third of a million young men and some young women in uniform went out from Flatbush and Bensonhurst and Bushwick to England, France, Italy, North Africa, Alaska, the South Seas, wherever the American armed forces penetrated. Even the calumny uttered by Noel Coward was, in the long run, a not unfavorable advertisement, for it called attention to Brooklyn's soldiers—soldiers, like other American boys, gregarious, adaptable, good-natured, a little careless, perhaps, but with plenty of guts. Mention of Brooklyn may start a smile in an odd and far-off corner of the earth or near home, but it is more often a smile of affectionate warmth than of derisive contempt.

Every great city has a distinctive atmosphere—a something in the air, an essence, a flavor—that belongs to it alone and marks it off from all other cities. You sense it as you walk its streets, breathe its air, sit in its restaurants, visit its monuments and parks, talk with its people. That atmosphere is no less real because it is intangible, no less powerful because you cannot define it exactly. It is, like the aroma and flavor of a well-blended liquor, peculiar to itself. Even if the elements are basically like those of another city, the proportions yield a special and unique blend. The lovable and laughable things about Brooklyn, even to the exaggerated vaudeville dialect, are part of Brooklyn's special quality, but the particular blend is much more than these, a subtle compound of peoples and places.

Brooklyn is vast and will not be bound in the tight

limits of a short definition, but above all its parts there
is unity. As in Manhattan and Chicago and New Orleans,
there are festering social sores and crime. In the slums
there are ill-housed and houseless waifs, while great housing projects go forward. As in many other cosmopolitan
centers, the springs of fanaticism and race hatred are not
sealed. But there is a much brighter side to the great
moving picture that is Brooklyn. Here you see the mingling of races in workaday relationships. There are vigorous plans of social rehabilitation. Quiet and peace live in
the streets. There are institutions where men of all sorts and
kinds and ranks meet on common ground. In Brooklyn the
discouraged observer of mankind may find some ground for
hope. It is the civilized world in microcosm; within its own
limits it is a demonstration of world peace.

Behind the miles of docks and basins, which stretch
along the waterfront from Newtown Creek far down East
River and the bay, there is a vast confusion of factories
and warehouses. And beyond the commercial and industrial rim lie the long residential streets, cutting some
eighty square miles in a great intersecting pattern.

There lie the Brooklyn neighborhoods, for though the
borough has certainly more self-conscious localism than
has any other part of the metropolis, the old country
villages are remembered in the neighborhoods. Each
neighborhood has its own self-consciousness, which per-
sists to a surprising degree in spite of waves of immigration that have transformed many areas, not once but many
times. New neighborhoods have been born within the
old. In some immigrant settlements old European customs have persisted even after the new immigrant color
has disappeared. In others, aggressive Americanism has
polished away the older habits and words and institutions.

The large sections of Brooklyn, which may in turn be

broken into smaller local units, are five in number: (1)
Brooklyn downtown—the busy shops of Fulton Street
and of the neighboring thoroughfares, the faded elegance
of Brooklyn Heights, and the boisterous vigor of the Navy
Yard and Fort Greene districts; (2) north Brooklyn—
comprising Williamsburg and Greenpoint, Bushwick and
Ridgewood, and Stuyvesant Heights; (3) central Brooklyn
—Bedford, Park Slope and the "Gold Coast," and Flatbush;
(4) western Brooklyn—Red Hook, the Bush Terminal
neighborhood, the Sunset Park district, Bay Ridge, Borough
Park, Bensonhurst, Bath Beach and Coney Island; and (5)
east Brooklyn—Brownsville, East New York and New Lots,
East Flatbush, Canarsie, Flatlands, and Sheepshead Bay.

A tour through the neighborhoods of these sections
would reveal much of the heart of Brooklyn. There, open
to sight, are vestiges of the city's past, conditions of its
present, hints of its future. Within a radius of a mile from
Brooklyn Bridge there are many architectural reminders
to mark successive stages of historical development.

Especially is this true of Brooklyn Heights, which over-
looks the skyscrapers of downtown Manhattan and the
curling waters where East River joins the bay. Here are
small three-story wooden houses, some of them graced
with dormer windows, built by Yankees a century and
more ago; prim brick and stone residences dating from
the 1820s, '30s and '40s; Gothic churches designed in the
forties and fifties by Upjohn and Lefevre; and relics of
each following decade down to the ornate hotels and
apartment houses of the early twentieth century and their
smoothly functional younger relatives of the 1930s.

On the Heights the Old Guard of aristocracy was in
full force in the last third of the nineteenth century. An
air of respectability and stalwart conservatism reigned
among the prosperous merchants, lawyers, and bankers.

Predominantly they were Yankees and Yorkers of old "American" stock, Protestants who supported the four-square churches which were apparently the most substantial and securely rooted in the City of Churches. Some of the Old Guard still stand valorously, but most of them have retreated before the onrush of newcomers, crowding in from everywhere—Manhattan, California, the Dakotas, New England, the South, Europe. The Heights has now been taken over by representatives of the various racial strains of middle-class America. Many of them are not even permanent residents, but unwilling city dwellers who eventually disappear into the suburbs, confirmed urbanites who move on to other city neighborhoods, and casual floaters who pause and then scatter again throughout the United States.

Young writers and artists, including a number of sculptors, have given the Heights a Bohemian tinge. Decayed mansions and inconvenient but solid dwellings now shelter an army of roomers. Aliens from Latin America and the Near East press close upon the once sacred flanks of the Heights. Strangers from apartment houses sit in the ancient family pews of Samuel Hanson Cox's First Presbyterian Church and Henry Ward Beecher's Plymouth Church. The old home of the Church of the Pilgrims, where Richard Salter Storrs once held forth, is now the Maronite rite Roman Catholic Church of Our Lady of Lebanon. Yet the buildings stand, reminders of the past, and the Heights itself—though not so thoroughly Brooklyn, perhaps, as Flatbush or Eastern Parkway—keeps its old identity. It is a pleasant region with a quiet charm not found in the other old neighborhoods of New York City.

The "Gold Coast" district, near Prospect Park, is totally different from the sedate Heights. This is where the substantially wealthy Brooklynites live. The region is dominated by Grand Army Plaza and the great Memorial Arch —an arch fairly alive with the facile sculpture of Mac-Monnies. Across the broad Plaza, at the corner of Eastern Parkway, the Brooklyn Public Library rears its concave front, and its giant bronze doors gleam in the sun. A short distance down the Parkway looms the bulky Brooklyn Museum, a democratic cultural focus for Brooklyn's diverse peoples.

From this impressive axis Eastern Parkway stretches all the way to the teeming streets of Brownsville. It is broad, with trees and bright belts of green between traffic lanes and along the walks, and it is lined by massive apartment houses and substantial private homes. It is, for the most part, comfortable middle-class Jewish Brooklyn, and it is very good to look upon.

There are other Jewish communities and communities that are largely Jewish, from the drab poverty of Williamsburg to the quiet respectability of Bensonhurst and Borough Park, with two- and four-family brick houses and clean-clipped hedges. Williamsburg, much described by the novelists, is perhaps best known. Its metamorphosis has been downward from its status as a self-contained, proud, independent community to the blighted region of factories and cheerless, dusty streets. Its story is one of great profit and great loss and of human persistence in the midst of dehumanizing living conditions. Greenpoint tells much the same story, perhaps in a more dismal tone, for Williamsburg has at least one splendid oasis in its desert—the low-rent housing project known as Williamsburg Houses.

Northeast of Williamsburg's Broadway lies the neat and self-respecting German-American world of Bushwick and Ridgewood. Beyond Prospect Park there is upper middle-class comfort, too, in Flatbush and the regions that border it, especially in Kensington, where wide private homes sit proudly behind close-cut lawns and look into shady streets. This is the very heart of the borough. In Flatbush and Flatlands old Dutch churches are reminiscent of Brooklyn's beginnings, though almost in their shadows students throng the cheerful campus of Brooklyn College and give testimony to the many peoples who have followed the forgotten Dutch farmers.

In the now predominantly Italian community of Gravesend, also, a few relics of the past still stand, but in newer sections there is little or nothing of the past. In Midwood, for instance, where a mixed population (Irish, German, Italian and Jewish) occupies modern apartment houses, or in East Flatbush, where vacant lots space out the more widely scattered two-family houses and the lawns, hedges, and gardens of a typically American neighborhood.

In some widely dispersed districts—some poor, some prosperous, racial segregation is the rule. Brooklyn's Harlem is in Stuyvesant Heights and Bedford. Here the uncertain lights and criss-crossing shadows of Manhattan's Harlem are repeated. High culture and distinguished talent are to be found in Stuyvesant Heights today. So is poverty. Poor Negroes, Puerto Ricans, and strays from other peoples also throng the dreary streets near the Navy Yard.

Down near the Gowanus Canal there is a small section where there has grown a rank crop of crime. Al Capone and other notorious gangsters were nurtured there. But recently this neighborhood has been partially redeemed.

In the overwhelming mass of Brooklyn it is easy to miss the little social islands where exotic customs are preserved. Gowanus—a name which, like Greenpoint, appeals to the flippant—was visited three hundred years ago by pious Labadist travelers, who were astonished by the enormous oysters there. It is impossible today to visualize the pristine Gowanus, and the oysters are all gone, but one can still find unexpected phenomena. Along the famous canal in the cold months one may come upon a Wintering colony of hardy Americans—the canal-boat folk who in the warmer season travel the State barge system. Astonishingly, Gowanus is the home, too, of another strictly American group, a colony of Mohawk Indians, whose men—even more astonishingly—are structural steel workers.

Southward from the Gowanus stretches Brooklyn's Scandinavia. Thousands of Norwegians live in the blocks east of Bush Terminal. A Norwegian newspaper, Norwegian churches and Norwegian societies promote the old traditions and encourage pride in the old folkways. More Scandinavians and Finns surround Sunset Park, and here are steam baths in the genuine rigorous Finnish style and Finnish restaurants where *kalisopa, liha pullia,* and *silli perunat* (respectively, cabbage soup, meat balls, and herring and potatoes) may be had. And in beautiful Bay Ridge there is a large neighborhood dominated by Swedes, Norwegians, and Danes.

Brooklyn is full of paradoxes and contrasts. The sweating thousands can find relief on Coney's sands from the merciless August heat of the city's streets; others can go with the Sheepshead Bay fishing fleets to the Jersey coast. The great boulevards, flung like giant arms across the borough, contrast vividly with dusty dinginess of meaner streets. Ocean Parkway cuts a wide swath through Flatbush, while to the west are Fort Hamilton Parkway, and still farther west, the Shore Road, which runs along the bay from Owl's Head Park to Fort Hamilton. Here be-

"The busy shops of Fulton Street" were busy in the 1890's too. This was a typical daily scene when Louis Loeb drew it for *Harper's New Monthly Magazine*.

Packer Collegiate Institute (successor of the Female Academy) is one of the educational institutions which have helped give Brooklyn "its shape and substance." More than fifty years ago *Harper's New Monthly Magazine* showed students saluting the flag.

"The German desire for good fellowship and conviviality" was and is strong, but not unique, in neighborly Brooklyn. This was a Dutchtown scene in the 1890's, according to *Harper's New Monthly Magazine*.

Henry Ward Beecher "kept the antislavery flame alive by auctioning slave girls in Plymouth Church." C. H. Wells sketched the church, in a city known for its houses of worship, for *Harper's Weekly* in 1866.

ence at the Academy of Music. It is fed by the chance
contacts and byplay of the streets. The teeming beach
at Coney, on a hot Summer day, is congenial to it. And it
finds expression—unconscious, robust and utterly sincere
—in the great commingled shout from 30,000 Brooklyn
throats at Ebbets Field when the Dodgers score a run.

side the sea is Brooklyn at its showy best, with the sting
of salt in the air and a view across the blue bay. Here one
knows that Brooklyn is a great sea city.

One knows it, too, by other evidence: the mighty,
awe-inspiring Navy Yard; the endless miles of docks
and piers; the Atlantic and Erie basins; the Bush Terminal conglomerate of warehouses and factories; the great
Todd and United shipyards; Sands Street, the. sailor's
naughty midnight paradise which stretches from lower
Fulton Street toward the Navy Yard under the very nose
of the Heights; South Brooklyn, where sailors from ports
the world over walk the streets and crowd the bars; Atlantic Avenue, where airy Arabic signs on Syrian shops
and coffee houses somehow redeem a wide and cheerless
street—all these things tell us that Brooklyn reaches out
across the seven seas to the peoples of every land on earth
and that the world comes to Brooklyn by a thousand routes.

Today's Brooklyn includes all the racial strains from
Brooklyn's beginnings to the present day. Descendants
of old families of the Heights, the Hill, and Flatbush min-
gle in business, political, and social relationships with
citizens whose ancestors came from County Mayo or
Odessa or Sicily. No matter how reverently the cultural
treasures brought to the New World may be preserved—
and they are preserved in rich variety—the "Americanization" process goes forward in a thousand ways.

The borough's downtown shopping center, Fulton
Street below Flatbush Avenue, with its great department
stores, its shops, and its restaurants, hastens the process.
So do the schools, the movies, the voluntary and involun-
tary associations of political and neighborhood clubs, and
the armed services. Democracy has many sources for its
nurture that the textbooks. have never heard of. It can
find an impulse in a politely applauding concert audi-

"Brooklyn Bridge is a fact in history . . . a great act of creation." It has also been an "inspiration of poets and artists" and looked this way to Childe Hassam when he drew it for *Harper's New Monthly Magazine* in the early nineties.

Students, including young ladies, at Pratt Institute took their work seriously, judging by this "corner in the physical laboratory" as seen by *Harper's New Monthly Magazine* in the last decade of the nineteenth century.

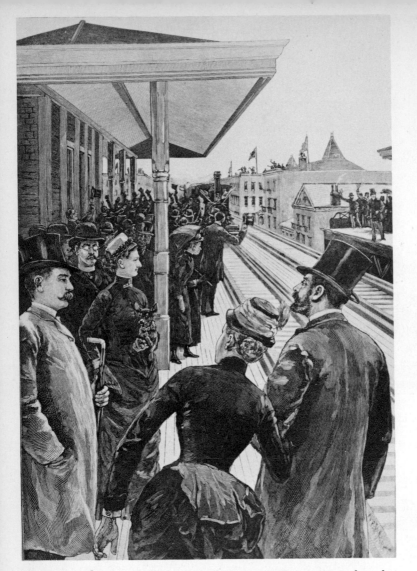

The latest in fashions vied with the newest in transportation when the Brooklyn Elevated Railway—"El" for short—was opened in 1885. W. P. Snyder paid less attention to the train than to Brooklyn's well-dressed citizens when he drew the scene for *Harper's Weekly*.

Brooklyn Bridge "became the very symbol" of the city and "changed the current its history." The central figure in this group at the Brooklyn anchorage of Jo Roebling's monument is Henry Cruse Murphy, civic leader and public official. T photograph is from *The Eagle and Brooklyn*.

In the nineties Brooklyn "proceeded along its four-track course—as a residential suburb, as an important shopping and business town, as a manufacturing center, and as one of the world's greatest commercial cities." This typical street scene appeared in *The Eagle and Brooklyn*.

Flatbush, Williamsburg, Greenpoint, Bushwick, New Utrecht, and other sections of Brooklyn were once separate villages and farm neighborhoods. Now Flatbush Avenue, shown in this *Eagle* photograph, is one of Brooklyn's world-famous streets.

"Every city has a distinctive atmosphere. You sense it as you walk its streets, breathe its air, sit in its restaurants, visit its monuments and parks, talk with its people." Prospect Park, in this Department of Parks photograph, is distinctively Brooklyn.

"Brooklyn is a great sea city," and the United States Navy knew it long ago when it established the Navy Yard. This Navy Department photograph shows a typical scene of hustle and bustle, where many of the Navy's ships have been built, refitted, and repaired after battle.

An aerial view of a section of Brooklyn shows the comfortable Norwegian Seamen's House on Hansen Place in the center foreground.

The Brooklyn part of what is officially the Port of New York is the biggest and busiest so far as freight is concerned. Ships of every nation, like these two Norwegian freighters, are regular visitors. Both pictures on this page are from the Norwegian Government Social Welfare Office for the Merchant Marine.

"The truest Americanization can be found in preserving a 'cultural solidarity' with the past." Different groups do it in different ways, and folk dances are one link. Here the Norskefolkdanslaget (Norwegian folk dancers of Brooklyn) commemorate National Constitution Day.

"The promotion of good citizenship and the preservation of great cultural treasures" are dual enterprises of many groups, partly through hospitality in pleasant meeting places. Typical is the Norwegian Seamen's Church. Photographs on this page by Rudy Larsen.

There are "all sorts of bridges to Brooklyn's common life." One of them is the community center. And behind all such organizations, as at the Stuyvesant Community Center, is a staff to plan and guide. Photograph by Julius A. Brown.

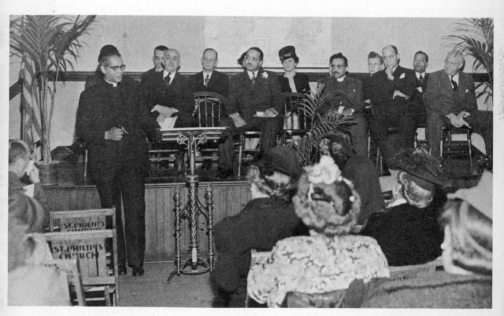

In Brooklyn "the discouraged observer of mankind may find some ground for hope" and "see the mingling of races in workaday relationships" in such events as this ceremony at the opening of the Stuyvesant Community Center.

"Each group grows to adult stature in the great democratic community as its members acquire the capacity to appreciate the cultural gifts of the other groups." Young artists at the Stuyvesant Community Center start from scratch, unhampered by dogma or rules. Bernard Ravitz took this artistic scene.

"The lovable and laughable things about Brooklyn . . . are part of Brooklyn's special quality," but boys are boys whatever the city or race. One play in a game in a recreation room can be the most important thing in the world, as it is to these opponents at the Stuyvesant Community Center. James Kavallines, of the New York *Herald Tribune*, snapped a dramatic moment.

Starting early, perhaps, to learn how to be true fans of "a remarkably efficient, yet colorful baseball team"—the Dodgers, of course—are these noisemakers at the Day Nursery of the Jewish Community House of Bensonhurst, photographed by Roman Vishniac for the Federation of Jewish Philanthropies of New York.

In early days the theater had to battle New York's competition and the "dour Yankee conscience." Now potential drama critics begin early with puppet performances at the Brooklyn Public Library—and the show was given four stars. Photograph by Rinaldi.

Brooklyn has always had, among a multitude of things, churches and pretty girls. One hundred years ago, there were 113 of the former, but there is no record of the latter. Here is a modern combination of the two: young members of the Norwegian Evangelical Lutheran Free Church attired for confirmation. Photograph by Rudy Larsen.

Some museums couldn't attract the small fry even with television. But the story hour, with an appropriate costume for everyone, brings Brooklyn's younger set to the Brooklyn Museum.

Pasadena has its Tournament of Roses parade, Manhattan has its St. Patrick's Day goings-on, but Brooklyn has the Sunday School Parade. Fashions change, and generations grow up, but it is always a great event, as J. N. Currie's photograph of a few years ago testifies.

"For after all, Brooklyn is one and not many, notwithstanding the impression of separateness inevitably conveyed. . . . The thousand ties—business, political, cultural, social—which bind each group to the whole society are matters of day-by-day experience. As time passes, they become more intimate. There is no deliberate plan to promote unity. It is a democratic process which began in this western tip of Long Island three hundred years ago and has continued with the growth of Brooklyn from its Dutch infancy to its present giant stature." One of the newest manifestations of this never-ending process is the housing development—privately or publicly financed. This one happens to be Marcy Houses, photographed for the New York City Housing Authority by L. Marinoff. In these developments all races, all creeds, all religions dwell in harmony, for Brooklyn is America, and America is people.

The Dutch Pioneers

In a farmhouse surrounded by peach trees, somewhere between the tiny village of Breukelen and Gowanus Kill, a woman sat quietly smoking her pipe. She was very old—her years were said to number one hundred, and her children and grandchildren certainly numbered more than seventy. She smoked pipeful after pipeful without interruption, as she sat beside the great fireplace. Sometimes she spoke to those around her in the French speech of the Walloons of the southern Netherlands. Sometimes her mind wandered a little.

This matriarch was owner of the farm. She had lived in the colony for half a century; much of the history of Brooklyn's early struggles was wrapped up in her small and shriveled form. On a September morning in 1679 two strangers tarried for an hour by her fireside. Their names were Jasper Danckaerts and Peter Sluyter, and they were followers of the mystic, Labadie. They had come from Wieward, in Friesland, to try to find an American refuge for members of their sect. The ancient lady's liveliness astonished them. They were given new cider to drink and smoked fish to eat. The fish was striped bass, called *twaelft* because it was caught next after the *elft* (shad). And the grandame proudly exhibited to the travelers some fine large apples, different from European varieties.

The Labadists listened eagerly and took careful note of all they saw. They were exploring a partly cultivated, partly wooded region which was one day to be Brook-

lyn. It was still shaggy and wild, but its soil was bringing forth fruit and grain in lush abundance. They came
upon other Walloon families, and Flemings, also, for
Brooklyn pioneers were not exclusively Holland Dutch;
they were Netherland folk, northern and southern, Dutch-
speaking and French-speaking, but intermarriage was to
make them essentially one people. Wherever the travelers
went, the farmhouse doors were opened to them and
West Indian rum, which the colonists called kill-devil,
was pressed upon them. They found it a miserable,
unpalatable drink and were more grateful for the cider,
the milk, the fruit, and tobacco, which was also abun-
dant.

At Gowanus they were welcomed by Simon de Hart
and his busy wife, and there they slept snugly in a "Kermis"
bed, in a corner of the hearth beside the fire. They enjoyed no such comfort at the home of Jacques Cortelyou,
in New Utrecht. But they found good conversation there.
Cortelyou could speak Latin and French, and had some
knowledge of mathematics and science, including medicine. His visitors discovered that he was not a Christian,
but a follower of Descartes. They were sorry for that, but
were candid enough to record their impression that he
conducted himself better as a Cartesian than did many of
those in the colony who were supposed to be pious. After
supper they had to content themselves with a pile of straw
in the barn. They pulled up their sheepskin covers, but
could not sleep. A cold north wind blew through the open
barn door. Fleas and vermin pestered them, and there was
a "continuous grunting of hogs, squealing of pigs, bleat-
ing and coughing of sheep, barking of dogs, crowing of
cocks and cackling of hens." Yet they felt they had no
reason to complain, for Cortelyou's son usually slept in

the same bed and had then "crept in the straw" behind them.*

At the time of Danckaerts and Sluyter's visit the *bouweries* (farms) were sending their produce in plenty to the little city across the river—watermelons, cabbages, carrots, turnips, butter and cheese, beef and pork. Tobacco was grown in large quantities for export to Holland, and pickled Gowanus oysters were sent in casks to Barbadoes. Thirty years earlier the colony's permanence had been threatened because the *boers* (farmers) were neglecting farming for fur-trading.

New Netherland was then a rough, tough trading outpost. Fortune seekers of all descriptions and many races had been drawn to it, adventurers whose only object was to get from the Indians the skins of the mink and the beaver, which were so easily converted into great wealth when sold in Europe. No colony could be built securely out of such material. Permanent settlers were needed.

It was Brooklyn's destiny to help save New Netherland by becoming a prosaic farm community, a region of plain *boers* and *bouweries*.

There had been scattered tracts in cultivation in western Long Island ever since the time of Governor Wouter Van Twiller. In 1643 an event occurred which emptied the countryside. Governor Kieft's reckless massacre of sleeping Indians caused an uprising of all the tribes of southern New Netherland. The panic-stricken farm people fled to the protection of the fort at New Amsterdam, while enraged natives were stealing cattle and burning houses, barns and crops. After the subjugation of the

* Jasper Danckaerts and Peter Sluyter, *Journal of a Voyage to New York, and a Tour in Several of the American Colonies in 1679–80;* translated and edited by Henry Cruse Murphy, Brooklyn, 1867, pp. 120–23, 126–29.

tribes, settlement was again undertaken, and the hamlet of Breukelen was laid out in an Indian cornfield a mile and a half from the ferrying point to Manhattan.

Among the settlers of Breukelen there was an enterprising man who knew that the colony was in a bad way—Jan Evertszen Bout, a member of the Governor's council. He was one of three colonial leaders who went to Holland in 1649 to try to get the home authorities to mend affairs. They were not very successful but one thing they did. They advertised New Netherland and its products by printed propaganda and by word of mouth, and as a result of their energy two ships, crammed with emigrants, many of them sturdy *boers,* reached New Amsterdam in 1650. For years thereafter scarcely a ship sailed from Holland for the Hudson without some passengers who intended to remain in the New World.

From that time there was considerable progress in Long Island. The sound of the ax was heard in Midwout and New Utrecht, in Boswyck and Breukelen, as the land was cleared of timber, and farmhouses and barns were built. The Brooklyn pioneers were full of hope, or they would not have ventured on the perilous voyage to the New World. But they had to endure many hardships. Fear of the Indians long persisted. Many of the colonists perished in the annual scourges of fever and smallpox. And when the plague struck, there was little that could be done to check its ravages or alleviate suffering. We owe to the Labadists' simple record a stark and pitiful picture of two children lying dead and unburied and three others sick with smallpox in a farmhouse in New Utrecht, another child having died the previous week.

But after making all allowances for primitive conditions and for lonely suffering far from kindred—conditions that have always been the grim incidents of pioneering

—it is impossible not to be impressed by more cheerful facts. We read of a thirty-pound haunch of venison bought from the Indians for a pittance, of wild turkeys and wild geese, of oysters at Gowanus, excellent in quality, "some of them not less than a foot long," of watermelons in profusion, of profitable tobacco fields at Breukelen and the Waal-boght, of good crops of wheat and other grains, of great fires of oak and hickory blazing up the farmhouse chimneys. According to the chronicler and poet of New Utrecht, Captain Nicasius de Sille, who wrote a trilogy on that hamlet, the very soil sang

> I now am satisfied by th' honor of my name,
> By grain and orchard fruit, by horses and by kine,
> By plants and by a race of men—all growth of mine.[*]

These good things meant security and permanence. They meant that a substantial Dutch civilization was thrusting down its roots, a growth that was little hindered by the English conquest. The chief symbols of that civilization were the Dutch farmhouse and the Dutch church.

The early farmhouse—ancestor of that familiar type of home which modern builders call the Dutch colonial —was a small cottage with a huge chimney and great fireplace. If the Labadists had been given to minute architectural description, they might have left an account of the appearance of the cottages of New Utrecht, many of which they noted had recently been rebuilt of stone, after fire had destroyed the village and impoverished some of the villagers.

At the time of their visit and for generations afterward, one might have found there and in the neighboring villages many charming little houses of the quaint

[*] Ellis Lawrence Raesly, *Portrait of New Netherland,* New York, 1945, p. 306.

type which Irving described in the *Legend of Sleepy Hollow*. Long and low, their sweeping rooflines ended in graceful overhanging curves both in the front and at the rear of the house. In some cases a rear lean-to brought the roof close to the ground. They were sided with clay and straw often protected by long, narrow, hand-hewn shingles, sometimes by brick or stone.

Historians were long puzzled over their origin, for it was impossible to find anything like these cozy picturesque dwellings in the farmhouses of old Holland, where as a rule the same great roof covered the farmer's family and his cattle alike. Professor T. J. Wertenbaker, of Princeton, has traced them to the farm cottage of the *Houtland* region of West Flanders. In his opinion they testify to the wanderings of Flemish refugees who, with many of their Walloon neighbors, fled to the northern provinces from a homeland devastated during the war with Spain.°

Failing to find farms to work in the already crowded fields of Holland, they turned to the New World, where there was virgin soil in plenty—resembling, the Labadists said, the garden mold of Holland. In New Utrecht, in Gravesend, in the Hackensack Valley, wherever they settled, they built their houses on the model of the Flemish farm cottage, with its "flying gutter" and overhanging eaves, and with the same interior arrangement.

There were no frills—the house was severely functional—and furnishings were scant. A large general room served as living room, dining room, and kitchen, its principal feature being a fireplace stretching across an entire side, sometimes large enough to permit the farmer's family to sit within the opening on either side of the fire. Across the ceiling were massive hand-hewn beams. The chief

° Thomas Jefferson Wertenbaker, *The Founding of American Cililization; the Middle Colonies*, New York, 1938, pp. 69 ff.

article of furniture was a great paneled chest. The "best room," a parlor and bedroom combined, opened off at one side, while under the eaves back of the kitchen there were two or three narrow bedrooms.

Many seasons of good crops and a growing market brought prosperity to the Brooklyn *boers*, and with prosperity came a desire for greater comfort and even a little display. So additions were built on at the sides and the back, or new and more substantial houses were constructed of better materials. Fireplace openings were reduced in size, and blue Delft tiles were placed around them. There were such Dutch refinements as the divided door and the *betse*—the bed-in-a-closet—which in the daytime was shut away like the modern apartment-house Murphy bed. Most important were the immaculate floors covered with clean sea-sand, which was decorated with arabesque patterns skillfully designed by means of the housewives' broom-handles.

These farmhouses reflected as in a mirror the simplicity, frugality, sobriety and integrity of the Dutch farm family.

Stranger to modern eyes than the farm cottages were the tiny octagonal churches at Boswyck and Amersfoort, harking back to the same extraordinary type in Holland. Breukelen's "small and ugly little church standing in the middle of the road" attracted the notice of Danckaerts and Sluyter in 1679. The first church built in the region which we now call Brooklyn was erected in Flatbush in 1654 by order of Governor Stuyvesant, who directed that it should be built in the form of a cross and that the rear of the building should house the minister.

The sermon was the chief feature of Reformed Dutch worship; hence the pulpit was the main architectural object in the interior of these churches. It was reached by a steep flight of steps and was surmounted by a sounding board, and from its height the Dutch domine looked down upon his little flock, the men ranged around the sides of the room, the women sitting in the middle.

The learned clergyman who first occupied the Flatbush pulpit was the Reverend Jacob Theodorus Polhemus, who was probably a native of Switzerland. Before coming to New Netherland he had had a brief experience of the hazards of colonial life in Brazil, where he had preached in French, Portuguese, and Dutch. In 1654 he began a long career in Flatbush.

Amersfoort and Breukelen were also under his charge, but after a time the Breukelenites became discontented. They felt they were not getting their money's worth and complained to the magistrates that fifteen minutes every two weeks on Sunday afternoons, with a prayer or a sermon that ended before it was well begun, was not enough. So in 1660 they received their own domine, the Reverend Henricus Selijns.

Selijns, like De Sille, a versifier, was only twenty-four when he came to Breukelen. He was a native of Amsterdam, his uncles and his cousins were clergymen and lawyers and schoolmasters, he had studied at Leyden University, and there could have been no doubt about his qualifications as a scholar. In Breukelen he proved to be zealous and efficient. He found twenty-four communicants in a hamlet of 134 souls and quadrupled their number during his four-year stay.

But Selijns was more than a competent clergyman. He was a lively young man and an ardent lover. He twanged his lyre and sang of mundane things as well as of things sacred. He had left a tall and fair girl behind him when he came to the New World, Machtelt Specht of Utrecht, "the sweetest creature of the town," according to a "Birthday Garland" * which he composed when she was twenty.

His Breukelen church was only a barn, but the villagers had built him a parsonage. It was a lonely place, and he begged Machtelt to cross the ocean to share it with him. For a time she hesitated, but in July, 1662, she arrived at New Amsterdam, and they were married. They were a happy couple. He continued to write verses to her, rejoicing over "Your soul of purest beauty, your sweet and fine proud face," in lines addressed to "Machtelt Specht, My House-wife." †

Unfortunately, the cost of living bore hard upon these young people. The Breukelenites had not been able to collect the full salary—in shell currency (sewan) and beaver skins—that they had incautiously promised. Governor Stuyvesant had helped out by engaging Selijns to preach on Sunday evenings at his "bouwery" on Manhattan, and he also made him Latin secretary of New Netherland. But inflation nullified this assistance. The purchasing power of pelts and sewan dropped sharply, and the domine and his wife found little cheer in their bare parsonage. Just before the English conquest of 1664 they sailed for Holland. After an interval Domine Polhemus took over again, and in 1666 the villagers erected their "small and ugly little church."

The bell which announced the hour of Sunday service was sometimes rung by an official whose duties extended from the teaching of the village school to the digging of the graves. Adrian Hegeman was the first schoolmaster and community handy man in Midwout. Such a one, also, was Carel de Beauvois, from Leyden, who in 1661 agreed

* Raesly, *Portrait of New Netherland*, p. 317.
† *Ibid.*, 319 f.

not only to perform these functions in Breukelen but to sing on Sundays, to act as court messenger, to serve summons, and to do "whatever else is required." For these services he was given free lodging and a stipend from the village, which was supplemented by an annual appropriation by the colonial magistrates of fifty guilders in wampum. For a time, when no clergyman was functioning in Breukelen, this accomplished scholar conducted the services and read the sermons of approved divines.

The domine and the schoolmaster composed the village intelligentsia. They were the custodians of Dutch culture, a sacred responsibility which was not lessened after the English conquest. The *boers* possessed few books besides the Dutch Bible, which was in every home; but there were few illiterates. The use of the English tongue became an issue in the eighteenth century, as generations of young people grew up who preferred the speech of their neighbors. By this time Kings County was a Dutch island threatened by a strong English-speaking tide, a tide which did, indeed, in time, sweep over it. But the Dutch language persisted in many family circles after the nineteenth century was far advanced. The imperfect English of the Reverend Martinus Schoonmaker, minister of the six collegiate churches of the county until 1824, made him a butt of ridicule. According to a story preserved by Henry R. Stiles, the Brooklyn historian, he attempted on one occasion to use the marriage service in English; instead of the solemn final words, "I pronounce you man and wife and one flesh," the astonished couple heard the declaration, "I pronounce you two to be one beef."

At the eve of the Revolution Kings County was a prosperous farm neighborhood. All along the region from the Wallabout down the bay, where the city now stretches its mighty bulk, one could see the substantial houses and ample barns of Dutch families, their wide fields and meadows, their orchards and grazing cattle.

The name Breukelen had passed through various evolutions, in the course of which it became Brookland, and finally Brooklyn. Boswyck had become Bushwick; the Waal-boght, sometimes called Ye Wale, was now Wallabout. Midwout, which had also been called 't Vlacke-Bos (meaning wooded flat), was now Flatbush. Amersfoort was Flatlands.

These changes were symptomatic of changes in the Dutch population, but they were surface changes. The essential character of the people remained. The Kings County Dutch were an orderly, industrious, practical people, with strong common sense and a spirit of tolerance and little disposition to join actively in the Revolutionary turmoil which was agitating their neighbors of British blood. They were the pioneers of that pleasant region. They had laid its foundations, and they had built a stable, literate, and soberly substantial civilization. They were content.

But Revolutionary ardor is contagious. There were Dutch patriots, some of whom were electors of delegates to the Second Continental Congress. Young Dutchmen joined the patriot army. And the Dutch people of Kings County suffered grievously when, in the summer of 1776, they were caught between the contending forces, and the full fury of war was let loose on their unoffending farms. No other populous community in the state had such a fearful experience during the whole course of the long-drawn-out struggle.

Before the invading British marched through New Utrecht and Flatbush, the American defenders drove the farmers' cattle into the eastern counties to keep it from the enemy. The helpless *boers* had to look on while Yankee soldiers put the torch to their grain. Many families, taking

their Negro slaves and a few belongings, fled in farm
wagons from the path of the oncoming British, oppressed
with the heavy foreboding that their houses and barns
would be burned. After the disastrous battle which nearly
wrecked the American cause, the Dutch farm folk had to
get along somehow with the British occupying force. It remained with them until 1783.

Most of them considered the war lost and made what
profit they could from the invaders. But there were patriots among them. In those long years when captured
American officers were quartered in the farmers' homes,
when British officers and Tories from the city and neighboring counties in New York and Jersey were betting on
the horses at "Ascot Heath" in Flatlands, and less genteel
sportsmen were reveling in bull-baiting, when royal birth-
days were celebrated by great feasts in Loosely's Tavern
at Brooklyn Ferry, and people were laughing over Gentleman Johnny Burgoyne's farce, "The Battle of Brooklyn,"
with its broad ridicule of General Washington and the rebel
chiefs, when the New York newspapers, Rivington's *Gazette* and Gaine's *Mercury,* constantly informed the people
of Kings County that the rebel cause was hopeless and the
confident demeanor of red-coated officers and men always
confirmed this view of affairs, it took an extraordinary
amount of faith to believe in American victory.

There were some who did. All through those years they
managed to smuggle out money to aid the patriot cause.
Perhaps their determination was strengthened by the sight
of certain black hulks in Wallabout Bay, the prison ships
in which the martyrs died whose bones now rest in Fort
Greene Park.

The flood of Yankees which set in after the war, followed
in the new century by the Irish and then the Germans, put
in motion great currents that created a new society. Over-

whelmed as it was, the Dutch culture of colonial Brooklyn persisted for generations. The Dutch Church was a very citadel of respectability. At the beginning of the city period a new church building was erected on Joralemon Street, to replace one that had been built in 1807. It was a large, classic structure, the city's finest church building, dignified and austere in its beautiful setting of lawn and great shade trees in a region that is now solid stone and brick.

It was a monument to the oldest community institution, around which had gathered the sanctity of age. It had been the social center of the landowners of the whole countryside stretching from the Wallabout through Cripplebush and Bedford to Gowanus—the Bergens, the Van Brunts, the Couwenhovens, the Suydams, the Tiebouts, the Ryersons, the Schencks, the Remsens, the Cortelyous. Chief among them, perhaps, was General Jeremiah Johnson of the Wallabout, son of Barent Johnson, Revolutionary patriot, and great-great-grandson of Jan Barentsen Van Driest, of Zutphen in Guelderland, who settled in Gravesend in 1657.

Some of the Dutch proprietors may have profited a little too willingly from the expansion of Brooklyn, cutting up their farms into building lots and retiring on their gains; others may have given way with extreme reluctance, and some may have attempted to block progress. Johnson was the most conspicuous of those far-seeing Dutchmen who rose above the spirit of mere gain, or caste, or race. Peppery, genial, fond of his pipe to the last hour of his life, he was long thought of as Brooklyn's first citizen. Sometimes he turned his hand to satirical verse, and he was regarded by the Brooklyn townsfolk as their chief authority on the local lore of the Revolution. As a boy he was an eyewitness of many events which were afterwards preserved in his notes. In the brittle yellow pages of a copy of Brooklyn's first newspaper, the *Long Island Courier,* one may read, under date of October 15, 1800, a portion of Johnson's "Topographical View of the Township of Brooklyn," written when he was a little past thirty. But his scholarship went beyond antiquarianism. For his own pleasure he translated passages from Erasmus, the great Dutch humanist, and also put into English one of the finest relics of the colonial period, Van der Donck's *History of New Netherland.*

His leadership served Brooklyn well at a critical time, for he led the fight for Brooklyn's city charter against New York's determined opposition, and he was afterwards mayor of the new city. He represented better than most of the Dutchmen of his day the transition from Brooklyn's pastoral period to its urbanization. His Anglicized name emphasizes the change that was going on. No one loved the past more than he, and no Dutchman welcomed the future more willingly. He symbolized both Dutch permanence and Dutch progress at a time when the Yankees and the Irish were pressing on and obliterating many an old landmark.

For many years Flatbush remained comparatively undisturbed by the alien tide. The satisfied farmers of that quiet tree-shaded village held on to their acres. For a century in colonial days the stone fences lining the village street had bloomed each season with primroses which grew from soil on their tops. A blight killed them, and the old stone fences gave way to wooden pickets, which in time stretched in unbroken lines down both sides of the street. The Dutch church, with its slender spire stood near the center of the village, like a New England meetinghouse. And so Flatbush appeared when its neighbor over the hill was noisily celebrating the acquisition of a city charter.

The Dutch plant which put down its roots in the 1630s, '40s and '50s was a tough plant, and the crowding growths of the centuries have not succeeded in destroying it. The pioneer blood-stream still runs strong in the veins of many families in Brooklyn and far away from Brooklyn. A Dutch or Walloon name today may be a mark of aristocracy; it may signify distinguished service to the city or the nation; it is pretty sure to imply solid respectability and worth. But the Dutch blood has been mingled with that of many other breeds, and may be disguised by an English, Irish, Scottish, German, or some other name.

At any rate, there is nothing more vigorously American than this foundation stock of old Brooklyn. Brooklyn's street signs call the roll of the pioneers—Lefferts Avenue, Vanderbilt Avenue, Cortelyou Road, Ditmas Avenue, Boerum Place, Vanderveer Street, Remsen Street . . . One could go on for some time longer. These names are repeated glibly every day in many accents—unconscious tribute which the heedless present pays to Brooklyn's past—to the sturdy *boers* and the men of learning and piety who came to a shaky and insecure trading post and built a long-enduring and sound society.

Yankee Enterprise

We KNOW the main facts of the story of the young Yankee printer of Sag Harbor, for he wrote them down long afterwards for his children. What we don't know, it is easy to imagine. One day—it may have been in the early spring of 1811, it may have been sometime in the winter, or even earlier—he got hold of some news that jarred him into thinking seriously about his own future. The news concerned two friends of his—young fellows of the village—and it is probable that they themselves broke it to him.

They had caught the fever that was then sweeping through the eastern states, carrying families off by the thousands. It was a fever that threatened to depopulate many eastern communities, but it was filling the new states to the westward with an energetic race of pioneers. The printer's friends had made up their minds to emigrate to Cincinnati, and they urged him to join them.

For him, Cincinnati was out of the question. But he knew that he had reached the limit of any possible success that Sag Harbor had to offer him. His paper, the *Suffolk Gazette,* could not earn enough to meet the needs of his growing family. He remembered what James Sowden, the papermaker, had been saying—that a printer in Brooklyn wanted to sell his weekly newspaper, the *Long Island Star.* Brooklyn was only as far west as the other end of Long Island, but the young man, after thinking it over carefully, probably guessed that the opportunity for success there was about as good as in Cincinnati. Finally he came to his decision.

His name was Alden Spooner. He was the son of Judah Paddock Spooner, who had carried a printing press into the Green Mountains thirty years before, and had started Vermont's first newspaper in the hamlet of Westminster. Just as his father had felt the lure of the frontier, he now felt the pull of the great port of which Brooklyn was a part, the same powerful magnet that attracted many another Yankee in that generation. In May, 1811, he took ship at Sag Harbor and sailed for Brooklyn with his young wife, Rebecca, and his two small children. He took along a press as primitive as the one on which his father had printed the *Vermont Gazette; or, Green Mountain Post-Boy.* It was an old battered wooden hand press, for which he had paid twelve dollars. He had to patch it up again and again, and the first issues of the *Star* that came out under his editorship were unevenly printed and sometimes hard to read. But there was a fresh wind blowing through those four small pages—a Yankee wind from the east. That wind was to furnish a powerful impulse to every forward step that Brooklyn was destined to take for years to come.

Alden Spooner was a direct descendant of a famous couple of the old Plymouth colony, John Alden and his practical wife, Priscilla. From them, from his restless father and his patient, resourceful mother, and from others in the line of printers and farmers and mechanics that stretched behind him, he inherited a fortunate mixture of common sense, imagination, humor, and aggressiveness. He needed all these qualities, for the *Star* had fewer than three hundred subscribers when he took it over—hardly worth the money he paid for it, he ruefully concluded, after taking stock of his new property.

The Brooklyn to which the Spooners came in 1811 was

not a rural Dutch village like the other small communities of Kings County. It was not a village at all, politically speaking. It was the fire district of Brooklyn Ferry, with a population of between three and four thousand. Its main street, the narrow, winding Old Ferry Road—one day to be renamed Fulton Street—was lined with taverns and shops and dwelling houses for a short half mile. It was an untidy, littered street.

One had to have a great deal of faith, then, to believe in the future of the place. The Spooners must have been cast down in spirit by their first sight of it. The next year, when war with England broke out, the Ferry was alive with excitement. When the British blockade closed in around the coast Brooklynites remembered 1776 and expected invasion. Men of every age and all occupations turned out to build fortifications. Volunteers by the hundreds came over the river and across the Bay to help. Spooner advertised a new song, "The Patriotic Diggers." It could be bought at the *Star* office for six cents, and in a day or two everybody in town was singing it and whistling its tune. It was the song of the Brooklyn citizenry—all patriots now— at work to repel invasion.

> To protect our rights
>   'Gainst your flints and triggers,
> See on Brooklyn Heights
>   Our patriotic diggers.

The author of the song was a Yankee named Samuel Woodworth, whose "Old Oaken Bucket" was sung in every schoolhouse in America for a century.

Invasion did not come, but sailors, mechanics, and laborers were thrown out of work by the blockade, and there was plenty of hardship.

The editor had moments of doubt and anxiety during his

first years in Brooklyn, but when news of peace came, early in 1815, and with it news of General Andrew Jackson's victory at New Orleans, his naturally buoyant spirits revived. The Ferry continued to grow in a disheveled, disorderly way, and its Yankee population, considerable before the war, was again on the increase. It was the nearest point to the city in Kings County, and the city was spilling over to the Brooklyn shore.

The port of New York teemed with Yankee enterprise. Its merchants were again sending their fleets to ports all over the world. It was the sea, and the trade that flowed over it, that gave Brooklyn its first industries. Ship carpenters and riggers and caulkers and painters were being kept busy on both sides of the East River. As yet Brooklyn's share in the port's business was very small, but it held a promise of future greatness. There was the infant navy yard. There were the warehouses along the waterfront crowded with tobacco, tar, and wine from the Southern States and the West Indies—the Red Stores of Kimberley and Waring —Samuel Jackson's stores—Jonathan Thompson's dock and his White Cotton Stores (holding, tradition says, bales used by Andrew Jackson in the redoubt thrown up in defense of New Orleans)—Treadwell and Thorne's stores —and Robert Black's warehouse where salt had been produced during the war, evaporated from the water of the East River. And in the midst of what had once been the old Rapalje farm there was a ropewalk—a part of the sea-inspired business of the Ferry that was to expand into a large Brooklyn industry. The farm and the ropewalk belonged to Joshua Sands, and over the farm's wide acres a large part of the village of Brooklyn was to be built.

In the 1780s and '90s Sands had been a merchant, in partnership with his older brother, Comfort Sands. The ropewalk was first established as an adjunct of their mer-

cantile business. They had had to import from England
the cordage and rigging for their vessels. They decided,
instead, to import machinery and skilled ropemakers. When
the Spooners came to Brooklyn, Sands was a man of great
dignity and influence. He was an active Federalist politician, and had been a county judge and a member of the
state senate.

John Adams had appointed him collector of the port of
New York, and Jefferson had removed him from that post.
He had served a term in Congress. He lived in a mansion
fifty feet square on Front Street, and watched the town
grow, street by street, over the acres which he and his
brother, Comfort, had acquired as a reward for their patriotism. This old farm of the Tory Rapalje, confiscated by
the state and bought up very cheaply, was a mine of gold,
yielding its purchase price many times over. The Yankee
merchant had received the inheritance of the Dutch farmer.

Joshua Sands was a "Yankee" whose grandfather had
settled Cow Neck, now Sands Point, Long Island. The word
Yankee, it must be admitted, is a rather elastic term. For
our present purpose it is convenient to apply it to all people
of British blood who have come to Brooklyn, from Lady
Deborah Moody's little band of Anabaptists, who settled
in Gravesend in the 1640s, to the latest family of Robinsons
or Smiths to lease an apartment house on Monroe Place
or Grace Court. In spite of this extreme inclusiveness in
our usage, a decided stress is laid upon the New England
element in Brooklyn's population and on the New England
influence which strongly affected many whose origins were
elsewhere.

Some day great merchants from Salem, owners of clipper
ship fleets, would build stately mansions on Brooklyn
Heights. In the first two decades of the century the more
modest residences of a few well-to-do merchants looked

out from the orchards and gardens of Clover Hill, as the Heights was then usually called, over the wonderful panorama which the sail-flecked bay, with its wooded islands, and the mast-bounded, many-spired city afforded them. The wealthiest of the Heights dwellers, Hezekiah Pierrepont, was a Connecticut Yankee, grandson of one of the founders of Yale College.

As a youth he quit his studies at Yale to seek his fortune in trade. In the quest he found penty of excitement. He saw a great deal of the world. He was in Paris throughout the Reign of Terror. While on a voyage to the Far East as supercargo, he was captured by a French privateer. A period was put to his life of adventure when he returned home and married the daughter of the land-rich merchant William Constable, from whom he inherited vast tracts in northern New York. He bought sixty acres on the Heights from the Benson, De Bevoice, and Remsen families and settled there. In time the development of the Heights as a pleasant residential district was to owe much to this quondam adventurer.

It was through Pierrepont's energetic leadership and that of Joshua Sands and a few others, aided and abetted by Alden Spooner's vigorous editorial pen, that Brooklyn Ferry became Brooklyn village in 1816. A scant two years before the village charter was acquired, Robert Fulton's steam ferryboat, the *Nassau*, made its maiden trip across the East River. Perhaps we can say that with that short voyage the nineteenth century began for Brooklyn. And yet eighteenth century habits and modes of thought held the village back for years. Population mounted steadily, new industries and business establishments were started, but there was little progress in administration and in the development of institutions. In 1819 a post-war economic slump brought the community nearly to a standstill.

During those years of dragging progress, Alden Spooner was not content to confine his activities to the village. He took a flyer in New York journalism. He held on to the *Star*, but handed its direction over to Erastus Worthington, a steady, conscientious Connecticut Yankee, and he gave his own editorial attention to the New York *Columbian*. During his sojourn as a metropolitan editor—which lasted for fifteen months during 1817 and 1818—he mixed with the literary and the political figures of the city and attracted the notice of two talented young men who wrote verses for the New York *Evening Post*—Fitz-Greene Halleck and Joseph Rodman Drake.

These "Croakers," as they called themselves, twice mentioned the editor in a bantering way in their satirical verses. When Spooner again gave Brooklyn the benefit of his "classic hand" (as the "Croakers" put it) he brought to his task a certain easy sophistication gained by his experience over the river.

The editor did much to stir up the village and to make the villagers conscious that Brooklyn was certainly going to be a town of considerable importance. There was, in fact, great progress in the early twenties. The community quickly recovered from the slump. By the mid-twenties population figures had mounted to 9,000. An Apprentices' Library was built in 1825. In that year Joshua Sands started a movement for a city charter, and Spooner beat the editorial tom-tom for it. They failed to make Brooklyn a city— that dignity was to be deferred for nine years—but the agitation bore fruit in a greatly improved charter for the village.

Anyone going through Brooklyn and its hinterland with an observant eye in the mid-twenties would have noticed that while the surrounding farms were owned by Dutchmen whose ancestors had planted them in early colonial days, the village itself was now dominated by the Yankees. Yankee editors, merchants, lawyers, businessmen, manufacturers, pedagogues, and preachers were driving the community along its course. It had grown in a decade from an easy-going, ill-regulated community of about four thousand to become a pleasant suburban town.

Wealth and fashion were in evidence on the Heights, but the greater number of the population, Yankee and otherwise, derived their incomes from Brooklyn's own industries: shipping, warehousing, ship repairing, ship and boat building, the ropewalks, white lead works, distilleries, tanneries, glass-making works, a whiting manufactory, a glue factory, a wool and cotton card factory, leather goods and "floor-cloth" factories, a furnace for casting iron, lumber yards, printing establishments, and other enterprises.

All these industries were small and intimate affairs compared with the great establishments one sees now in Brooklyn, but they were portents of a great change in the lives and habits of the people. The factory and the wage system were displacing the old master-apprentice system, but the old ways survived in some crafts, such as the making of hats, coaches, wheels, and other articles. The industrial revolution was hastening on its Brooklyn course. Each year new enterprises sprang up. Each year Yankee mechanics, tradesmen and clerks in growing numbers were drawn to Brooklyn to live in the trim, boxlike houses that were springing up endlessly on twenty-five-foot lots in the ever-lengthening streets.

The more well-to-do of the Yankees—the merchants, the rising manufacturers, and the lawyers—were likewise increasing in numbers as the town grew. David Leavitt had made a fortune by shipping and selling arms and ammunition to Colombian revolutionists in South America. Augustus and John B. Graham—those mysterious "brothers" who were not brothers—began in Brooklyn as distillers and then laid the foundation of Brooklyn's, and America's, great white lead industry.

Peter W. Radcliff, a Yale graduate who rose to the top of the legal profession in New York, became a Heights resident in 1825 and later drafted Brooklyn's first city charter, with the assistance of a keen young lawyer whose name was John Greenwood. There were many other Yankee lawyers, and Cranberry Street was hung thickly with their signs. The Yankee schoolmasters could not afford pretentious mansions on the Heights, but there were men among them who had the town's deep respect. One, Theodore Dwight, Jr., was an intellectual of the purest Yankee strain, whose mind was mellowed and made cosmopolitan by wide acquaintanceship and travel abroad. His great-grandfather was Jonathan Edwards, mightiest of Puritan theologians. His father was one of the "Hartford Wits," a long-forgotten group of poets who had immense reputations in the 1790s. His uncle was president of Yale. When he came to Brooklyn he had already published books of travel and scholarship, and while living in Brooklyn he edited his *Dwight's American Magazine.*

Another schoolmaster, Theodore Eames, of Eames and Putnam's Classical Hall on Washington Street, was one of the chief boosters of general culture in Brooklyn in that generation. He was an active promoter of the Brooklyn Lyceum, perhaps the most zealous of its founders.

The Yankees and the Dutchmen of the village got on well together, on the whole. But there was some friction. Brooklyn editors and essayists sometimes ribbed their Dutch neighbors, not always very gently. Alden Spooner once wrote a few paragraphs for the *Star* which became famous, in which he ridiculed Jacob Patchen, a long-winded Dutch butcher whose legal maneuvers exasperated the village for years. In reference to the costume of the Brooklyn butcher clan of a by-gone day, which the eccentric Patchen persisted in wearing, Spooner entitled this piece "The Last of the Leather Breeches." Another Brooklyn writer referred to "the war which has always been kept up among us," a war between "house lots" and "cabbage gardens," caused by "Yankee innovation" and "Dutch tenacity." * He continued, with amused irritation:

With what pertinacity have the old paralytic fences, which seemed ready to tumble down of their own superannuation, resisted the assaults of village and legislative enactments! How often have they made improvement cower and lie down at the feet of their rotten posts!

Such criticisms were not intended to be taken very seriously. Probably the young Yankee essayists were more concerned with style than with subject matter. The truth is, of course, that the Yankees were by no means the only friends of progress. The Dutch were more phlegmatic, but they certainly did not stand still. The number of Dutch politicians, businessmen, lawyers, and schoolmasters was always large in proportion to the Dutch population.

No Yankee in the village was more highly respected than was Adrian Van Sinderen. He is remembered today as the first president of the Brooklyn Savings Bank. Like General Jeremiah Johnson, he was descended from an old Dutch family of Kings County and was, again like Johnson, a conservative, cultured, pious gentleman, with high ideals and a certain touch of Dutch obstinacy. He was one of those men who are indispensable to organizations, and as new reform agencies appeared, he became the first president of one after another of them—the Long Island Bible Society, the Brooklyn Temperance Society, the Brooklyn branch of

* "The Scribbler's Budget," *Long Island Star,* March 27, 1834.

the American Colonization Society (an antislavery enterprise which proposed to encourage gradual emancipation and the colonization of free Negroes in Liberia, on the west coast of Africa).

There were, of course, many other Dutchmen of prominence. Isaac and Jacob Van Doren were schoolmasters from New Jersey. They set a new high mark for the education of girls in their Young Ladies' Collegiate Institute on Hicks Street, advocating thorough training instead of the then-prevalent program of "female accomplishments." Tunis Joralemon was a village landowner and politician. And there were also non-Yankees such as Andrew Mercein, philanthropic businessman of Swiss parentage, and the prominent Irishmen Peter Turner, who led the movement for the building of St. James Roman Catholic Church, John Garrison Murphy, inventor and political leader, and Cornelius Heeney, the rich fur merchant, one-time partner of John Jacob Astor.

But Yankees were predominant. Their innovations prevailed. And many of the non-Yankees were very much under the influence of Yankee ideas. Van Sinderen's Temperance Society had its inspiration in a campaign launched by Lyman Beecher—father of Brooklyn's Henry Ward Beecher—in Litchfield, Connecticut. It mushroomed into a great national organization with headquarters in Boston and branches in every town and village.

In Brooklyn the ministers of all the Protestant churches unfurled the temperance banners, and the Reverend John Farnan, of St. James Catholic Church, announced a temperance sermon. The newspapers came out strongly for the reform. It was part of a movement that swept down from New England after the mid-twenties, filling the air with zeal for better manners and a passion for moral improvement. Spirituous liquors were renounced by many prominent citizens, who were careful to make a distinction in favor of wine and beer. Brooklyn's poorer districts were overcrowded with grog shops, and these became the targets of the temperance forces.

In most communities the early temperance movement was nonpolitical, but in Brooklyn, George Hall, a young Yankee who had come over from the city, made it his personal battle. He campaigned for village president as an enemy of grog shops and of the swine then roaming and rooting without hindrance in the village streets. The practice of free range for swine was by no means peculiar to Brooklyn. These beasts enjoyed the liberty of New York's streets, also, and nothing was to prevail against them for years to come.

Hall had the support of the clergy, the Brooklyn Temperance Society, the Brooklyn Young Men's Temperance Society, and Alden Spooner's *Star*. He was elected by a rather narrow majority and was afterward Brooklyn's first mayor under the city charter granted in 1834.

By the mid-thirties Brooklyn had become a neat little city of 25,000, already noted for its steady habits, a city of homes and churches and seminaries and lecture courses, a city with "a character for morals," as Alden Spooner put it. Its cosmopolitan character was becoming more and more marked, but in very many important respects the Yankees continued to call the tune. The temperance crusade was matched by other enthusiasms, which enlisted recruits quite as devoted.

One of these was a remarkable wave of popular enlightenment set in motion by a Yankee named Josiah Holbrook. He had gathered groups of farmers and mechanics in New England villages into local lyceums, to study and discuss the arts and sciences. These groups multiplied rapidly, and an elaborate organization such as that of the temperance

movement was planned, with county, state, and national societies. When a New York Lyceum convention was announced, Brooklynites promptly called a meeting, which
was presided over by Joseph Sprague—himself a Massachusetts Yankee. Delegates were elected and duly attended
the affair, where they listened to a stream of talk about
education and general culture, the very latest Yankee notions in the field of enlightenment.

One of the delegates was Gabriel Furman, the Brooklyn
annalist. Furman was nothing if not an industrious note-
taker. He took notes coolly and methodically, with the combined instincts of a reporter and a scholar, wherever anything of interest to him was happening—in the street when
crowds were surging through Brooklyn to the Jamaica race
course, on the ferryboat, along the waterfront, in the quiet
of his study. At the Lyceum Convention he recorded the
revolutionary ideas of the speakers with an amused skepti-
cism. He was not the man to be bowled over by New England enthusiasts.

Others, however, were more susceptible, and the Brooklyn Lyceum was organized in 1833. Its zealous promoters—
including Peter W. Radcliff and Theodore Eames—believed that the citizens of a democracy ought to be well-
informed. Although they professed a great interest in the
public schools, it was really an adult education movement, and its favorite method was the popular lecture.
Brooklyn's Yankee intellectuals—the lawyers and the
schoolmasters with degrees from Yale and Dartmouth and
other New England colleges—got behind it with enthusiasm, and in the first year of its existence lectured throughout the winter in Eames and Putnam's Classical Hall. The
Lyceum flourished for a number of years, and a granite-
front building to house it arose on Washington Street. But
it had little or no endowment, and the disastrous panic

which hit the country in 1837 killed it. The building remained, however, to furnish a home for its successor, the Brooklyn Institute, which was made secure by a substantial gift from Augustus Graham.

There were currents running deeper than those which carried the temperance movement and adult education to their partial successes. One of them—it proved to be the deepest and most powerful of all—was the antislavery passion.

The Colonization Society, headed by Van Sinderen, furnished a rather feeble outlet for that feeling. There was an air of harmless respectability about it. Benevolent citizens could automatically set aside a little portion of their incomes for it, feel virtuous, and concern themselves no more. Practically all Brooklynites were against slavery, but few wished to make a fuss about it. For some good citizens the Colonization Society was a way out. It satisfied their consciences, and it disturbed nobody.

Yet not all the citizens of Brooklyn in the early '30s shared this view of sunshine and calm. A little band of abolitionists, most of them Yankees, began to stir things up. In numbers they were few, but they were well educated, high in social standing, and loud with the zeal of holiness. They cried out that slavery was immoral, a monstrous crime, a sin in the sight of God. They denounced slaveholders as creatures of evil. They proclaimed the failure of colonization, pointing out that only some 1,200 free Negroes had been sent to Africa in the fifteen years since the Society was founded—fewer than the number of Negroes born into slavery in America every week. The slave system was meanwhile, the abolitionists said, more firmly intrenched in the South than ever before, and the demand for slaves in the cotton states was insatiable. Colonization, they insisted, was futile.

The Brooklyn abolitionists were inspired by the unrelenting propaganda of William Lloyd Garrison, of Boston, and other zealots. In 1833, in Philadelphia, the American Anti-Slavery Society was launched by the extremists. Its program challenged the gradual policy of colonization at every point. Branches of the new society sprang up throughout the eastern and middle states, and in the new West. Lectures, sermons, and the printing press spread the abolitionist gospel. Garrison, who pursued the slaveowner in the columns of his *Liberator,* was the brightest of the firebrands, but by no means the only one.

Other propagandists of the reform, such as the flaming evangelist Charles G. Finney, were spreading the seeds of radical antislavery in New York State and Ohio. The young farmer-poet of Amesbury, John Greenleaf Whittier, wrote stanzas lamenting the bitter wrongs of the slaves in rice swamps and cottonfields. Enthusiasts and poets in Brooklyn took fire, and spoke, and wrote, and kept up a constant agitation.

Moderate Brooklynites—steady, cool-headed men like Alden Spooner—were alarmed. They wanted, they expected, gradual reform, and they were sure that abolitionism would only rivet more firmly the chains of the slaves. But the abolitionists continued on their way.

In 1835 a Brooklyn antislavery society was formed. Most of its members—not all of them—were Yankees. One was David Leavitt; another was Arthur Tappan, a wealthy New York merchant, of New England origin, who had recently moved to Brooklyn. He and his brother Lewis supplied a large part of the funds which sustained the movement in New York. A third was Elizur Wright, a young Ohio college professor who darted around the country to promote the cause.

The ranks of the reformers in Brooklyn were split wide

apart, as conservative stood against radical, coloniza-
tionist against abolitionist. The quarrel was, so to speak,
between prudence and conscience, not only in Brooklyn
but throughout the country. Prudence spoke in the years
that followed through the voices of tolerant men of varying shades of opinion. Some were community leaders,
such as Van Sinderin; some were more obscure men, such
as the young Illinois legislator Abraham Lincoln. Some,
like Lincoln, hated slavery, but could not hate the slave-
holder. All threw their influence against the enthusiasts,
and by their prudence gave the Union time to prepare
for its great test in the sixties.

But conscience spoke ever more insistently in the pro-
vocative tones of the abolitionists. It spoke raucously in
the columns of the Boston *Liberator* and the New York
Emancipator. It spoke tenderly and even sentimentally
in the lines of verses written by Lucy Hooper, of Brooklyn.

Miss Hooper, a Massachusetts girl who came to Brooklyn in the '30s, was the heroine of one of those misty and
pathetic romances dear to the nineteenth-century heart.
Just what happened between her and John Greenleaf
Whittier no one knows. For a time she saw much of Whittier, who came to New York as secretary of the American
Anti-Slavery Society in 1837, and sought rest in Brooklyn's quiet, shaded streets. She was heart and soul with
the movement and was dedicated to poetry. Whittier, a
sympathetic young man, encouraged her.

Whether with a moralist's gift he combined a rigid
sense of duty with a fondness for female company and
thus broke Lucy Hooper's heart, we do not know. The
affair, if one can give it so definite a name, was incon-
clusive. A few years later Lucy Hooper died. Whittier,
hearing the tragic news, wrote an elegy for her. Whether

he loved her or not is a mystery. His connection with
her was her chief claim to fame.* Yet her verses had
their own modest worth, apart from her possible love for
the dark-eyed poet. Her lines had the genuine ardor for
emancipation. In 1838, when Great Britain, carrying out
the gradual emancipation of the Act of 1833, freed the
last slaves in the West Indian islands and New York
abolitionists held a meeting to celebrate the event, Miss
Hooper wrote:

> It was not mine to meet
> In the full temple, while the closing day
> Shone through the sacred aisles, and wildly sweet
> From many a heart the swelling hymn found sway
> Praise and Thanksgiving—that the galling chain
> Has melted from the Islands of the main!
>
> .   .   .
>
> Nor was it theirs to see
> Who met in that full temple, how the sun
> Looked down that morning, glorious on the free,
> Whose bitter days of toil and stripes were done;
> When the loud bell, that tolled their bondage out,
> Was lost in Freedom's overwhelming shout! †

Earnest abolitionists were relatively few in Brooklyn
in the thirties, but they had one great advantage. They had
faced the issue squarely and were sure that eternal right
was on their side. Alden Spooner, the aging editor, was
deeply disturbed. He feared the consequences to the
Federal Union of such deep passions. He spoke the sentiments of most of the stanch, solid, dependable, respectable Yankees in Brooklyn society. Some of them endorsed

---

* *See* Samuel T. Pickard, *Life and Letters of John Greenleaf Whittier,*
Boston, 1894, I, 204, 210, 211–14; Albert Mordell, *Quaker Militant: John
Greenleaf Whittier,* Boston, 1933, pp. 89, 109–13.
† *Poetical Remains of the Late Lucy Hooper,* New York, 1842, pp. 280–84.

the assurance which many New Englanders and New
Yorkers gave to the alarmed slaveholders—saying that
all but a handful of Northerners were friendly to the
South and despised abolitionists as heartily as Southern-
ers did.

Irish Sons and Daughters

THE YEAR was 1847. Brooklyn was a city of 70,000, or thereabouts, and growing so fast that population figures were out of date as soon as they were compiled. One enthusiast, pointing to its trees and gardens, declared that it was the "most beautiful city in the world." In early May a Brooklyn journalist by the name of Walt Whitman, strolling indolently through the streets, noted that the horse chestnuts "had burst out their bright green leaves" and that the peach and early cherry trees were in bloom. Brooklyn would soon be "in its pride and glory." *

It was to a large extent a city of small and moderate-sized homes. To that fact Whitman ascribed much of Brooklyn's remarkable growth. New York was for the rich and for the poor. There was no medium there, he declared (somewhat hyperbolically), "between a palatial mansion and a dilapidated hovel." In Brooklyn "men of moderate means" could find homes "at a moderate cost." In consequence, Brooklyn had a large number of middle-class people, and "the most valuable class in any community," commented this writer of moderate means, "is the middle class." †

In that year of 1847 Brooklyn's middle class included many Irish people. In its upper social strata there were a dozen or so well-to-do Irish families. Two or three were

* Brooklyn *Daily Eagle*, May 3, 1847.
† Brooklyn *Daily Times*, May 13, 1858.

very wealthy. Yet most of them were newly come and poor.

In '47 the well-to-do Irish belonged to well-established families who had first come to Brooklyn decades earlier. As old settlers, they had watched the Irish population grow steadily and had aided in its growth. The stream of Celtic Irish to New York, a mere trickle in the early years of the century, swelled in the decade after the War of 1812 and became a flood in the thirties and forties. The side flow to Brooklyn was at first very small, but it grew rapidly after the mid-twenties. Now the Irish were crowding in so rapidly that an end to the Dutch-Yankee monopoly in the management of Brooklyn affairs was unmistakably foreshadowed.

The Irish came to America because conditions on their native island were intolerable. In the land of tiny farms and great English-owned estates the growing population found no outlet. Landlord and tenant were pitted against each other. Hatred of English control had not died in the Irish people, who remembered Cromwell with clear bitterness. Tithes were exacted from a Catholic people to support a Protestant state church. Irish ambitions were sternly repressed, and rebellion lay always beneath the surface. It broke out in the rebellion of 1798, which ended in a fiasco, and again feebly in Robert Emmet's uprising, which flickered only for a moment in the streets of Dublin in 1803.

Discontent and hopelessness lay over Erin. Looking for an escape and a chance, more and more Irishmen set out across the North Atlantic, getting their passage in any way they could. America called them, and as the decades wore on, thousands followed Irish thousands in search of liberty and a decent living. When the potato famine came as an unspeakably tragic climax of misery,

many starved in the green island, and the thousands of
immigrants increased manyfold.

This movement was, of course, but a single chapter
in the westward migration of Europe's restless peoples, but
the Irish chapter had its own special meaning and characteristics. It is, perhaps, not fanciful to see that the
Irish movement took a special color from the Celtic
imagination, which fired readily to enthusiasm in re-
sponse to stories of Irish success in the United States.
The stories of boys who had left Ireland with nothing except their own wit and courage and had shortly won comfort and luxury in the New World were told and retold
about the firesides of Ireland.

There were many such lads. Though the stories of the
husky immigrants varied immensely in detail, there was
a certain likeness of fortune in the general outlines, a
sort of type story of a typical Irishman who won typical
success in Brooklyn. Let us imagine one such immigrant,
who was not an actual man, but rather one hundred men
melted together to make a fictional character. Let us
call him John Curran.

John Curran, then, was a native of Galway. When he
had grown to be eighteen, he looked about him and
found his prospects narrow, and his discontent was increased when he read a pamphlet entitled *Hints to Irishmen Who Intend to Make a Permanent Residence in
America.* One of its sponsors was Thomas Addis Emmet,
elder brother of the martyred Robert Emmet, and the
very name was greeted with deep emotion by the many
young Irishmen who read it. John, dissatisfied, was more
and more enticed by the golden light that seemed to
shine across the Atlantic, until finally he made his way
to Dublin with his hard-earned passage money in his

pocket. He boarded an American packet for the hope-filled voyage across the ocean.

His expectations may have been shadowed by some doubts during the voyage on the crowded and not-too-clean ship, and when he landed in New York he was surrounded by a horde of petty criminals—vultures who lay in wait for innocent immigrants, ready to strip them of all they possessed. John Curran may have been given a helping hand by Thomas Addis Emmet, who helped many such young men to escape the parasites. Probably when he went to Brooklyn he was aided and befriended—at least with good advice—by some Brooklyn men who took an especial interest in promising young Irishmen: Peter Turner, George S. Wise, and Robert Snow. And in a little while he was hard at work, for labor was needed in Brooklyn in the years following the War of 1812, and John was a hearty man to swing a pick.

He did not long labor with his hands. He was ambitious, and before long he was a clerk in a grocery store. By the time he was ready, a few years later, to send back to the Ould Country for his sweetheart, Katie Phelan, he had saved very little money, yet he was looking forward to buying a store of his own. When Katie arrived, the two were married by Father John Power in St. Peter's Church on Manhattan, for Brooklyn did not yet have a Roman Catholic church.

It was not until 1822 that Peter Turner, a grocer who lived at the corner of Washington and Front Streets—Peter Turner, whose son was to be vicar general of the Diocese of Brooklyn—took the first step leading to the founding of a Catholic church in Brooklyn. At his home a small company gathered to make plans. They found that seventy persons could be expected to help: some

could give money, and others (such as the imaginary John
Curran) could give only the labor of their hands and
brains.

Cornelius Heeney offered to give an acre tract at the
corner of Court and Congress streets, on the outskirts of
the village, but this was considered too far out for the
convenience of the parishioners. Instead, a spot was chosen
nearer to the heart of things, at the corner of Jay and
Chapel streets. Eight lots were bought. In April the ground
was consecrated by Bishop Connolly, "in the presence,"
said the *Star,* "of a large concourse of respectful and atten-
tive listeners."

St. James Church, as it was called, was dedicated in
August, 1823. The occasion, which marked the introduction of Catholicism into a community that had been exclusively Protestant for two centuries, attracted the interest of all Brooklyn. Bishop Connolly officiated, and
Father Power, of St. Peter's, very popular in Brooklyn,
spoke eloquently. Spooner, the Yankee editor, took note,
commenting that "our country is happily blessed with
proper feelings on the subject of religious toleration."

As a bookseller, he marked the beginning of the new
church by stocking his bookstore with prayerbooks and
missals and Catholic religious books, such as *Paths to
Paradise.* He showed in that same year his own sense of
the balance of religious toleration by offering Dwight's
metrical version of the Psalms to the Presbyterians who
had just dedicated their first Brooklyn church, on Cranberry Street.

Our fictional John Curran could not give money for the
erection of St. James, but a few years later his fortunes
had improved, and when a branch of the Friends of Ireland was organized, he was able to contribute to the gifts
sent to aid Daniel O'Connell, who was fighting for Catho-

lic Emancipation in Ireland. He was not only better off, he was also a well-integrated member of the Irish-American community. He had marched with his brother members of the Erin Fraternal Society in a parade on July 4, 1825, to welcome the visiting Lafayette, who graciously assisted in laying the cornerstone of the Apprentices' Library in Brooklyn. John Curran, in his own way, had a genius for friendship and for politics. In national politics he was a stanch Democrat, and helped to bring out the vote for Andrew Jackson. In local politics he was an adherent of the brilliant Brooklyn lawyer Henry Cruse Murphy. His connections helped John Curran immeasurably on his climb up from laboring man to prosperous grocer.

Prosperous he was in 1847. He was a respectable pew-holder at St. James, and every Sunday he and his wife and the youngest Curran boy went to 10:30 mass. Some of the five older children, now all married, would sometimes sit in the old family pew, too, and all the neighbors would recognize the solidity of the family front. The Currans lived in a three-story brick dwelling with a strip of green before it and a deep garden with fruit trees behind. Beyond the garden towered the steepled and weather-vaned stable, large enough to house a phaeton and two carriage horses. The whole home was one of middle-class comfort and content. And the faces of John Curran and his Katie, in a stiff daguerreotype likeness taken by Corduan and Fay on Fulton Street, also showed middle-class comfort and worthy content, though little of the personalities of the two.

Many versions of the story of John Curran could be told, and were told, over and over again by the firesides of Ireland. The stories sped the coming of the Irish. At the beginning of the century there had been a few Irish families on Vinegar Hill, between the ferry and Wallabout, and a few Protestant Irish at the ferry. The name Vinegar Hill commemorated one of the gallant stands in the Irish rebellion of 1798, and attracted to the region refugees whose blood was stirred and whose hearts were warmed by such an association. One of the Irish immigrants at the ferry was Thomas Kirk, a Methodist printer, who in 1800 started Brooklyn's first and unsuccessful newspaper, the *Long Island Courier,* and in 1809 tried again, with the *Long Island Star,* which he sold two years later to Alden Spooner. Another was the gentle, guileless Robert Snow, also a Methodist, a friend of youth and the first president of the Apprentices' Library. A handful of Irish enlisted under Captain Joseph Dean in the War of 1812, and in August, 1814, when British invasion was feared, 1,500 Irish troops from New York marched into Brooklyn to help man the trenches at Fort Greene constructed by Brooklyn's "patriotic diggers."

In the era of Governor Clinton's Great Western Canal project high wages for mechanics and workers lured many Irish, and some of them settled in Brooklyn. By 1822 there were Irish tavernkeepers, grocers, and shopkeepers, as well as many Irish newcomers who did the back-breaking and dangerous work at docks and in the ropewalks and the distilleries. Some were licensed cartmen. One milkman, George McCloskey, had a son who was to be Bishop of Louisville. Other sons of laborers and mechanics were to become famous, and many new settlers themselves arrived at some local standing, while still later arrivals took over the harder work. By 1847 St. James Church had some four thousand communicants.

The Brooklyn Irish did not lose their Irishness by their transplantation. On the great celebrations on July 4 and on Saint Patrick's Day the members of the Erin Fraternal

Association drank sincere toasts to "America, the Land of Our Adoption" and to "Ireland, the Land of Our Nativity." The "fair daughters of Ireland" were praised along with the fair daughters of America. The revelers saw no contradiction in their two loyalties, and indeed there was none. The Protestant Irish joined with the Catholic Irish in the celebrations that ended at Duflon's Military Garden, and Yankees and Dutchmen contributed also to the funds raised for Daniel O'Connell by the Friends of Ireland. Yet the Irish felt still, to a great extent, that they were "foreigners," and in the list of subscribers for the O'Connell fund the label "American" was written beside the names of all the non-Irish donors except one, and that was firmly noted as "English." *

The Catholic immigrants had their own institutions, not only St. James Church but also a parochial school run by the Sisters of Charity in the basement of the church and an orphan asylum started by Peter Turner, J. Sullivan Thorne, and others. These foundations were not, of course, anti-American or un-American, but they did mark off the Irish as "different" from their neighbors.

Brooklyn had other "foreigners" too—Germans newly arrived, French dancing masters, Italian musicians. The older settlers viewed them as "odd," and the editor of the *Star* did not hesitate to call William Knight Northall, a rival editor who had been an English dentist, a "foreigner," as a term of opprobrium. But the Irish were the principal targets of a fanatical wave of antiforeignism that arose in the thirties and forties.

There had been warnings of it in minor incidents in Brooklyn, New York, and other cities. Hostility had been shown toward Irish workers, who would often underbid in the highly competitive labor markets of the port cities. Re-

* *Long Island Star*, February 26, 1829.

sentment had been expressed because the Jackson Democrats successfully corralled the Irish vote. Some Protestants were concerned over the influx of Catholics into the
cities, a flood which threatened sometime to swamp the
prevalent Yankee culture.

The greatly increased immigration of the thirties and
forties accentuated all these factors. Nativism, however,
was only one of the emotional currents that swept through
the country in those decades. Fears of many kinds were
making the people jittery. Fears that Andrew Jackson's
"dictatorship" would ruin the country troubled many
solid citizens. The fear of secret orders fed the fanaticism
of anti-Masonry. Fear of abolitionism, fear of the slave
power, and fear of the prospect of disunion were all felt
by different groups of citizens in Brooklyn.

Some of these fears were in reality the fear of democracy. The old order was instinctively seeking to ward off
the changes that seemed to be impending. The Nativist
movement, at any rate, was definitely undemocratic.

People who had looked upon the Irish with friendliness in the twenties began to take alarm in the thirties,
as these fears were played upon by skillful agitators.
Editors gradually changed their tunes to suit the shift-
ing tempers. Whigs made use of Nativism for substantial political reasons, just as they had made use of anti-
Masonry. Spooner, the self-confessed "friend of Irishmen,"
gradually became an alarmist and raised the hue and cry
against all "foreigners," but quickly lost his heat after election day.

The Native Americans several times proved strong
enough to elect candidates in Brooklyn, running either
as Nativists or on both Nativist and Whig tickets. They
reached their maximum strength in the mid-forties, and

then subsided, to be revived again in the fifties as the
Know-Nothing party.

The badgered and bewildered Irish citizens of Brooklyn had a difficult role to play during the successive waves
of Nativist hysteria. They did not in any proper sense op-
pose it. They just lived through it. They were not, however, without friends who kept faith with the American
principles of toleration and freedom of worship. One of
these friends was the plainspoken rector of St. John's Episcopal Church, the Reverend Evan Johnson.

Brooklynites were fond of calling him Dominy Johnson. On Thanksgiving Day, 1835, he preached a sermon
which aroused a storm of controversy in Brooklyn and in
the City of New York. It was a root and branch condemnation of Nativism and a trenchant exposition of "the nature and duty of religious toleration." Perhaps the sermon was an act of expiation, for Dominy Johnson (not
understanding what was afoot) had permitted Brownlee
and Bourne of New York, two of the chief hatchers of
the mischief, to open their Brooklyn campaign in his
church, in the spring of 1832.

Whitman noted with satisfaction, in 1846, that the
Native American party was losing public confidence.
He wrote in the *Eagle,* "Our good friends the 'Native
Americans' (we humor them to that title) are determined
to die game. They have made up their minds—at least
their organs say so—to nominate a candidate for next
fall's gubernatorial contest—and here and there for assemblyman. Well, be it so. We could wish that the Natives
had withdrawn from a field where the people are so evidently against them. If, however, they insist on being
beaten beyond the possibility of hope, those who disagree
with their political principles are doubtless content . . .

The Natives may nominate governors and assemblymen
for an age; they will hardly get any decent vote for
them." *

While the Nativist agitation was going on, the lives of
distinguished Irishmen in Brooklyn were in themselves
the best answer to their enemies. Many of them were
"making good" in a way their neighbors could understand
and admire—by making money and going forward in
business and politics. William Baird and James Collins,
active Democratic politicians, made fortunes as contractors on the public roads. Jeremiah O'Donnell also got rich
as a road contractor. Francis O'Brien was a Whig, with
business and political interests in New York. The Buck-
leys, the Callaghans, the O'Haras, the Kearneys, the Mc-
Brides, the McFarlans, and the MacGuires were all well-
to-do in the mid-forties. Some of them had great wealth.

Cornelius Heeney, who had offered St. James Church an
acre of land, was a philanthropist, and as true an American as any man in Brooklyn. His career had been of the
very stuff of adventure. He had sailed for America soon
after the Revolution. His ship was struck by lightning and
wrecked in Delaware Bay. He was picked up by an oyster
boat and got a job in Philadelphia with a Quaker lumber
dealer. He had extraordinary qualities—those natural gifts
which enable a man to take advantage of circumstances
and achieve business success. He soon went to New York,
where he rose rapidly in the firm of another Quaker merchant, a dealer in furs named Backhouse. While thus employed, he became acquainted with a shrewd young German immigrant named John Jacob Astor. He and Astor
went into business on their own account, as partners. The
partnership soon dissolved, but Heeney continued in the
fur business for many years.

* Brooklyn *Daily Eagle,* June 26, 1846.

He was a bachelor all his days, but he was no misanthrope. He opened his house and his orchard in South Brooklyn to orphan children, and he opened his pocketbook to their needs. When he died, little of his wealth was left. It had gone to the poor and the struggling, to the building of Catholic churches and orphanages, and to the endowment of The Trustees and Associates of the Brooklyn Benevolent Society, which was to distribute millions in relief.

If the story of Heeney's wealth could be put in terms of the lives it affected, it would be a thrilling tale and a long one. It would tell, for instance, of a young couple, Patrick and Elizabeth McCloskey, of County Derry, Ireland, who came to the Ferry in the early years of the century, and of their boy John, who was born in 1810. It would tell that Patrick McCloskey secured employment as a clerk with one of the Ferry's chief men of affairs, Hezekiah B. Pierrepont; that a few years later he died; that Cornelius Heeney became the boy's guardian; and that in the year 1875 the boy, now a distinguished clergyman, became the first American cardinal.

As altruistic, perhaps, as Heeney, but differing from him in nearly every other respect, was Henry Cruse Murphy, the Democratic leader. In 1847 he was still in his middle thirties. His grandfather Timothy Murphy, a physician, had come over from Ireland before the Revolution and had settled in New Jersey. Early in the nineteenth century Timothy's son John Garrison Murphy, a skilled mechanic and millwright, moved to Brooklyn. Like the Irish-born Brooklynites Robert Snow, first president of the Apprentices' Library, and Thomas Kirk, the printer, John Garrison was a Protestant. He won local fame as an inventor, devising an improved horse ferryboat. Before coming to Brooklyn he had married the daughter of an old Dutch family in New Jersey; hence Henry Cruse Murphy had the blood of the colonial race in his veins. In his case the meeting of the two blood streams—Irish and Dutch—was most fortunate.

He was resourceful and conservative, brilliant and methodical. His public career began before he was admitted to the bar. After being graduated from Columbia at the age of twenty, he studied law with Peter W. Radcliff, and simultaneously wrote political editorials for the Brooklyn *Advocate*. At twenty-four he was city attorney, at thirty-one he became mayor, and he was sent to Congress before his term as mayor expired. Meanwhile, he was associated with Isaac Van Anden in the establishment (in 1841) of the Brooklyn *Eagle* and helped to edit it for a time.

This busy editor, lawyer, and politician was also a scholar, engaged in the collection of one of the finest private libraries in America. By 1847—aged thirty-seven —he had already done far more for his city than most public men manage to achieve in a lifetime. In that year, fortified by his experience in Brooklyn politics, he went to the state constitutional convention and fought, without success, for constitutional provisions which he believed would improve city government. His greatest achievements still lay far ahead of him.

Heeney the Catholic and Murphy the Protestant were both American in the spectacular dramas of their careers. Most of the Celtic Irishmen of Brooklyn had lesser individual roles, but collectively their performance was impressive. They—the John Currans and hosts of others— had already done much to make the town what it was. They could take pride in it. In the spring of 1847 they could read in the *Eagle* that summer was near and that their town was worth living in. "Then, in all the blocks between Fulton St. and the Heights," wrote the editor, in anticipatory mood, "will lie a dreamy shady quiet, under the trees that line the walks there, and through the ample yards. Then Brooklyn will have its green robes about its shoulders, and its skirts will be not a little draggled with the wet dews when it walks out in the morning." *

* *Eagle,* May 3, 1847.

Yankee Heyday

FROM THEIR GARDENS on the Heights, Yankee merchants, in the mid-century, could watch their own fast, graceful clippers glide proudly down the bay, bound around the Horn to California and China. At that time, one of the most enterprising of the alert fraternity of traders was Abiel Abbott Low. The first clipper in the Low fleet, the "Houqua," named for an old "hong" merchant of Canton, had then earned its cost over and over again, and already it had some famous successors. In 1850 one of them, the "Oriental," had broken the record from Hongkong to London, making the run around the Cape of Good Hope in ninety-seven days.

The Heights merchants swept the bay with their long glasses, but their vision and their calculations swept the globe. By birth and training they were fitted for a grand era in American commerce. In Low's blood, when he came to Brooklyn as a boy of nineteen, were the seafaring traditions of Salem. He had packed plenty of excitement into the twenty-odd years since he had left his clerk's stool there. His father, Seth Low, moved his East Indian drug house to New York in 1829, and took up his residence in Brooklyn. Young Low spent about three years with him, but in 1833 he sailed to China for a seven-year stay in the Canton foreign settlement, and there he became a partner in Russell & Company, the largest American house at the Chinese port. When he returned to the United States he set up his own New York firm.

Now he was in his forties, and his business was rising

to a great pitch of prosperity. Like many another Brooklyn merchant, he was a man of two cities. New York knew him as a prince of traders, but Brooklyn knew him as a promoter of education and general culture. There were hopeful movements that were given the breath of life and nurtured into full institutional status by men such as Low, not merely by their money benefactions but also by their shrewd and careful counsel.

A man like Low in some respects, and very unlike him in others, was Gordon Lester Ford. Ford was also descended from that hardy breed of New Englanders who believed in plunging a boy without delay into the practical business of life. He was Connecticut-born, of a line descended from a Massachusetts settler of 1654. In the middle 1830s, when he was eleven, his schooling and childhood were both over, and he was sent to New York to work for his uncle George Burnham, a well-to-do merchant. The boy got a good training. In his case there was a variation from the usual Yankee pattern, for in his early years in New York he acquired from the John Gray family, with whom he lived, a decided Quaker slant.

He worked with exemplary zeal and rose to be a substantial businessman at a time in life when many young fellows of today are looking for their first job. At twenty-nine he returned to Connecticut for a few years, to be president of a new railroad line that cut through the eastern hills of that state. While in New England he married the daughter of an Amherst professor, a young lady who was also the granddaughter of Noah Webster. The Fords returned to New York in 1856, and soon afterward moved across the river to Brooklyn.

This remarkable couple and their remarkable sons were lively factors in Brooklyn's business, political, social, and cultural life for a half century. In spite of his lack of formal

schooling, Ford had all the instincts of a scholar. In spite
of his practical, rigorous training and habits and the natural aptitude for business which inevitably made him a
rich man, he was much more than a money grabber. He
was an idealist, a humanitarian, and an abolitionist. Like
Low, he took his civic responsibilities very seriously.

But the merchants and the scholarly men of business
were not alone in making Brooklyn what it was in the
mid-nineteenth century. There were many ingredients in
the mixture that the genius of Brooklyn's Yankees was
concocting. Conscience and enlightenment and business
enterprise were stirred in with vigor. Indefatigable lecturers from transcendentalism's holy places, prophets of
science and of temperance and of abolition, capitalists,
manufacturers, "Shakespearean readers," amateur actors,
tuneful melodists, scholars, editors, preachers, philanthropists—all of them made their contributions. Brooklyn, to
a considerable degree, became an outpost of New England.

But it was also closely tied to New York City, and it
was influenced in a thousand ways by its neighbor. It was
an integral part of the great port, and the tides of population that flowed into the port encroached ever more
deeply upon the Brooklyn shore. Yankee enterprise came
from other points of the compass than New England—
from the new West, for instance, and from upstate New
York, in the persons of a breezy popular preacher, Henry
Ward Beecher, and the imaginative and daring city planner Colonel Daniel Richards. Richards had surveyed the
empty shore line of South Brooklyn in the early 1840s,
and in his mind great vessels were already moored in
Atlantic Basin and new streets were already teeming with
life. These things he and others after him brought to pass,
men who could think and plan and act,

Many leaders who were neither Yankees nor Dutchmen were coming rapidly to the front in Brooklyn's affairs, but Yankees were still dominant in business and manufacturing in that period of rapid expansion. Brooklyn-made hats were covering the heads of nearly every man in America and were a considerable export item, the city's farm machinery, glassware, brass, and copper goods, chemicals, white lead, and cordage were finding expanding markets. Greenpoint shipyards had begun to rival those on the Manhattan shore above Corlaer's Hook. The first vessel which went out from Eckford Webb's Greenpoint yard—soon one of the busiest in the port—was a little river steamboat named the Honda, which for many decades carried passengers up the Magdalena River into the deep interior of Colombia. In 1855 Greenpoint, Williamsburg, and Bushwick were absorbed by the City of Brooklyn.

The first mayor of the "consolidated" city, as it was called, was George Hall, the champion of temperance who had been first mayor of Brooklyn under its original charter, more than twenty years earlier. When he took office, he addressed the Common Council and surveyed Brooklyn's material condition.* He was proud to report that the city, swollen by consolidation to a population of two hundred thousand, had become the third in size in the Union, that it now had an area of twenty-five square miles, and that it boasted eight and a half miles of water front. He informed the city fathers that there were thirty miles of railroad track in the corporate limits, by which he meant tracks for the horsecars. This was looked upon as substantial progress; but twelve lines of stages and omnibuses remained in operation to form a link with the

* Henry R. Stiles, *A History of the City of Brooklyn*, Brooklyn, 1869, II, 418–20.

past. Editor Walt Whitman had little to say about horse-cars, but he wrote with gusto of the Brooklyn stages and their drivers and of rolling down to Fort Hamilton through miles of open country. For the most part, gas lights had superseded oil lamps in the city's streets, but there were still districts where the lamplighter made his rounds, cleaning chimneys and filling lamps by day and lighting each one as twilight approached.

It was not until 1859 that a modern water system became a fact, and Brooklyn staged the biggest celebration in its history up to that time. The affair rivaled New York's gigantic fete of the previous decade, when the miracle of Croton water was hailed by an excited populace. In Brooklyn twelve thousand people and three thousand horses paraded, fountains cascaded, orators thundered, and three hundred thousand spectators cheered —half of them New Yorkers who crossed the ferries to share the excitement.

But let us return for a moment to Mayor Hall and his prideful statistical summary. In addressing the Common Council, he took note of the fact that Brooklyn then had twenty-seven public schools and more than 30,000 "scholars," in addition to its numerous private day and boarding schools. He pointed out that the spires of one hundred and thirteen churches pierced Brooklyn's sky. He boasted that thirteen ferries provided constant communication with New York and promoted Brooklyn's prodigious growth as a residential suburb. Brooklyn, it was evident, had become quite a town.

One of the truly Yankee features of the city was Beecher's Plymouth Church. Its new building stood on Orange Street. It was more like a great lecture hall than a church, offering a striking contrast to some of its neighbors on the Heights—Upjohn's and Lefevre's Gothic creations, with their elaborate symbolisms. But it was exactly the right setting for the forty-two-year-old preacher orator from the West. All he needed was a platform, one that would put him close to the crowd. The crowds came, and Beecher thrived on them. In that decade he made Plymouth a great national forum.

The biting, uncompromising accents of Wendell Phillips, Yankee apostle of abolitionism, were heard there. The abolitionist Congressman from Ohio, Joshua R. Giddings, lashed out against slavery there in his bitter, acid tones. More urbane, but powerful in his denunciation of the national evil, the self-made scholar and essayist, George William Curtis, stood on Plymouth's platform. Senator Charles Sumner, of Massachusetts, spoke there—the statesman whose blistering scorn, directed against Senator Butler of South Carolina would provoke a caning at his Senate desk which would come near to killing him. These men and others—but most of all Beecher himself—made Plymouth Church a powerhouse, a generating center for the tides of opinion which swept the nation on toward war. They did not seek war, but they were busily fostering a national temper which would at last make compromise impossible.

In May, 1850, a tense and expectant audience heard Phillips there for the first time. In that year California was asking to be admitted as a free state, and Southern extremists were threatening dissolution of the Union unless all agitation against slavery came to an end. Certainly, a great majority of Brooklyn's Yankees had agreed with the reasoning of Daniel Webster's "7th of March Speech" in the Senate, in which the great champion of the Union had coolly weighed the issues and declared himself for compromise. But the speech had maddened the abolitionists and had provoked Whittier's bitter "Ichabod."

In New York a mob had broken up the May meeting of

the American Anti-slavery Society, and every hall in the
city was closed against discussion of the dangerous theme.
It was in this atmosphere—charged with passion nationally
and locally—that Beecher opened Plymouth Church to
Phillips, to vindicate, as he explained, "freedom of speech
and freedom of conscience."

While New York's officials were failing to protect these
American principles, Brooklyn's mayor, Samuel Smith, upheld Beecher by attending the affair. Hundreds of other
Brooklynites who had no use for abolitionism, but thought
that its advocates ought not to be muzzled, were there.
Phillips, wrote Beecher, "seemed inspired, and played with
his audience (turbulent, of course) as Gulliver might with
the Liliputians." He was amazed at the unagitated agitator,
"so calm, so fearless, so incisive—every word a bullet." *

Later in that year Congress passed the famous Compromise, including a fugitive slave act which apparently left
no loophole for the release of an accused Negro. Two
Yankee preachers of Brooklyn took opposite stands on this
measure. Dr. Spencer, of the Second Presbyterian Church,
upheld the law with vigor, denounced half allegiance, and
declared that Government must be obeyed or abolished.
Richard Salter Storrs, the scholarly young pastor of the
Church of the Pilgrims, who was very far from being an
abolitionist firebrand, solemnly asserted the duty of civil
disobedience when a law so plainly contravened conscience. These preachers made articulate the conflict that
was going on in the minds of the people.

Many sober-minded Brooklynites who had no patience
with extremists on either side of the slavery question were
shocked by the glaring injustice of the fugitive slave law.
Against their will they were being driven to take a stand in
opposition to the South. In 1852 sympathy for the victims

* Carlos Martyn, *Wendell Phillips: The Agitator,* p. 231.

of slavery was roused to a new high pitch in Brooklyn and throughout the Northern States. The cause of this was a book published in that year and called *Uncle Tom's Cabin;* its author was the sister of the pastor of Plymouth Church.

Excitement rose higher still when the Kansas-Nebraska bill inaugurated a struggle between "Free State" settlers and "border ruffians" for the control of Kansas. More and more people became convinced that there was no satisfying the slave power—that it intended to force slavery into the territories and then to press on for further gains. The Emigrant Aid Society, which was organized to send Northern "Free Staters" into Kansas, began to equip them with breech-loading Sharpe's rifles to enable them to cope with the Missourians, who crossed the border with Springfield muskets taken from the Missouri state arsenal. Beecher, at a meeting in New Haven in 1856, gave his blessing to this Yankee enterprise to protect freedom in Kansas, and from that moment the Sharpe's rifles were known as "Beecher's Bibles." With his instinct for drama, he kept the antislavery flame alive by auctioning slave girls in Plymouth Church. And when John Brown's raid at Harper's Ferry alarmed the country, in 1859, and spread a dread of the future throughout the North as well as the South, he again invited Wendell Phillips to speak in the Orange Street forum.

The fame—many would have said the notoriety—of the church and its pastor had spread into the remotest parts of the country since Phillips appeared there in 1850. He now spoke to an audience that had been going through the successive shocks of the most ominous decade in the country's history. He himself had changed. He had been opposed to violence hitherto, but now defended Brown's act in a burning, slashing speech that struck the audience with a terrifying impact.

It was the first of November, 1859, that Phillips spoke.

A few months later a prairie lawyer named Abraham Lincoln boarded the train in Springfield, Illinois. He thought, then, that his destination was Brooklyn. He expected to make a speech in the famous church of the great preacher, a speech that might be of critical importance in his career, for he was a candidate for the Republican Presidential nomination, and he knew that many eastern city dwellers were not taking his candidacy very seriously. He had, indeed, attracted national attention by his skillful handling of issues in a series of debates with Senator Stephen A. Douglas, the "Little Giant" of Illinois. Although he had failed in his attempt to unseat the Senator and go to Washington in his stead, the newspapers had reported the debates, and there was widespread admiration for the manner in which he had cornered Douglas and forced him to make admissions that would later cost him many Southern votes in a Presidential contest.

Nevertheless, while there was undoubtedly great interest in the Illinoisan in Brooklyn, there was probably little feeling that he would be particularly honoring the church or the city by his presence there. Plymouth had heard too many national figures to be overly impressed. Besides, the candidate favored by Brooklyn Republicans was Senator Seward.

When Lincoln reached New York the arrangements were altered. It was decided to have him speak in Cooper Union, in that city, instead of in Brooklyn. Nevertheless, he went to Plymouth Church on Sunday, the day after the memorable speech that helped to make him President. He wanted to hear the most generally admired orator in the country, the man who was idolized by thousands throughout the North and bitterly hated by other thousands, North as well as South. Some historians have built rather fanciful structures on this event. It was dramatic enough as it was.

When the tall, lank prairie lawyer—a rural, awkward figure—walked in Brooklyn's streets, it was mid-winter and the Heights was not at its best. Nevertheless, even a less sensitive visitor than Lincoln could tell that it had many things that were yet lacking in the West. One could appreciate that without entering any of those square, massive, red brick and brownstone houses. There were residences of well-to-do Dutchmen and of a scattering of other breeds, but most of them had been built by Yankees. Civilization, in its transit westward from Europe, had undergone modifications, but it had left a deposit in Brooklyn that could be exceeded or matched in few places in the country. Material evidence of its refinements were in every nook and corner of these houses, with their heavy hangings, thick carpets, bulky furniture, shining silverware, oil portraits, libraries rich with morocco bindings, tinkling pianofortes, and gas illumination. Some of them could show also exotic trophies from the Orient, silks, china, idols of teakwood, and articles of ebony inlaid with mother-of-pearl.

There was plenty of evidence that was not material. Brooklyn's Yankee civilization of the mid-century was full of vigor. All the serious minded and many of the frivolous flocked to the lecture halls. Several lecture courses were going on at the same time during the winter season—Brooklyn Institute courses, Athenaeum courses, courses at the Female Academy. The lecturers—many of them New England Yankees, some of them Brooklyn's own variety of Yankee—delivered themselves on an enormous variety of subjects, ranging from natural science to women's fashions. Ormsby McKnight Mitchel, apostle of astronomy, came from Cincinnati and stirred up so much enthusiasm in Brooklyn that an Astronomical Society was formed. Samuel Hanson Cox, antislavery pastor of the First Presbyterian Church, was made its president, and for a time he seemed almost on the point of persuading Brooklyn's wealthy citizens to build an observatory on one of the city's hills. This enthusiasm faded before others which took firmer root and resulted in permanent institutions.

Down from Concord came Emerson to talk about "Books," and "Natural Aristocracy," and other high matters. During one season at the Female Academy he was billed to repeat his lecture on "England," which had been rather fully reported in the newspapers of other cities. The *Star* warned Emerson that his praise of foreigners was a bit irritating. The editor was ready to back, for size and weight, "our Assembly at Albany against an equal number of beef-eating Englishmen."

Yet there were Yankees in Brooklyn—hundreds of them —who were quite ready to lionize one famous beef-eater— an Englishman who in size and weight could match the best in the Assembly. His name was William Makepeace Thackeray. He visited the Female Academy in 1852. *Henry Esmond* was then just out, and all Brooklyn was reading it. For three memorable nights, in the packed Academy lecture hall, the great satirist talked about Sterne and Goldsmith, Steele, Addison, Swift, Congreve, Prior, Gay, and Pope. Later in the decade he was in Brooklyn again. His theme was "The Four Georges," and Plymouth Church was filled to the doors.

There were no American novelists who could match Thackeray for popularity in Brooklyn's lecture halls, but there were many Yankees who could draw good audiences to hear discussions of American themes. One of them, now long forgotten, was Edwin P. Whipple, a Boston literary critic, who talked on the "American Mind" at the Institute. Another Institute lecturer—one who is still well remembered—spoke with the authority of experience on his theme, "Self-Culture." He had left school at fourteen, and he had become an American oracle. His name was Horace Greeley.

These and others like them were heard with enthusiasm, season after season, by audiences which were predominantly Yankee. But a more intense enthusiasm than most of these could excite greeted the efforts of the great temperance lecturer John B. Gough. Alcohol had been denounced in Brooklyn by a long succession of temperance propagandists, editors, politicians, versifiers, and preachers. Temperance was more than a reform; it was a popular amusement. People crowded to the lectures for the excitement of the thing.

The same audiences found less nervous tension, and more pleasing entertainment, in such affairs as the concerts of the "Hutchinson Family." The Hutchinsons were Yankees from New Hampshire, and they sang homely American melodies of the farm and the old home, of the sailor and the soldier and the Red Man, of California and the Plains— "Zekle and Huldy," "Jamie's on the Stormy Sea," "Where Can the Soul Find Rest?" Miss Abby and her three brothers could always pack the house in Brooklyn. Year after year they came to sing at the Institute and at Plymouth Church and at other Brooklyn halls, and during the Civil War they did more for morale than can be easily calculated.

Their influence may be inferred from the fact that editors soberly discussed their political affiliation. Walt Whitman, while conducting the *Eagle,* remarked that the *Globe* of New York, "in speaking of the singers Hutchinson 'suspects they are rather Whiggish in their politics.' We happen to know," he insisted, "that this is not the case. The H's are true sons of the Old Granite State; they are Democrats." *

Somewhat less democratic, perhaps, but still popular, was the music rendered by the Brooklyn choral societies.

* Brooklyn *Eagle,* March 13, 1847.

They had been flourishing for a generation. They had two distinct lines of derivation—the village singing schools of New England and the cathedral choirs of old England. In the days of Brooklyn village, Cyrus P. Smith, the Yankee lawyer who had led country choirs in Connecticut, joined with S. P. Taylor, St. Ann's choirmaster, and Fanning C. Tucker, Joshua Sands' son-in-law, in organizing choruses which sang Handel's oratorios and other sacred music.

Favorite singers drew large crowds to the churches, Gothic Hall, the Institute, the Female Academy, and the Athenaeum. In 1845 Julia Northall, a young and attractive soprano—sister of William Knight Northall, editor of the Brooklyn *Daily News* and an ambitious dramatist of some fame in New York—sang when Ole Bull appeared before a Brooklyn audience. The famous Norwegian violinist played Paganini's "Carnival of Venice" and some of his own compositions. Newspaper musical criticism was frank and unabashed. The Yankee editor of the *Star* liked the Brooklyn singer. She was good to look at, and her voice was pleasing. But he, like Whitman a few years later, found the "foreign" music hard to take.

Julia Northall, in her progress as a singer, helped to train the Yankee ear to appreciate operatic music. So, also, did such favorites as Mrs. Emma Gillingham Bostwick and Mrs. Laura A. Jones. Yet, when Isidora Clark, the "American Prima Donna," sang in Italian at the Athenaeum in 1854, there were many protests. The evidence is strong, nevertheless, that Brooklynites in great numbers were both singing and listening to music of a higher order than the Hutchinsons' simple melodies. On this foundation of musical appreciation and participation—a foundation which included solid Yankee blocks—was built, in the early sixties, the Brooklyn Academy of Music.

Somehow, the theater languished in Brooklyn for decades, in spite of the efforts of Gabriel Harrison, Brooklyn's tireless promoter of the drama. It had to battle the stiff competition of the New York playhouses. Worse than that, it had to contend with the dour Yankee conscience. Beecher —afterwards much more liberal—let loose his fluent rhetoric on the Brooklyn Museum (a theater and not to be confused with the present Brooklyn Museum) when it was struggling for a foothold, in 1850. With the willing aid of other Yankee parsons, he probably helped to kill that enterprise of the actor managers Francis Chanfrau and Charles Burke and of their successors, Lovell and King. Brooklyn's Yankees, however, would listen conscience-free to "Shakespearean Readings" at the Institute, and a decade or so later a large proportion of them shed all their qualms.

Not only the Academy of Music but also most of the other institutions which gave the City of Brooklyn its shape and substance took root at this time—the Institute, the Athenaeum, the Y.M.C.A., Packer Collegiate Institute (successor of the Female Academy), the Polytechnic Institute, the Long Island Historical Society. These and the public schools and the press derived much from breeds other than the Yankees. Certainly the Dutch contribution cannot be ignored. But they were chiefly Yankee in inspiration and origin, and without Yankee dollars most of them could not have lived.

Partial Eclipse of the Yankees

AFTER THE CIVIL WAR the Yankees gradually gave way before the Irish, the Germans, the Italians, and the Jews. On the other hand, the last decades of the nineteenth century witnessed the seasoned maturity of Brooklyn's Yankee civilization. It may have been more difficult than it had been a generation earlier to tell just who was Yankee and who was not. Intermarriage had considerably complicated the matter of definition. But the main lines of descent were plain enough in many a big house along the broad avenues of the Hill and the pleasant streets of the Heights and in many a smaller house in the various neighborhoods of Brooklyn.

In 1870 Brooklyn had 400,000 people and was growing at a rate that only the mushroom cities of the West could rival. All along its waterfront it had felt the stimulus of Civil War industries and war business. Now, from Red Hook, where Erie Basin was nearing completion, to Newtown Creek, where new construction was under way, the docks and the basins, the warehouses and the factories were teeming with the enterprise of an era of peace.

The storehouses were filled with sugar, molasses, coffee, wool, naval stores, hides, fish, East India goods, and other products. Between the South and the Hamilton ferries were the grain elevators of the United States Warehousing Company and the Pacific Stores. Beyond the Hamilton Ferry was the great Atlantic Basin, with its busy docks and its storehouses. Along the shore above the Navy Yard were distilleries, sugar refineries, and shipyards. The one-time swampland along Bushwick inlet was being reclaimed and covered with manufactories, shops, and dwelling-houses.

During the remainder of the city period of its history Brooklyn proceeded along its four-track course—as a residential suburb, as an important shopping and business town, as a manufacturing center, and as one of the world's greatest commercial cities. It was not a port in its own right. In that respect its identity was submerged in that of the port of New York. But sailors from everywhere knew its real importance in world trade.

By the nineties the Brooklyn waterfront was nearly twice as long as in 1855, when Mayor Hall made his boast of it. It was many times twice as busy. New York, Jersey City, and Hoboken were receiving most of the passenger liners, but the actual number of vessels arriving and departing annually along the Brooklyn shore now exceeded those at Manhattan's piers. Evidence of mammoth business enterprise extended from Greenpoint, all along the East River waterfront, and far down the harbor. One could stand on Brooklyn Bridge—new, then, and one of the wonders of the world—and see, beyond the Navy Yard, the grimy bulk of the massive sugar refineries looming darkly over the river. Brooklyn was then receiving almost all the raw sugar and molasses that came to the port, and its sugar plants were refining half the sugar consumed in the United States.

It was receiving, storing, and transshipping an enormous quantity of other goods. It was the chief terminus of those freight liners—steam and sailing craft—from South and Central America, and from Europe, which carried goods of a bulky nature. It was also one of the major terminal depots of American goods, especially of the cereals of the Great West.

Just as the huge refineries compelled the attention of the observer who looked up the river, down along the Bay it was the grain elevators which held the eye. They had been significant enough twenty years earlier, but here again superlatives were in order, for the elevators at the Erie and the Atlantic basins, used principally to store grain to be shipped abroad, were the largest in the United States. There were still others on Gowanus Canal, and at the foot of Atlantic Avenue, and at the end of Pacific, Degraw, Second, and Furman streets. Few Brooklynites realized their city's importance as a storage and transshipment center of grain. Fewer, perhaps, were conscious of the existence of the hardy barge folk who wintered in the Gowanus Canal, whose business it was to bring the grain to Brooklyn.

In fact, one of the curious aspects of Brooklyn was that countless thousands would daily pass the tremendous commercial area which rimmed the city and give it scarcely a thought or a glance. They were preoccupied with their jobs in Manhattan and their homes along Brooklyn's pleasant streets. In spite of its commerce and its industry, Brooklyn's pervading atmosphere at the century's end was not that of a great world center. Its later cosmopolitan character was clearly foreshadowed. Already a considerable proportion of the population was foreign-born. But at that time Brooklyn did not by a wide margin rival New York in its racial diversity. To the casual observer—and to many of its residents—it was still a nineteenth-century Yankee town.

A very large proportion of Brooklyn's salaried people and wage earners, as well as a sizable flock of bankers and brokers and businessmen, spent most of their daylight hours in New York. This had been going on ever since Robert Fulton's steam ferry *Nassau* and the improved horse boats invented by John Garrison Murphy began their shuttle service after the War of 1812. The ferries—fourteen of them now—were supplemented by the bridge. Horsecars persisted in the face of the new smoothly gliding trolleys. The elevated was a modern wonder, and the rush across the bridge in mornings and late afternoons was something for country cousins to gape at.

But when the Manhattan office worker who lived in Brooklyn—he who gave Brooklyn its sobriquet as "the bedroom of New York"—took his country cousin to his home, he was proud to show him suburban comforts—rural luxuries—homely and pleasant reminders of the country—which could not be enjoyed by his fellow workers who lived in Manhattan. Walt Whitman would have said of the city in the nineties exactly what he said a half-century earlier, that it was the favored home of the great middle class. The reason now was the same as then—for a moderate rental it offered elbow room which Manhattan denied.

But the Brooklyn of the nineties had its Yankee and Dutch upper-crust social level, descendants of the merchants and the landowners of earlier days. It had clubhouses with plate-glass windows and heavy Richardsonesque stone trimmings. It had prosperous and famous churches. The Heights was more placidly conscious of its social superiority than it had been before the Civil War. Charles Cuthbert Hall, the urbane Brooklyn clergyman who had gone to England as a young student, noticed in the Heights as it then was something of that blending of cultures which he had himself experienced. He summed it up in a sentence:

Wealth, tempered by a sense of public duty; learning, leavened by love; social station, calmly certain of its own rights; the simple customs of New England finely blended with the flavor of European influence; the prevalence of broad-minded Christian sentiments, have made these Heights sweet to dwell upon and have bred a race of minds clean and kind and strong.*

* *The Fiftieth Anniversary of the Installation of Richard Salter Storrs*, Brooklyn, 1897, p. 103.

That was the Heights as a Heights-dweller saw the district in the nineties. It was not a democratic social viewpoint, and not all Brooklynites would have been so complimentary in their references to the region. There were some who might have remarked that with the growth of wealth and complacency there had been a certain loss in moral passion. They might have missed the clash of opinions that characterized the time when Wendell Phillips and Charles Sumner and Joshua Giddings stirred the blood and roused the sleeping consciences of the respectable church- and lecture-goers of those quiet streets. Nevertheless, one could not altogether dispute the justice of Dr. Hall's characterization of the neighborhood he loved.

If the Heights people felt their superiority, no one could say that they were very ostentatious or offensive about it. The New England flavor on the Heights was stronger than in any other part of Brooklyn. It was a flavor that made for strongly marked individuality rather than for uniformity, so that the story told of any one of the old houses along Willow or Hicks or Columbia Heights would be strikingly different from the story of its neighboring house. And yet in each tale there would be striking similarities, enough to reveal much of Yankee Brooklyn.

One of the biggest and solidest and squarest of all the Heights homes was No. 3 Pierrepont Place. It had been built by Abiel Abbott Low in the 1850s, and it was faced by carefully selected, beautifully grained blocks of brownstone. When it was brand-new an excited boy had looked out from one of its great tall windows to see a beautiful clipper ship moving in full sail up the Bay. The boy was Seth Low. The ship belonged to his father, and it was his first sight of it. It was the world-famed *Houqua*.

Seth was eleven years old when the Civil War broke out. Although he was keenly alive to the stirring events of that decade, like every other boy in Brooklyn, he attended to his schooling with more than average concentration, and in 1870 was graduated from Columbia College at the head of his class. As was the case with his father, the smell of the sea had never been far from his nostrils; so it was natural that he should go to work, on graduation, in his father's office at No. 31 Burling Slip, New York, close to the South Street shipping. There he learned the business, and soon rose to prominence in the silk trade.

The young businessman had a winning, straightforward personality, a keen and clear mind, and an inclination to work hard. The fact that he was born of a prosperous mercantile family in a city moving strongly in the tide of progress made his success a matter of course. Having such advantages, when he interested himself in politics, he became a leader. He was the first president of Brooklyn's Young Republican Club, and he led the club in campaigning for Garfield in 1880.

When the Young Republicans and the regular Republican organization backed different men for the mayoralty in 1881, Seth Low was accepted by both factions as a compromise candidate. He held office as mayor of Brooklyn for two terms, and gave the city a clean-cut, business administration—too businesslike, indeed, to suit the party hacks. During his second term, when Blaine was nominated for the Presidency by his party, the young Republican mayor supported Cleveland. Such independence was too much for the organization; the politicians could not understand Low's theory that the efficient administration of a city was a thing apart from state and national politics and the spoils of office.

His political career in Brooklyn was ended for the time, but his record as mayor carried him to the presidency of Columbia University and afterwards to the mayoralty of

Greater New York. A planner and a builder, he moved the university to Morningside Heights, and he gave it a noble library building as a memorial to his father.

This was the story of one of the big Yankee houses on the Heights. Other houses had other tales to tell. The Ford house was around the corner from Columbia Heights, on Clark Street. In 1891 Gordon Lester Ford died, at the age of sixty-eight. His home had become not only a social center but one of the chief resorts of Brooklyn's intelligentsia, especially of writers and of artists. Ford had been one of the group of well-to-do Yankees interested enough in the cultural progress of the city to give money and time and careful thought to the building of institutions. On the eve of the Civil War he had been one of the most active and generous in starting the Academy of Music, the Art Association, the Historical Society, and the Brooklyn Library. He had been prominent in the Hamilton Club, which succeeded the Hamilton Literary Association in 1882. He had also mixed in journalism and in politics. In Civil War days he had been leader of the group which sought to strengthen the Federal cause by establishing a new daily paper, the Brooklyn *Union*. During Grant's administration he had been removed from office as collector of internal revenue because he would not permit his subordinates to be assessed to build up the party war-chest. He had gone as a Brooklyn delegate to the Cincinnati convention of the Liberal Republicans in 1873, and had supported Charles Francis Adams for the nomination which was strangely and perversely given to Horace Greeley.

His mixture of Yankee and Quaker idealism had led him into such activities. Something deeper in his nature had made him a lover of books and a discerning collector of Americana. A zest for American history, an innate sense of values in the selection of its printed and manuscript materials, and an ever-ripening, self-acquired scholarship in the field had led him throughout his intensely active life to build up one of the largest libraries ever acquired by a private American citizen. When he died it was one of Brooklyn's richest treasures. It overflowed into many chambers of the Clark Street house, but its chief repository was a room more than fifty feet square at the rear.

But it is not of him that one thinks in picturing this huge room, with its orderly shelves and its disorderly tables, strewn with manuscripts, books, and proofsheets, but of his sons, the scholarly Worthington and the precocious Paul Leicester. Especially of Paul Leicester Ford, because of his handicapped childhood and youth, his striking talents and prodigious industry, and his tragic death. He was dwarfed by a spinal injury in early childhood, but the library which his father had collected with such intelligent zeal was a perfect school for the development of the boy. He read with eager, consuming interest. As health returned he became an expert in the field of rare Americana and bibliography. Both he and his brother Worthington eventually did immensely valuable work in American history, and scholars have been greatly indebted to their researches and their innumerable publications.

The public, however, knew Paul Leicester Ford as a different kind of genius. His chief historical interest had always been the Revolutionary and early national periods. In the 1890s he began to write novels and popular biographies relating to those times—*Janice Meredith,* the *True George Washington,* and the *Many-sided Franklin. The Honorable Peter Stirling,* however, dealt with contemporary politics. Famous now as the writer of best-sellers, he left Brooklyn for Manhattan at the turn of the century, produced a succession of light romances, and led an active social and club life. In 1902, when he was thirty-seven, his brilliant career was cut short by a pistol shot fired by his disinherited brother, Malcolm, who then turned the gun on himself.

Three years before his death he and Worthington had presented the great Ford collection to the New York Public Library as a memorial to their father. Other talented Yankees—and others than Yankees, it should be emphasized— came to Brooklyn to write and to paint. A couple of blocks from the Ford home, on Orange Street, Edward Eggleston wrote his American classic, *The Hoosier Schoolmaster*, in the early seventies, a novel which is brilliant social history. Years later Ernest Poole found inspiration on the Heights for *The Harbor*, and Joseph Pennell came to the Hotel Margaret to make etchings of the waterside, the shipping, and the vertical city.

Frederick MacMonnies, the sculptor whose flamboyant fountain at Chicago's World's Fair in 1893 won him fame in his twenties, was born on the Heights. And to the old-timers the Heights recalls the names of other artists—William Hamilton Gibson, who portrayed nature as accurately as Charles Dana Gibson portrayed the American girl—Edwin A. Abbey, known today for his *Quest of the Holy Grail* in the Boston Public Library rather than for his remarkable pen and ink illustrations of Goldsmith and Shakespeare— the still-famous caricaturist, Thomas Nast, who invented the Tammany tiger, the G.O.P. elephant, and the Democratic donkey, and who did so much to doom the Tweed Ring.

All of these things and much more could be said about the district in the generation that spanned the closing period of the nineteenth century and the early years of the twentieth. And yet, in the last decade of the dying century the odor of decay could be faintly detected already, here and there. It was the Hill and not the Heights that seemed the more characteristic and the more promising to the average Brooklynite. The massive, square houses of the Hill, stretching along wide, tree-shaded Clinton and Washington avenues, stood out each from the other in detached, wide spacing, behind spreading lawns. They were the sort of house which the typical Brooklyn suburbanite aspired to own if he were ever rich enough to afford it. But the Hill was not by any means the only region where such solid comfort could be found, where croquet and tennis could be played on the lawn, and where flower gardens were cultivated in full view of the street instead of behind houses, as in the Heights. Along New York Avenue, Brooklyn Avenue, and St. Mark's Avenue in the Twenty-fourth Ward the same standard of living prevailed. In less pretentious form, but in comparable degrees of comfort, it could be found in many other streets.

Countless thousands of folk with incomes ranging from moderate to low lived in rented houses. Householders in this category formed the great majority of the hurrying thousands who in the nineties crossed the river morning and evening by the fourteen ferries and the bridge. They lived in streets of small houses which stretched away for endless miles. Yankees and Germans and Irish and others shared these houses, sometimes in mixed neighborhoods, sometimes in neighborhoods where people of one stock prevailed. Many and many a small-townsman who got a job in the great city sooner or later crossed the river to live in Brooklyn. He could feel at home there. He could find in the friendly streets something of the neighborly quality of the village in which he grew up.

German Builders and Householders

"AMERIKA DU HAST ES BESSER." A Brooklyn Yankee with little or no knowledge of German could appreciate the significance of that line of Goethe's, written in 1831. All Yankees in Brooklyn knew that America's way of life was better than that of the benighted German states, where tyranny crushed out the liberties of the people.

Many a Fritz and Wilhelm and Karl along the Rhine shared the belief. Over and over again, between 1830 and 1860, political unrest, crop failures, cold winters and the distress of peasants and townsmen alike gave such point and urgency to the belief that thousands upon thousands of German emigrants crowded Bremen and Hamburg and the French port of Le Havre to escape to America. There were many in that generation who were convinced that Germany was done for, and they turned westward quite naturally to the young and cocky republic across the Atlantic, where jobs were plentiful and land was cheap.

When the uprisings of 1848 and 1849 were crushed, the flood of emigrants became a torrent. For a brief moment the delegates who met in national assembly at Frankfort thought that free government for Germany was won, but stupid reaction supported by sharp bayonets ended their dreams. The refugees of '48 who crossed the ocean—especially those democratic reformers whose faith in free institutions was deep-seated and ardent—brought over many talents. Their high idealism, thorough scholarship, and technical skills could be used in America. The plodding industry of the great mass of emigrants who were not so much political as economic refugees could also be used.

America's West beckoned to many of the wanderers. There, in the great unpeopled wilderness they could plant a new Germany. But there were others who did their pioneering in the midst of the Eastern cities. A few of these in the thirties and fourties trickled into Williamsburg and Brooklyn. As decade succeeded decade, they came in greater numbers, sometimes penniless but hopeful young men traveling alone, sometimes fathers with their strapping sons, sometimes whole family groups.

So far as they could, they preserved in their Brooklyn neighborhoods the social customs of the Fatherland. "You will feel at home here," they wrote in the countless letters that were read and reread in Germany, letters whose magnetic force drew more and more Karls and Wilhelms and Fritzes—and Wilhelminas and Minnas and Lauras—across the ocean. These letters, written in angular German script, told about the singing societies and *Turnvereins* and dance halls and beer gardens that helped to make life pleasant in the good old German way.

But they also stressed and underscored other things. In Brooklyn, they said, German youths could get a good start in life without squandering years in enforced military service. Employment was regular, and wages were high. Every one who would work and use his wits had a chance to rise in life. The strict supervision and hampering restrictions of Germany were unknown. Encouraged by such good news from friends and kinfolk overseas, and driven by hard conditions in their own land, the home-loving Germans continued to crowd the immigrant ships, and new families came every year to Brooklyn's German colony.

In the late '50s, after the Eastern District had been absorbed, Brooklyn had a substantial body of German citizens. Few had wealth; many were poor; most of them were industrious people of small means. There were, for example, shoemakers, bootmakers, weavers, coopers, "segarmakers," cabinetmakers, brass molders, glasscutters, watch crystalmakers, engravers, and upholsterers. There were liquor sellers and tailors by the dozen. There were barbers, butchers, grocers, bakers, confectioners, druggists, and jewelers. There were carpenters, masons, lathe-workers, milkmen, and gardeners. There were policemen, clerks, nurses, and midwives. There were teachers, doctors, lawyers, engineers, businessmen, Catholic priests, and Lutheran pastors. And there were representatives of many other occupations, some of them skilled in techniques and arts that were new to Brooklyn and to America. Among those whose fortunes were above the average were a few brewers, merchants, manufacturers, and speculators.

Life in Brooklyn was not free from discouragement. Hard work was the rule, and hardship was not uncommon. Not all the rosy dreams of a better life in America came true. Many longed for their old homes. Like the Irish, the Germans found themselves the targets of Nativism and Know-Nothingism. They were surrounded by a population which spoke a language which to them was alien, and which many had no wish to acquire. On the other hand, they were courted by politicians who wanted their votes; and in 1861, when their sons responded to the call of the German Turner societies for volunteers, and the "Turner Rifles" (Companies I and K of the Twentieth New York Volunteers) marched to the defense of the Union, a new and deep emotion stirred them—an emotion which they held in common with the Dutch and Yankees of the oldest Colonial stock.

The first sergeant of Company I was a 20-year-old lad from Williamsburg. We can understand better, perhaps, what was happening to the Germans of Brooklyn in that generation if we follow the course of this German youth for 15 or 20 years of his busy career.

He was wounded in a skirmish in Virginia in December, '61. Promotion to second lieutenant came to the boy on his recovery, and the next summer he was with the Army of the Potomac in the "Seven Days Fight" before Richmond. He was stricken with fever, recovered to fight again, and served in Virginia and Maryland campaigns until the late spring of 1863. His enlistment period over, he went home to Williamsburg as first lieutenant. But he was ready to return to the field as captain when an attempt was made to reorganize the Twentieth Regiment. The attempt failed, so the young officer started a printing shop in Williamsburg.

His name was Henry Roehr. He had already served an apprenticeship as a printer. His education had been practical rather than academic, but it was a good training. It would have been different if he had grown up in Germany. He had a vivid memory of the outbreak of the Revolution of 1848. He was a boy of seven then, in the little principality of Reuss in southern Germany. His father, Edward Franz Roehr, a military officer, had turned against his prince and become a leader in the revolutionary movement in the little state. The rebel officer had helped to organize the Landwehr (militia) there, and when the uprising collapsed, like countless others, he fled the country. For him Williamsburg was the final haven, and there he worked with his hands as an unskilled mechanic until he had earned enough to send for his wife and his four children. So it was that in 1850 the boy who had already seen so much excitement in his short life found himself in Williamsburg.

This son of an officer in the tiny army of Prince Henry LXII would certainly have experienced strict and methodical school training if he had remained in Germany, and would afterwards have gone to university or technical school. His education in America began on the streets of Williamsburg. His father had secured an agency for the *Abend Zeitung* of New York, and the boy peddled the paper among the German people of the little city which was soon to become part of Brooklyn.

By this time Roehr the elder had managed to save enough money to stock a bookstore on Montrose Avenue with German books and papers. This was the very heart of German Williamsburg, afterwards Brooklyn's 16th Ward, a district so completely Germanized that it came to be called "klein Deutschland" or "Dutchtown." The boy worked in the store, and when his father, in 1854, started a small four-page newspaper, the *Long Island Anzeiger*, young Henry learned the printer's trade. The paper died the next year, but it had served its purpose. It had determined the direction of the boy's career.

At the age of 17, this hard-working lad went forth to see the country as an itinerant printer. He worked on the Albany *Freie Blaetter,* and then went on to various other cities, getting as far west as Cincinnati. For him, it was work and education and adventure combined. Afterwards his campaigning with the Army of the Potomac piled up new experiences. When he went back to Williamsburg, aged 22, he was seasoned in two trades, soldiering and printing, and ready for another venture.

During his absence "Dutchtown" had grown enormously. In ten years the German population of Brooklyn had quadrupled. There were now at least 40,000 in the city. Culturally, the Germans were still largely cut off from the great mass of Brooklynites. But the German boys in the army, the native and German politicians, and some of the businessmen were helping in one way or another to overcome their isolation. A German-language newspaper, if well edited, could also help to bridge the gap, and young Roehr was equipped to do the job. He looked about him and decided that the time was ripe for such a venture.

The small weekly he brought out was given the name his father had used ten years before, the *Long Island Anzeiger.* It was Williamsburg's newspaper, a local sheet. Roehr found it tough work to keep it alive at first. By main force he drove it along to success, working early and late. In a few years the Anzeiger grew into a daily and Roehr moved it out of Williamsburg to Myrtle Avenue, near the city hall, and changed its name to the Brooklyn *Freie Presse.*

By 1875 the German lad who had seen the hopeless uprising of 1848 and who knew the blood and fever of Virginia campaigns was a man of wide influence in Brooklyn. Like other American editors of that generation, he was addressed as "Colonel." Unlike some of them, he deserved the title, for he had served as commanding officer of the 32d Regiment of the National Guard.

The *Freie Presse* told German Brooklynites about what was really going on in their city. It helped to make them active citizens by making them really well informed. While Colonel Roehr was performing this useful service, Germans of many other sorts were doing an infinite variety of things; Paul Weidmann, a Bavarian, who came to Williamsburg in 1852, got a job in a brewery, and afterwards built up a large cooperage business in that part of Brooklyn; Louis Bossert, a lad of eleven years when he came to Brooklyn, manufactured interior house fittings on a grand scale and, like Roehr, became colonel of the 32d Regiment; Frederick Herr, who came to America in 1845, opened a bakery on Bridge Street in 1857 and afterwards built hundreds of houses in Williamsburg and Bushwick; Julius Rueger, who

was brought to America in 1847 when he was a boy of
seven, and at twenty-four was a portrait artist in Brooklyn;
Martin Worn, a Wurttemberger, who came to Brooklyn in
1852 and became a large furniture manufacturer; Hermann Wischmann, a farm boy from Hanover, who was
taken into Waring's coffee house and was later head of his
own large wholesale coffee and tea business; Nicholas Seitz,
who came over from Bavaria in 1843, and in 1848 started a
brewery in Williamsburg which grew to immense size;
Julius Meyer, a pupil of Mendelssohn in Leipzig, a violinist, baritone, vocal teacher and composer, who brought his
own many talents to Brooklyn and became the first teacher
of Brooklyn's Emma Thursby, one of the greatest concert
singers of her day.

These men, and scores upon scores of others—obscure
workers and pushing, prosperous men—were in their various ways builders of the city. In certain respects they were
changing its character and modifying its habits, and they
themselves were being changed by the city. A German engineer brought about the greatest change of all. He did it
by dreaming of a bridge. It was a lifelong dream, but it
finally materialized in steel and granite. No dream of any
other man in the history of Brooklyn influenced the city
so profoundly.

John Augustus Roebling had studied bridge construction, hydraulics and architecture at the Royal Polytechnic
in Berlin. He had studied philosophy there, too, and had
been a pupil and a favorite of the great Hegel. That was
early in the century, before the revolutionary movement
of 1830. There was a little chain suspension bridge at Bam-
berg in Bavaria. To Roebling it suggested possibilities yet
unsuspected by other engineers. He made a meticulous
study of it and presented his findings as a thesis for his state
examination.

He was no ordinary student of engineering. He differed from the great majority who learn their lessons and carry out what they have learned with reasonable skill. There was a fire that burned deep within him, a passion to create, a tireless inventive drive. But there was no chance for original ideas to live and breathe in the deadening official atmosphere of the Prussia of the 1820s. In 1831, like so many others whose hopes for liberalism were disappointed, he sailed for America.

At first his career followed a pattern that was common enough in American pioneering. He wanted to help Germans to establish an ideal German agricultural colony in the New World. So he and his brother went to western Pennsylvania and bought 7,000 acres of land for refugees to develop. He himself tried farming; but he was an engineer, not a farmer. In America there were great streams that were still unbridged; new states and cities growing at an incredible rate. Roebling's destiny was tied close to that of the expanding republic. He was to be, not a German settler, but a great American engineer.

He named his American-born son, Washington. His inventive genius was turned to the development of the steel cable, and he began manufacturing it at Trenton. Finally he undertook that great series of bridges which led straight to the crowning achievement of his life. The suspension spans at Niagara Falls, Pittsburgh, and Cincinnati were engineering triumphs, but they were, in a way, preliminary studies. He knew, when he set out to do it, that the bridge over the East River would be his greatest work. Here was the summation of his inventive genius, his engineering skill, and his architectural mastery. It became a world wonder; but he, himself, did not live to see the materialization of his dream.

It cost him his life; and it was in Brooklyn that the end

came. In July, 1869, he climbed to the top of some piles at Fulton Ferry in order to take observations to determine the location of the Brooklyn tower. He was intent on his work and took no notice of a ferryboat which was entering the slip. The boat crashed against the piles, and Roebling's foot was crushed in the grinding timbers. Amputation was followed by lockjaw, and he died at the home of his son, Washington, on the Heights.

But his monument rose high over the river. The prodigious work was pushed to completion by the labor and devotion of the son. The plan and architectural design of the bridge had been John Roebling's. Washington Roebling was responsible for its actual building and for the masterly solution of many technical problems. He had inherited his father's inventive powers and his dogged tenacity. But he was put to a fearful test, for in 1872, during one of his inspection trips down into the pneumatic caisson at the Brooklyn end, he was stricken with the "caisson disease." From that day until the completion of the bridge eleven years later he was an invalid. There are many instances of moral courage in Brooklyn's long history, but nothing, perhaps, to equal the performance of this man, who during those years of pain never relaxed his grip on the great work. The picture of Washington Roebling lying on his bed in his Columbia Heights residence and watching the progress of the work through a spyglass is one that Brooklyn can never forget.

The bridge—which came in the fullness of time when the two great engineers, the father and the son, had discovered its principles, and a city was ready for it—became the very symbol of Brooklyn and changed the current of its history.

It was during this period of achievement—the long years when the bridge was slowly rising—that other Germans were becoming outstanding leaders in the city's affairs. Such successful business men as Frederick A. Schroeder and Charles Adolph Schieren went into politics in order to rescue the city from the hands of bosses and public plunderers.

Schroeder's background resembled John Augustus Roebling's, and that of many another son of prosperous and intellectual German parentage who came to this country because of the collapse of liberal hopes in Germany. He was an immigrant of the 1848 migration. He was only fifteen when he came over, and he worked with zeal to gain a firm economic footing, starting his own cigar-making business. By the time he was twenty-one he was employer of a dozen workers, and at thirty he was a rich man.

At thirty-four he was founder and president of the Germania Savings Bank. When Brooklyn needed a political house-cleaning, he became a reform politician and was elected city controller in 1871. The Tweed Ring had just been exposed in New York. Both cities had been robbed by their officials. Schroeder recovered many thousands of the Brooklyn loot and reformed the city's bookkeeping system. After this methodical, clear-headed business administrator had served a term as mayor, he renewed his fight for good city government in the state senate, where he worked valiantly to put through a "reform" charter for Brooklyn.

This new charter was known as the "Schroeder charter," and was hailed by political reformers everywhere as a great advance in city government. It reduced the number of elective offices, giving the mayor the sole power of appointing the heads of city departments. Responsibility for government was thus centralized. It meant that honest citizens who wanted good government need only keep their eyes on the mayor. The "Schroeder charter" became effective in January, 1882, and young Seth Low was the first mayor to take office under its authority.

Although he was not an aggressive fighter of the Schroeder stamp, Charles Schieren was also a reformer in politics. His father had been a political refugee. Like Schroeder, Schieren built up a prosperous business and became a wealthy man. He developed and manufactured leather belting capable of withstanding the strain of the highspeed electric driven machinery which was then rapidly coming into use. Like Schroeder, also, he took business methods into politics, and when he was elected mayor in 1893, he pulled the city out of bankruptcy.

He was like Schroeder in still another respect, for Schieren was one of those German-born Americans who were so completely identified with the general cultural and public affairs of the city and country that their foreign birth was seldom thought of. As mayor, he pushed the development of the park system and the Shore Drive, and as a citizen of Brooklyn he was president of the Academy of Music. When Brooklyn was consolidated with New York he served on the Greater New York Charter Commission, which was appointed by Governor Theodore Roosevelt.

At that time Brooklyn had reached the million mark in population. Great business organizations were rising under German leadership. Havemeyer and Elder's monolithic "sugar castles"—to use an expression of Julian Ralph's—loomed over the East River. The large German population now included great numbers whose interests took them into the general affairs of the city. They were Americans of German origin, not transplanted Germans trying to maintain a separate German culture in the New World. For many the old pattern of German life was broken down effectively by intermarriage with the Irish, Yankees, or other stocks.

While men of German birth were serving their city so effectively in the field of reform politics and others were distinguishing themselves as bankers, or lawyers, or educators, or clergymen, a new flood of German immigrants was pouring into the city. It was the biggest migration of all, and it kept up at an ascending rate until 1882, when the curve went sharply down. It brought no ardent apostles of democracy and political liberalism of the sort who came over in '48, but it furnished thousands of workers for Brooklyn's expanding industries, and it tended strongly to preserve German ways of life which might otherwise have been forgotten.

The people of this migration fitted into Brooklyn's democratic political and social system readily enough. They were determined to be good citizens, more than ready to be Americans. But they were also determined to hold on to their cultural background. They intended to remain German. Deeply ingrained family customs, the German mother tongue, and habits imported from the fatherland were cherished. And yet the pervasive atmosphere of Brooklyn could not be resisted, nor was there any desire to resist it entirely. As with the Italians and other groups, friction and misunderstanding sometimes arose between children who had absorbed "American" ideas and parents who did not like the new notions. Boys and girls, for instance, sometimes resented the strong tradition of paternalism in the German family; they wanted the greater freedom which their Irish and Yankee friends enjoyed. Sometimes, as with other peoples, ties were broken because of such stresses. But the German family bond as a rule was a strong one.

When the City of Brooklyn became one of New York's five boroughs, its German population could show every social grade from extreme poverty to opulence. One of the most interesting expressions of this complex society was in the field of music. Here the Germans had a native talent which most of the Yankees lacked. There were many organizations, such as the Arion Society and the Saengerbund, which gave frequent concerts. The restaurants and taprooms of these clubs gave them a peculiarly German tone.

The German societies scattered through the borough were potent factors in conserving traditions and customs. Hundreds of them, of various descriptions, came into existence. The walls of one of them, Schwaben Hall, standing at Knickerbocker and Myrtle, were lined with murals illustrating German history. Plattsdeutsch House, a social club, was located in Franklin Square. These two clubs and many others served German dishes in their restaurants.

The German desire for goodfellowship and conviviality was gratified by target clubs, dance halls, and beer gardens. Typical German food stores—pork butchers, pastry shops, delicatessens—catered to German tastes and tempted the palates of non-Germans.

Beer, especially, was important to the German worker, and Sunday was a day of relaxation and enjoyment. It was at this point that the Germans of Brooklyn found themselves in direct collision with Yankee austerity. For many years they fought the state excise law. They considered heavy license fees and Sunday closing to be direct invasions of their liberties. To them there was no conflict between beer drinking on Sunday and the teachings of religion. Most of them were adherents of Catholic and Lutheran churches, although a few had drifted from strictly German associations and become members of other communions.

But there were descendants of Brooklyn's mid-century Yankees—Presbyterians and Methodists and Baptists who had flocked to hear Gough—who were shocked by the German championship of the "Continental Sabbath."

Mayor Seth Low was not one of them. There was no doubt about his Yankee descent, but he understood the German viewpoint and sympathized with it. He put an end to the warfare between the Excise Board and Brooklyn's German people by enforcing a "rule of common sense." The incident was a good illustration of the sort of thing that necessarily happened whenever cultures so various as those represented in Brooklyn came into conflict. The "rule of common sense" usually meant a recognition of the other fellow's point of view—a smoothing away of friction by mutual accommodation.

In many other respects the German Brooklynites were quite in line with old ways of life in Brooklyn. The earlier-established groups recognized this, and respected them accordingly. Like the Colonial Dutch, they were sticklers for cleanliness and order. The neat and trim brownstone residences which spread through the quiet streets of Bushwick and Ridgewood were models for middle-class America. They represented a German ideal—the ideal of respectable social standing in a well-regulated community.

In 1917–'19 and 1941–'45 thousands upon thousands of Brooklyn boys and scores of Brooklyn girls of German descent went overseas. They were like any other Brooklyn boys and girls in their devotion to their country—and as large a proportion of these boys as of any other breed gave their lives in the battle against Germany.

A Jewish Community Takes Root

AFTER MONTHS AT SEA the good ship *Saint Charles* arrived at New Amsterdam in September, 1654. It brought twenty-three weary, half-starved passengers. They were refugees fleeing from Pernambuco, in Brazil, which had been reconquered by the Portuguese after being for a quarter of a century in the hands of the Dutch.

The twenty-three refugees were Jews. It was their misfortune that Peter Stuyvesant, the peg-legged Director General of New Netherland, although not without many rugged virtues, was an intolerant man. He objected not only to Jews, but to Lutherans and Quakers and any other adherents of "dangerous heresies and schisms." Domine Megapolensis, pastor of the church at New Amsterdam, was fully as zealous. Both the governor and the domine regarded the newcomers with cold disfavor.

This inhospitable attitude was not particularly remarkable in the mid-seventeenth century. One could go on a long hunt in Europe and America without encountering much real charity in the matter of religious opinion. There were few exceptions to the general rule. But in Stuyvesant's own homeland a more tolerant practice did, in fact, prevail.

Holland had long been a refuge for harried folk who had been persecuted elsewhere. French Huguenots and English Separatists (including the Mayflower Pilgrims who settled Plymouth Colony) had found a quiet haven there. And Jews, expelled from Spain and Portugal, lived in peace in the Dutch provinces. So it is not surprising that Stuyvesant's peevish request for authority to turn away the hapless refugees got an unsympathetic hearing. It was curtly denied by the directors of the West India Company, and the Pernambuco Jews remained at New Amsterdam.

Other Jews came over from Holland in 1655 and in later years, and a small Jewish community gradually took shape. Freedom to worship openly, however, was not granted during the Dutch regime. To the English authorities belongs the credit for that liberty; for public worship first took place in 1674, after the English for the second time had taken over the colony from the Dutch.

Among the more active of the Jewish pioneers was one Asser Levy. He had bought land far and wide in the colony. One of his purchases was made in the vicinity of Albany, another across the East River from New Amsterdam, in what is now Brooklyn. A century later the records show Jews in possession of property in New Utrecht, Gravesend and New Lots; but little or no traces of Jewish activity remained after the social upsets of the Revolution and British occupation.

It was not until almost two centuries after the arrival of the pioneer Jews at New York that a permanent Jewish settlement in Brooklyn began to take shape. In the 1830s, at the very beginning of Brooklyn's history as a chartered city, a few Jewish families bearing the names Levy and Moses were living on or near Fulton Street. These early Brooklyn Jews, few as they were, represented various levels of prosperity. One was a cartman, another a junk dealer; there was an auctioneer at 79 Fulton Street whose name was Benjamin Levy, and another Benjamin Levy had a variety store a little farther up the street.

The settling of these Jewish families in Brooklyn constituted a very simple, unpretentious beginning—but it was the beginning of a mighty migration, for a century later Brooklyn was to contain the largest Jewish community in the world. It remained a very small community during that generation. There were, in fact, two small communities, for while Jews were settling in the young city of Brooklyn, other Jews began to cross the East River to the village of Williamsburg. As their numbers gradually increased in both places, certain occupational tendencies became evident.

A number of Jewish butcher shops appeared along Hudson Avenue in Brooklyn. In 1851 a kosher slaughterhouse was established in Williamsburg. The Jewish tailors and cigarmakers in both Brooklyn and Williamsburg and Jewish clothing manufacturers, capmakers, and small drygoods dealers in Brooklyn were the advance guard, not only of a great army of humble workers, but also of industrial leaders and great merchants.

The stories of individual enterprise in that day of small beginnings are full of interest. Levi Blumenau, who emigrated from Germany in 1845, established a real estate business which became a firmly rooted enterprise; Abraham Cohen, of Williamsburg, was an importer with a New York office; Bernhard Schellenberg, a native of Frankfort-on-the-Main, who crossed the Atlantic at the age of nineteen, at twenty-three opened a merchant tailor shop on Myrtle Avenue, and during the Civil War was head of a thriving business which turned out soldiers' uniforms.

Michael Heilprin, born in Poland and afterwards a resident of Hungary, where he joined Kossuth's revolutionary movement, was one of the highly gifted intellectuals who found their way to the United States because of the collapse of European liberal hopes in the mid-nineteenth century. He became a resident of Brooklyn at the time events were fast leading the nation toward Civil War. He gave himself with ardor to the antislavery cause.

There were others who found adventure in America, if not immediate success. For instance, Elias Isaacson, who had come over from London in 1838, joined the "gold rush" to California a dozen years later, and came back to Brooklyn with nothing to show for it but experience.

For years there was no public worship by Jews, either in Williamsburg or in Brooklyn. Those who desired to observe the ancient rites had to cross the East River and worship with their brethren in New York. There is a tradition that some of the faithful in Williamsburg went across every Friday night in rowboats. In 1851 eighteen or twenty of the Williamsburg community formed Congregation Kabal Kodesh Beth Elohim. Five years later the Jews who had settled in the Fulton Street area of Brooklyn organized Congregation Beth Israel. In both Brooklyn and Williamsburg the congregations at first met for worship in the homes of their members. The Brooklyn group dedicated, in 1862, the first synagogue to be built on Long Island. The brick building was situated a few blocks from the city hall, at the corner of Boerum Place and State Street.

An active young man by the name of Solomon Furst was president of this congregation. He had come from Poland in the early '50s. He was a tailor by trade, but he invested his savings in real estate in the growing Atlantic Avenue neighborhood. When war broke out in '61, he joined a company of cavalry in the National Guard. Although he was never called to the front, he had a period of stern duty when New York was torn by draft riots.

The Civil War was a powerful stimulus to Jewish patriotism. It gave the Brooklyn community an enthusiasm which it could feel in common with its neighbors. Jewish boys in the ranks and officers such as Colonel Leopold Newman and Captain Coleman Cohen shared the hardships as well as the easy comradeships and intimacies of army life with their Irish and German and Yankee brothers in arms. In Brooklyn, Morris Hess helped to roll up support for Abraham Lincoln.

Meanwhile the Jewish population of the city was increasing steadily. By 1870 nearly half the tailors and manufacturers of clothing in Brooklyn were Jews, and there were numerous Jewish manufacturers and dealers in the boot and shoe fields. Jewish shopkeepers and especially drygoods merchants were growing in numbers year by year. The number of manufacturers and dealers in the cigar and tobacco lines had reached half a hundred in 1870, and there were almost as many butchers and slaughterers. A district on Johnson Avenue in Williamsburg, east of Bushwick Avenue, grew into a huge wholesale kosher meat market. All of this indicated healthy growth and prosperity, yet the Brooklyn Jews remained few in numbers in proportion to Yankees and Irish and Germans.

Until the closing years of the nineteenth century most of Brooklyn's Jews who were born abroad were natives of Western Europe. They came to the New World from Bavaria, the Rhine provinces, and Alsace, and few came entirely empty-handed. They were not particularly city-minded, for they had always lived in small towns. In fact, a large majority did not tarry in New York, but scattered widely, and were soon engaged in little business enterprises in villages and towns throughout the country—enterprises which sometimes grew to large proportions with the growth of inland cities.

Perhaps some of those who came to Brooklyn were attracted because Brooklyn, compared with New York, had something of a small-town aspect. Until the new migration from Eastern Europe set in, a Jewish boy growing up in the eighties and nineties could know by sight most of the Jews in the city. He could know many others, too, for there was a captivating friendliness in the air of the place. By nature the Jewish boy was open-hearted and friendly. Fulton Street was congenial to him. It is no wonder that he prospered when he went into business or took up a profession. He was alert and industrious, and the conditions for success were favorable.

He could look around him and see Jews who had been important factors in the general business and political concerns of the city. Politics at that time was not considered as fertile a field for the Jews as business, but there were some who were engaged in it in Brooklyn with the skill and astuteness of any Yankee or Irishman.

Ernst Nathan, a native of Brandenburg, was Republican leader of Kings County and one of the chief figures in Republican councils in the state. Nathan was a self-made man. His father had died when he was ten. The boy got a job in a tobacco factory, saved all that he could, and at a very early age had his own tobacco business. As soon as he got solidly on his feet, he began to interest himself in politics. The Dutchmen and the Yankees of the old Twenty-third Ward finally elected him supervisor. He had ideas about ending political corruption that appealed to many of them. He cleaned up the county penitentiary and put an end to certain dishonest voting practices in Flatbush. In the course of years he became so influential that

President Harrison made him Collector of Internal Revenue. For many years after that he was the chief Republican figure in the county.

Nathan was not the only Jew who was prominently identified with Brooklyn politics in the '90s. Israel Fischer, a New Yorker, who had moved to Brooklyn in 1887, when he was twenty-nine, was also high in Republican party councils. In 1894 he went to Congress. In later years Israel Fischer succeeded Nathan as county leader, and rose high in the Federal judiciary as chief justice of the United States Customs Court.

The bright Jewish boy of the nineties, growing up in the cheerful atmosphere of Brooklyn's Fulton Street, could not help being impressed by the success of Jewish retail merchants. No journalist at that time was better known than Julian Ralph. In 1893 Ralph surveyed Brooklyn with a critical and appraising eye, and recorded his judgment, in *Harper's Magazine,* that Brooklyn's retail establishments were second to none in New York.* That interesting fact was due, the ambitious young Jew would note, to the merchandising skill of such men as Abraham Abraham.

Abraham was one of the first of the great Jewish merchants in America. His business career can be compared with those of Wanamaker and Field. He had a novitiate in retailing in Newark. Having learned the fundamentals, he set up for himself, in 1865, in the lower part of Fulton Street. For twenty-eight years he had a partner whose name was Joseph Wechsler. Abraham's genius as a merchant caused the business to grow at an extraordinary rate. The building of the Brooklyn Bridge threatened to throw a giant shadow over all that part of Fulton

---

* "The City of Brooklyn," *Harper's New Monthly Magazine,* April, 1893, pp. 659–60.

Street, and the prosperous establishment was therefore moved to a fine new modern building at the corner of Hoyt Street. A new retailing center was thus established. From that day the district has been one of the greatest shopping hives in the nation. After Wechsler's retirement the business became known as Abraham and Straus, with Nathan Straus, Isidore Straus, and Simon F. Rothschild as members of the firm.

The great merchant was a native of New York City, born in 1843. His parents had been immigrants from Bavaria. As a boy he was not very rugged, and he did not have the kind of schooling that Jewish parents like to give their sons, but from the time he started to work as a youth he set out energetically to make up for the lack. In his maturity his tastes and his activities were those of a man of exceptional culture and enlightenment. His interests extended to many fields. Among other acquisitions was the library and collection of the German Egyptologist, Professor Eisenlohn, which he later handed over to Cornell University. He made many benefactions to charities and to institutions of all kinds, Jewish and non-Jewish. One of his greatest interests was the Brooklyn Institute of Arts and Sciences. His wealth came from the community, and he returned to the community his wise leadership and his devotion to its cultural growth.

Such stores as Abraham and Straus gave Fulton Street a gay tone in spite of the nerve-racking vibration and the ear-splitting roar of the elevated railway. Probably the young man of the nineties enjoyed the racket, as well as the gaiety of the scene.

Across the East River a phenomenal increase in the Jewish population was taking place. It had started in the 1880s. Early in that decade a major exodus from eastern Europe began, and floods of anxious, bewildered immigrants poured into New York's East Side. It was an urban migration, with no tendency to spread broadcast throughout the country like the earlier migration from western Europe. The reason for this concentration of rabbis and people in solidly Jewish communities was that the new migration was orthodox. The strictly orthodox Jew could not exist detached from his people. The imperatives of kosher diet and legal and ceremonial observances—imperatives that combined religious, economic, and sanitary factors—held him close to his brethren.

The people of the new migration were on the average much poorer than their predecessors had been when they first came to New York and Brooklyn. They came directly from a mediaeval feudalism into modern democracy. They had had to endure harsh and primitive conditions of life. Many had been victims of cruel and fanatical persecution. In Russia they had been confined to the Pale of Settlement established by the Empress Catherine. If permitted to live outside the Pale they had had to submit to harsh conditions and restrictions from which other Russian subjects were free.

Some had fled in fear from the insane, fanatic fury of Russian pogroms, which were frequently instigated and abetted by the police. None of them, whether from Russia or Rumania or any other part of eastern Europe, had had any experience of the civil liberties which were symbolized by the colossal bronze Goddess on Bedloe's Island, that reassuring and welcoming figure at America's gateway upon which they gazed as their ships moved up the harbor.

The statue was erected in 1886, in full view of the Brooklyn shore. Engraved on its pedestal were lines written by Emma Lazarus, a richly talented American woman of

Sephardic Jewish descent, who had exerted herself to aid immigrants, and knew their hopes and fears:

> Give me your tired, your poor,
> Your huddled masses yearning to breathe free,
> The wretched refuse from your teeming shore,
> Send these, the homeless, tempest-tost, to me:
> I lift my lamp beside the golden door.

The door, wide open then, has since been all but closed by a generation which did not share Emma Lazarus' concept of America as a haven for the oppressed. For decades, however, hundreds of thousands passed through it annually.

Thousands of these newcomers from eastern Europe came over the river into Williamsburg during the eighties and nineties, and proceeded to develop their own community life. Russian and Polish Jews established synagogues in the Moore Street area, Rumanian Jews built a synagogue on Hopkins Street, and there was a Hungarian congregation on Cook Street.

The older Jewish residents of Williamsburg gave way before the invasion and began to move into other districts. Some of them went to Bedford, some went to Stuyvesant Heights, and some scattered elsewhere. The newly developed elevated lines aided this dispersion, for they opened up new districts and made a general fanning out of population possible.

The invasion and the dispersion of these years was only a small upheaval compared with the mighty surge that followed it at the turn of the century. Soon after the corporate union of Brooklyn with Manhattan and the other boroughs of Greater New York, an event occurred which sent a tidal wave of population into Williamsburg and

inaugurated a great series of waves in the borough of
Brooklyn, a sort of chain reaction which is still felt. The
event was the building of Williamsburg Bridge. A wide-
sweeping scythe cut down block after block of tenement
buildings in Manhattan to provide room for the immense
span which was to thrust deep into the East Side. This
caused a human displacement on a huge scale.

The people from the once-swarming streets—thousands
upon thousands—crossed the river into Williamsburg, and
inaugurated a new era in the checkered history of that
part of Brooklyn. It was also a new era in the history of
the borough. The Jewish boy of the nineties, who could feel
that he knew every Jew in Brooklyn by sight, would now
find his world completely changed. In 1910 Brooklyn
had nearly 400,000 Jews to Manhattan's 600,000. Within
twenty years Manhattan's Jewish population had dropped
to 400,000 and Brooklyn's was fast climbing to the million
mark. So far as Jewish neighborhoods were concerned
there was little of the old-time small-town atmosphere left.

City transportation facilities were developing just in time
to provide for the great influx. During the early decades
of the twentieth century the new city subway system
tunneled under the East River and gradually spread out
to the confines of Brooklyn. It was a big factor in reliev-
ing overcrowded areas and in building up neighborhoods
along the borough's periphery. Not only prosperous business men but also poor factory workers could live in pleas-
anter districts miles from their jobs in Manhattan. Within
a few years Jewish people in small groups and in larger
communities dispersed far and wide throughout the borough.

Some of the new Jewish communities grew rapidly
into large, crowded neighborhoods. Brownsville is the
most striking illustration of such a development. In the early

eighties it was far outside the city, a country village surrounded by farms. It was called Brown's Village. Jacob Cohen, a merchant tailor from New York, bought a house in Brown's Village in 1885. His wife was ill, and he thought that the fresh country air would be good for her. Soon other Jews from New York's East Side followed him. They were, for the most part, tailors and garment workers.

A real estate boom set in. Farmers sold their property to East Side speculators, who subdivided the land and advertised the advantages of the new suburb. East Side Jews by the thousands eagerly purchased property in Brownsville in order to escape from the narrow ghetto-like streets in which they were crowded. The early inhabitants enjoyed for a brief period the advantages of the suburbs and low land prices. Gradually a good-sized town took shape, with a substantial retail section and several synagogues.

The opening of Williamsburg Bridge was the signal for a tremendous development to the remote neighborhood. As the multitude from over the river poured into Williamsburg, thousands moved from that section to Brownsville. Immigrants newly arrived from Europe also joined the current. In 1904 Brownsville had 25,000 people. During the next ten years came a steady stream from abroad, from the East Side, and from the Williamsburg area. The increase from Europe was reduced by the war and immigration restrictions, but from other sources population continued its upward curve until in 1940 it had reached nearly a quarter of a million, and Brownsville had become the most densely peopled section in the great borough.

The garment trades were the biggest economic prop for the Eastern European Jews. The sewing machine and the needle were the tools they used in their climb up-

ward from poverty. For the most part the industry was
Russian Jewish in its ownership, its management, and its
labor—though not exclusively so. In Brooklyn, as in New
York, it held out the promise of a livelihood to the newly
arrived immigrant. Even the sweatshop, of evil repute,
had this much to its credit—it gave an immediate job to
the penniless newcomer.

The industry grew to great size in both New York and
Brooklyn. Jewish manufacturers, wholesalers, and retailers,
employing Jewish workers, acquired comfortable fortunes.
The enormous expansion of Jewish neighborhoods brought
wealth to Jewish real estate owners and speculators.
Many Jews of the great Eastern European migration went
into the professions. The ceaseless drive for betterment
brought a large and ever-growing middle class into existence.

The story of Jewish expansion in Brooklyn is one of
epic dimensions. Through the years the trek from Williamsburg to Brownsville continued to other districts—
to New Lots, to Bath Beach, to Midwood, Bensonhurst,
and Borough Park—and then strongly to Flatbush. A
sense of well-being, of friendliness, and contented family
life pervaded the pleasant Jewish neighborhoods in the
south of Brooklyn. And along Eastern Parkway, stretching from Grand Army Plaza to Brownsville—a broad,
tree-shaded avenue lined with massive apartment houses
and spacious private homes—a street fairly redolent of
good living and good will—here also Jewish Brooklyn
found free and untrammeled expression.

Orthodox Jews in these neighborhoods observed with
careful strictness the ancient festivals and fasts. In September (Tishri in the Jewish calendar) the festival of
the New Year began with Rosh Hoshanah, and lasted for
ten days. Yom Kippur, the tenth day, the most solemn of

all Jewish holy days, was a day of fasting. Late in the fall came the harvest festival, Succoth, the Feast of Booths, a time of rejoicing. Gifts were exchanged in December at the time of the festival of Hanukkah, the Feast of Lights. Candle lights twinkled from the Hanukkah Menorah in the windows of Jewish homes, an added light for each of the eight evenings of the festival.

Purim was a festival dedicated to hilarity. It celebrated Queen Esther's triumph over Haman. At each mention of Haman's name during the reading of the scroll of Esther in the synagogue, noisy rattles were zipped through the air by the children to symbolize the cutting off of the tyrant's head. Three-cornered cakes called Hamantaschen, meaning Haman's ears, were made for the occasion. Purim merrymaking was an inheritance from the days of persecution and the ghetto life of the past. In the revelry and the Purim plays the Jews could poke fun at one persecutor who was completely foiled.

In the spring came Passover and Shabuoth (Pentecost), when all the Brooklyn Orthodox remembered the suffering of the Jews in Egypt, their deliverance from the land of bondage, and the giving of the Law to Moses on Sinai.

One of the notable aspects of the feasts was that they brought the family together. The solidarity of the Jewish family was a fact of great importance in Brooklyn's society. It made for stability and order. For a time, however, there were deep cleavages separating the Brooklyn Jews. Differences in culture, in wealth, in religious affiliation—whether Orthodox, Conservative, or Reform—differences in origin—whether Eastern European, Western European, or Sephardic—ran in crossed lines through the whole community.

In such an immense population the kinds and degrees of difference were, of course, almost infinite. There was a tendency toward isolation and aloofness among the neighborhoods. Instead of the Jews of Brooklyn, people spoke of the Brownsville Jews, the New Lots Jews, the Bath Beach Jews, the Borough Park Jews, the Williamsburg Jews, the Greenpoint Jews.

But, if there were divisive tendencies, there were also tendencies toward co-operation. These became more and more evident as the years went by. Extension of the subways made it possible for people to get around the borough and mix more freely. Families moved from section to section more frequently. Children ceased to speak the various Yiddish dialects of their fathers, and conversed in the English of the school and the playground. The differences between the Jewish peoples of the Western European and the Eastern European migrations tended to fade out. And there were common efforts which tended to bring the Jewish people together as members of a great community, as citizens of Brooklyn, and as patriotic Americans.

Another chapter will deal with some of these constructive movements.

The Irish Take Over

MOST GENERALIZATIONS about Brooklyn, even some of the cleverest and apparently most shrewdly aimed of them, fall far from the mark. Brooklyn is too big and too endlessly varied in the expressions of its social life to be summed up neatly in an aphorism. Certainly few sweeping generalizations are applicable to Brooklyn's Irish people. One, perhaps, we may venture: an assertion that the Irish have mirrored Brooklyn's vast complexity more perfectly than any other race.

Today there are many thousands of them who are the very epitome of Americanism. In every impulse they are as American as Yankee Doodle, they are as native as apple pie, and as widely different from one another in attitudes and ambitions and talents as the far-flung descendants of the Mayflower Pilgrims. On the other hand there are still Irish in Brooklyn whose conciousness of their Irishness is acute and ever-present. There are aesthetes devoted to the Gaelic revival, and Irish patriots whose temperatures rise at the bare mention of England. There are still those who can remember their childhood homes in Ireland. There are many who hold their Americanism and their Irish consciousness in even balance. There are also those untold thousands who can boast of Irish blood in their mixed ancestry, Brooklynites whose inheritance includes Dutch or Italian or German or Yankee or Polish or other ingredients. The Irish story is complex indeed, and he who endeavors to tell it should approach the task with humility.

The Irish strands in Brooklyn's social fabric were long ago interwoven securely and in many colors. Decades ago it could have been said that none were stronger or more pervading. By the early days of the twentieth century the Irish were furnishing in every sphere of activity a large part of the borough's motive power. They were in all strata of society, in all types of occupation, and could be found on all sides of all questions. Many were prominent in business and industrial management, and many were equally prominent in labor. Among them were distinguished figures in journalism, education, religion, social service, scholarship, science, the arts, and sports. In politics, the Irish were pre-eminent. In sober fact, they were the Yankees of modern Brooklyn, occupying much the same position that the New Englanders had held in the preceding century. And when, in 1946, a Brooklynite named William O'Dwyer, a native of County Mayo, Ireland, took the oath of office as mayor of New York, he seemed to the whole city the very model of a hundred percent American. The fact that he had been born in Ireland had nothing to do with the case—if, indeed, it were not taken as confirmation of his hundred percentism rather than otherwise.

It is easy to recall the deeds of big men. In fact, the Irish have furnished so many outstanding figures that it is embarrassing to make a choice. They have almost made a specialty of leadership. But the characteristics of leaders have merely reflected in heightened fashion the qualities of the rank and file. Irish people of varying degrees of social prominence and obscurity have lived throughout the borough—in Heights mansions, on the Hill, in Flatbush, Kensington, Park Slope—in Greenpoint and Williamsburg—in the neighborhood of Erie Basin's docks. The memories of some cling to one neighborhood, some to another. But from an early day there have been sections that were largely, if not exclusively, Irish. One old neighborhood should be mentioned in passing, because it long bore the Irish name.*

In after years Irish people widely scattered over the borough looked back to childhood days in Irishtown with nostalgia. They were wont to say that in those days, when the old city of Brooklyn was dying and the borough was coming to birth, the section was a "little bit of Ireland" transplanted to the New World. Some who were born there, and whose later prosperity made it possible for them to live in much finer parts of town and to put on considerable style, would talk appreciatively and a bit wistfully of the simplicity of life in the old days, when people were not ashamed to go buggy riding to Coney on Sundays behind any kind of hack, when there were no night clubs or movies, and when neighborhood parties broke up at nine o'clock.

The boundaries of Irishtown were a little indefinite in their memories. It lay between lower Fulton Street and the waterfront. Some would place its western line at Bridge Street and its eastern bounds at the Navy Yard, and would set Sands Street and the East River as its southern and northern limits respectively. Others would stretch its boundary far beyond Sands Street. They recalled McIntire's candy store, McLean's livery stable, Sweeney the harness-maker, the Adams chewing gum factory on Sands Street, the No. 8 Engine House on Front Street, the Congressman Clancy saloon, Martin Connolly's saloon on one of the Sands Street corners, Catherwood's meat market,

* The paragraphs on "Irishtown" in this chapter are based on articles and letters by George Hawkins, W. J. Monsies, James P. Canning, and others in the New York *Times* and the Brooklyn *Eagle: Times,* July 3, 1930; *Eagle,* January 28, 1946; August 17 and 31, 1947; January 4, 1948.

and many other spots. They remembered the alleys—
Fleet Alley, Harrison Alley, Hart's Alley, Cornell's Alley,
Gothic Alley, Shinbone Alley, and others. They remembered how as boys they smoked American Beauty ciga-
rettes, four for a cent, and how the brown nicotine stain
clung to their fingers. They thought often of their free
range in the neighborhood, of baseball in the streets, and
the space they had to play in, which their children and
grandchildren in more prosperous neighborhoods often
lacked. Some of them went to public school; a good many
went to St. Ann's parochial school at Water and York
Streets. Weddings, christenings, and wakes floated in
their memories. There were good times and hard times.
There were many good people whom they recalled with
tender appreciation, and a few others, perhaps, whom they
were willing to forget.

But Irishtown had long ceased to be Irish when such
memories were evoked. The name stuck to it for many
years after it was no longer descriptive. The sign "Irishtown Barber Shop" adorned a window in the heart of the
old section as late as the 1930s, when the racial mixture
there was such that no one national group could claim
predominance. Its scattered people, in many cases, saw
their sons and daughters climb to places of prominence.
Others were content with modest living. Some remained
poor.

One of the happy memories of Irishtown was connected
with the Smith Street open trolleys which ran to Sands
and Washington streets. In those days there were no
subways, and the wooden cars of the elevated lines were
drawn by miniature steam locomotives. No one then considered the "L" an antiquated nuisance. Brooklyn's first
line opened in 1885. Electric power came in 1900. Then
many things began to happen.

With the new century a new era in transportation dawned. Brooklyn had already become a Borough of Greater New York. In 1898 the merger, long broached, and stoutly resisted by many Brooklynites, had become an accomplished fact. It was the culmination of a series of consolidations. In 1886 New Lots had been added to the city of Brooklyn. Flatbush, New Utrecht, and Gravesend were absorbed in 1894. In 1896 Flatlands, the last remaining township of the county of Kings still outside the corporate limits, was drawn in. Brooklyn took approximately a million people into the greater city. During the following five decades it tripled in population and became the largest borough by a wide margin, its boundaries containing nearly one-fifth the people of the most populous state in the Union.

The elevated, the new bridges, and the subways with their five tunnels connecting Brooklyn with the other boroughs helped to accomplish this miracle of growth, not to mention Brooklyn's own fast-developing industries. Every morning, from the far limits of the borough the fast trains of the transit systems carried their packed loads of clerks and workers, of business and professional people, of college students and miscellaneous travelers, young and old of both sexes, sitting and standing and swaying as they held on to straps, instinctively leaning to restore balance as the train lurched around curves, reading the morning papers in spite of lack of space, an adaptable crowd that had learned from experience to manage the trip to daily work with minimum discomfort. Every evening they returned to Brooklyn's far-flung streets, tired but happy to leave Manhattan for the wider spaces of a borough which still had room for growth in its eighty square miles.

Brooklyn was more "the bedroom of New York" than ever, but the myriad bedrooms of Brooklyn were much

more widely dispersed over the face of Kings County
than in the '90s. The long reach of the subways was the
magic carpet which was largely responsible for that. For
the magic nickel (lately superseded by the dime) swung
the turnstiles of the Interborough, the BMT, and the
Independent to the hundreds of thousands, and carried
them from the inner recesses of Brooklyn to Wall Street
and on to mid-Manhattan in a matter of minutes. The
new age of the borough was an age of speed. The subways were making the slower ferries and the elevated lines
obsolete. Speed in transit brought great changes and
portended greater changes. Brooklyn, just beginning to
be cosmopolitan in the '90s, was pre-eminently the home
of Americans of all nations in the 1940s.

Meanwhile, the swift electric trains of the railroad lines
were taking a large proportion of the old-time families,
Yankee, Irish, Dutch, and others, to suburbs beyond the
borders of the borough. They became out-of-town commuters. Some of Brooklyn's chief businessmen were in
this category, living in Garden City, perhaps, or in some
other pleasant Long Island town, or even in Westchester,
and spending only the business day in Brooklyn. The process inaugurated in 1814 by Robert Fulton's *Nassau*, Brooklyn's first steam-powered ferryboat, was thus reversed,
and the shift of the well-to-do from the Heights reduced
its population. The subways had the same effect on less
pretentious regions, such as Williamsburg and Greenpoint, making it possible for many families to relocate
in remoter parts of the borough. On the other hand, they
caused the populations of other districts to mount rapidly:
Flatbush, Park Slope, Eastern Parkway, Borough Park,
Bensonhurst, Bay Ridge, and many other neighborhoods.
But one fact remained constant—Brooklyn continued to
grow.

In this borough of the heightened tempo and of increasing racial complexity the adaptable, skillful, resourceful, inventive, adroit Irish leadership counted for much. This leadership was based on more than a century of history. And for all of the diversity in opinion and occupation and social status of the Irish, there were certain unifying factors. Of these the Roman Catholic Church was chief, and the cause of Irish freedom took second place only because its object had been won.

The membership of the church was racially diverse, but its outstanding leaders had been Irish from the beginning. The Diocese of Brooklyn was created in 1853, and the Right Reverend John Loughlin became Brooklyn's first bishop. He found twelve churches in the city, and a Catholic population of 15,000. During the four decades of his episcopate the Catholic population mounted to several hundred thousand, Irish people forming a large proportion of the total.

In that time more than a hundred churches were erected. Scores of parochial schools, two colleges, and a diocesan seminary were established. The development of charitable establishments, including hospitals and orphan asylums, was in proportion to the advance along other lines.

But figures of growth do not tell the story. It is told, rather, by the character and deeds of such men as Father Malone, who flew the American flag from the spire of his church during the Civil War. Sylvester Malone was a native of Ireland, born in the town of Trim, twenty miles from Dublin, in 1821. As a young man he came to America, studied for the priesthood at St. John's Seminary, Fordham, and in 1848 became pastor of the Church of Saints Peter and Paul on Wythe Avenue in Williamsburg.

He was a tireless patriot during the Civil War. He labored for his country's cause, for the soldiers' welfare, and for their families. When the flag which he hoisted to the church's mast was carried to the front by Williamsburg men, it was promptly replaced by another one. This wise, broad-visioned man of cultivated tastes was one of Brooklyn's first citizens throughout a long life.

Bishop Loughlin died in December, 1891, and was succeeded by the Right Reverend Charles Edward McDonnell, a native of New York, who dedicated many new parishes and continued to build up the church's charitable and educational enterprises. In 1921 he was in turn succeeded by the Right Reverend Thomas E. Molloy. Bishop Molloy, in the 1940s, was guiding the tremendously intricate and varied concerns—religious, cultural, and philanthropic—of a Catholic population of nearly a million.

Back of Mayor O'Dwyer in Brooklyn's political annals ran a long line of stalwart figures. Among the Irishmen in that procession were practical politicians, old-time city bosses, and reformers: Henry Cruse Murphy, Hugh McLaughlin, John F. Hylan, William J. Gaynor, and many others, little and big.

The learned and polished Murphy narrowly missed a Presidential nomination as a dark horse candidate in 1852. In that year the Democratic National Convention was deadlocked. It proved to be impossible to pick a candidate among the great factional leaders—Lewis Cass, William M. Marcy, James Buchanan, and Stephen A. Douglas. Murphy had strong backing in the Virginia delegation, and might conceivably have been nominated and elected to the Presidency if one delegate had changed his mind. The delegation, however, impressed by the personal charm and the political conformity and inoffensiveness of a Mexican war general named Franklin Pierce, decided by one vote to support him.

Therefore Pierce, instead of Brooklyn's Murphy, was introduced to the convention by the Virginians, and in the Presidential campaign that followed, he defeated a more famous general, Winfield Scott. Murphy would certainly have defeated the bumbling Scott—an able soldier, but a pitiable politician—if he had been nominated. A brilliant and an astute man, he might have changed the course of history.

In 1857 President Buchanan sent Murphy to the Netherlands as American minister. After Lincoln's election, in 1860, when Southern States were tumbling over each other to quit the Union they could no longer control, Murphy explained the crisis and the Federal viewpoint to the Dutch in one of the ablest public papers produced in that troubled time. At home, during the war, he supported the fight for the Union while certain other powerful Democrats in the state were dangerously near to treason. After the war he lost the support of the dominant factions in the Democratic party of the state.

But his career was by no means over. His influence in Brooklyn was still so great that the original projectors of Brooklyn Bridge turned to him as the natural leader of the great project. He drafted the legislation necessary to build it, and pushed it through the legislature. He was made president of the original private bridge company, and also of its successor, a public corporation of the two cities of Brooklyn and New York. Over and over again he had to beat down jealous opposition from New York, and he had to conquer many legal and political obstacles. The two cities found that he could be a grim and relentless fighter. There is a bronze plaque on the bridge with his name on it, but not many who read it know what manner of man he was. The great structure is, in fact, a monument to this determined Irish scholar in politics as well as to the German engineers who planned and built it. Between them they carried through Brooklyn's greatest civic enterprise.

Back in the 1840s Murphy had noticed a young fish merchant who had a market down near the waterside. He was an active fellow, always ready if challenged to square off for a fight, and he became a leader in the Democratic party in his district. He had physical stamina, but there was something in his steely blue eyes which made men recognize a moral sway as well. Murphy was leader of Brooklyn's Democracy then, and he picked the young man as one of his lieutenants. His name was Hugh McLaughlin. He had been born in Brooklyn twenty or so years before, the youngest of ten children. As a boy he had gone to work in a ropewalk. For a time he handled barrels on the docks. Afterwards he joined an older brother in the management of the fish market, and he became its sole proprietor when his brother died. The volunteer fire forces of both New York and Brooklyn had political potency in that period. McLaughlin joined the force. In 1855 his political leadership was strengthened by an appointment as master foreman of civilian labor at the Navy Yard.

In the 1860s this young man became "boss" of the Democratic party in Brooklyn, and he remained at the head of the party until Patrick McCarren dislodged him in 1903. During his long lease of power he directed party affairs from Kerrigan's Auction Rooms on Willoughby Street, near the City Hall. Hugh McLaughlin was a very practical politician, like most of the party leaders of his time. He had the good judgment to gather able men around him. One of them was William C. Kingsley, a valuable liaison officer who maintained contacts with the more fastidious Murphy wing of the party. Another was the wealthy, cultured Alexander McCue, who later became Solicitor of the Treasury and Assistant Treasurer of the United States under Grover Cleveland. Governors Horatio Seymour, Samuel J. Tilden, and Grover Cleveland considered McLaughlin a valuable ally and maintained close relations with him. From time to time, however, he had to fight to maintain his leadership. On one of those occasions he was sharply challenged by Thomas Kinsella, editor of the Brooklyn *Eagle*. Kinsella, a native of the County of Wexford in Ireland, had served his apprenticeship as a printer in the little up-state New York village of Cambridge, in Washington County. From Cambridge he had gone to Troy, and then to New Orleans and Vicksburg. From 1854 to 1858 the keen, observant young man had appraised the deep South and its jealously defended institution of slavery. Evidently it did not appeal to him, for he was a strong supporter of the Union cause when war broke out in '61. By that time he had come to Brooklyn and had joined the staff of the *Eagle*.

His ability and his convictions made him editor when Van Anden reluctantly separated Hugh McCloskey from the responsibilities of that post. McCloskey had the misfortune to believe in the right of secession in the wrong place at the wrong time. Kinsella suffered from no such intellectual handicap. He carried on with the *Eagle* for a score of years, served on Brooklyn's Board of Education, and went to Congress. His savage editorial attacks on the McLaughlin forces, in 1880, led to the formation of a rival organization, the "Jefferson Hall Democracy," which rocked the McLaughlin boat for a time, but did not capsize it.

The boss's power in the city government finally came to an end in 1893, when the Republicans took over, but he retained control of the Democratic organization until 1903. Patrick McCarren, his successor, had been his lieutenant. Once installed as leader, the lean-visaged McCarren, who played the game of politics with extraordinary skill, fought successfully to keep the Brooklyn Democratic organization independent of Tammany Hall.

In McCarren's day and in the years when his successor, John H. McCooey, was directing the Democratic machine, the influx of eastern and southern Europeans had the inevitable effect of cutting down the relative importance of the Irish vote. For many years, however, the Irish political leaders held their own. The Irishman could work with the Yankee, the Dutchman, the German, the Italian, and the Jew with urbane efficiency. Indeed, for a time the power of the Irish boss increased, and McCooey was able to roll up a tremendous Democratic vote in Brooklyn when, in 1917, his choice for mayor of New York, the red-haired Brooklyn Irishman, John F. Hylan—a man of the people if there ever was one—overwhelmed the silk-stockinged Manhattan Irishman, John Purroy Mitchel.

Mitchel had given the city one of the best nonpartisan administrations it had ever had, but he lacked the common touch, that *rapport* with the masses which was absolutely essential for lasting political success in Greater New York. The Irish bosses knew how to maintain the common touch. They had an innate ability for political organization. The long struggle of Irishmen in Ireland to wrest political control from the hands of the English should be borne in mind in any attempt to account for the skill of the Irish in municipal politics. In the old country, townsmen and peasants, the educated and the illiterate had learned to work together for political ends in well-articulated organizations. Generation following generation, the Steelboys, the Whiteboys, the United Irishmen, the Fenians, and many another desperate and zealous cabal or political association had given them training. This inherited skill was not lost when its objectives were success in municipal politics rather than freedom from foreign control.*

In Brooklyn the Irish leaders adapted themselves with

* See Edward F. Roberts, *Ireland in America*, New York, 1931, p. 126.

ease and assurance to local conditions. For instance, they were able to carry on effectively with leaders of the Jewish community. They were good mixers on all levels of society. The retail liquor business of the borough for years was largely in German and Irish hands, but the Irish saloon was more of a general meetingplace of all races and all types than was the German. It was often called the "poor man's club," and it was an important factor in machine politics. The Irish bosses were as familiar with the rich man's plushier hangout, knowing everybody whom it was worthwhile to know, no matter what their social rank.

But the McCarrens and the McCooeys and the Kellys do not comprise the total Irish contribution to politics in the twentieth century. It is worth bearing in mind that Brooklyn has given four mayors to Greater New York and that three of the four have been Irish. Irish leaders of great ability have given themselves to reform and expert municipal administration. One of these independent operators began to make himself known back in the days of Boss McLaughlin. He was destined to rise higher in politics than most of his contemporaries in Brooklyn. His name was William J. Gaynor. He was a reformer by instinct, and he loved a fight.

Gaynor was born on a farm in Oneida County, New York, near Oriskany. His parents were very poor, but the boy was ambitious. It took him a number of years, after he left home, to discover his true vocation. For a time he studied for the priesthood. He traveled to Panama, Mexico, and San Francisco. Then, for a period, he taught school, and finally he studied law. He began his law practice in Flatbush in the late seventies. It was not much more than a country town then, still separate from Brooklyn, but it was there that the young lawyer's career as a reformer began. During his brief residence in the township, he reorganized the local government, and in his year as police commissioner he gave an instructive demonstration of what that office could be in the hands of an aggressive, keen-witted official who really believed in doing his duty.

When he moved from Flatbush to the city of Brooklyn, in 1885, he carried on in the same high-spirited fashion. He was of decidedly different mettle from the sort of reformer who had high ideals, but who did not know how to translate them into action on the level of practical city politics. He knew where to look for trouble and how to meet it. His method was to carry on reform by aggressive actions in the courts. He applied this method in his first big fight in Brooklyn when he prevented the sale of a private water company to the city for a figure amounting to several times its actual value.

Another reform for which he was responsible was the cleaning up of Coney Island, which had sunk into vice and corruption under the notorious John Y. McKane. In 1893 Gaynor became a Supreme Court judge, and he remained on the bench until 1909, when he was elected mayor of New York City.

Judge Gaynor was the kind of man who is sometimes called "picturesque." He made many bitter enemies, and attracted many friends. In the summer of 1910 he narrowly escaped assassination when a discharged city employee shot him in the throat when he was taking ship for Europe. A master of direct expression, he spoke his mind in terse, vigorous English. Sometimes his remarks were spiced with references to Cervantes and the first century Stoic philosopher Epictetus. He died in 1913, before his term as mayor expired, on board the steamship *Baltic*, six hundred miles off the Irish coast.

While Gaynor's fame as a reformer was on the rise, Edgar M. Cullen, from his Supreme Court bench, was

steadily building up a reputation for learning, wisdom and
integrity. Judge Cullen was a son of Dr. Henry J. Cullen,
who lived on Montague Street, at the corner of Clinton.
His mother was a sister of Alexander McCue. He had
graduated from Columbia at sixteen, had studied engineering at Rensselaer Polytechnic, and had gone to the
front in the spring of '62 as second lieutenant, when he was
barely eighteen. He had commanded a brigade before he
was twenty-one and had served with Grant at Corinth and
Vicksburg, and in the Virginia campaign which ended the
war.

After the war the energetic, talented youth entered Alexander McCue's law office, and was admitted to the bar at
the age of twenty-four. His career on the bench began in
1881. Although he was first elected to the Supreme Court
as a Democrat, the Republicans joined in renominating him
in 1894, and in 1900 Governor Theodore Roosevelt, a Republican, appointed him to the Court of Appeals. In 1904,
when Alton B. Parker resigned from the chief judgeship of
that court to run for President, Cullen became his successor.
It was the highest judicial office in the state. In 1914 he was
elected president of the Brooklyn Bar Association. At that
time people were still talking about his courageous act of
the previous year, when he left the bench at the impeachment trial of Governor Sulzer, and argued against Sulzer's
removal. He did not condone wrongdoing, but he con-
tended that the acts of which the governor was charged had
been committed before he took office, and therefore did not
furnish legal grounds for impeachment. It was an unpopu-
lar point of view in the politics-charged atmosphere of the
impeachment court.

Yet the opinions of Judge Cullen expressed from the
bench over a long period of years were fully appreciated
by the legal profession. A learned and high-minded judge,

he was a defender of personal liberty—a man who, according to his friend Henry Watterson, editor of the Louisville *Courier-Journal*, "would not lie to obtain office and . . . was never afraid to speak the truth."

Long before Cullen died in his home on Willow Street, in the Heights, in 1922, an infinitely complex pattern of Irish society had been woven in Brooklyn. The pattern was the work of so many hands in so many fields of endeavor that it is possible to see only a little of it at a time. The resourcefulness of the Irishman in business and industry had been hardly less spectacular than in politics. Some of them had been builders of the city in a literal sense. William J. Moran spread firehouses and public schools broadcast in the '80s and '90s, and constructed huge factory plants in the Eastern District. James F. Carey, a graduate of the Columbia School of Mines, during the seventies and eighties lifted the faces of New Utrecht, Gravesend, and New Lots, and performed an act of re-creation at Sheepshead Bay.

By way of variety, the inventive John J. Kiernan, a pioneer in his field, developed "Kiernan's Wall Street Financial News Bureau." Timothy Hogan, a native of Liverpool, started life as a sailor and climbed the ladder's rungs to a chief officership on an Atlantic steamship line. In the course of his exciting early career he went to New Orleans and contracted to build fortifications there for the Confederates, an enterprise which was interrupted by Farragut. After the war, he settled in Brooklyn and engaged in many enterprises, becoming an owner of steamship lines and a bank director. Hogan and Moran were both prominent yachtsmen.

Just as interesting was the career of Stephen McKeever, a native of Brooklyn's old Second Ward. At the age of ten he apprenticed himself to a plumber. Before he was twenty he was in business for himself, and while still a young man he secured the contract for the plumbing, gas, and steam-fitting work on the Brooklyn Bridge, then under construction. The new elevated lines gave him another big opportunity. He went into the general contracting business with his brother Edward, and in the '90s the McKeever brothers laid many miles of pavement over Brooklyn's lengthening streets.

But big contracts and corresponding profits were not their only interest. In 1912, when Ebbets Field was being built, they saved Brooklyn's tottering baseball club from bankruptcy. Charles Ebbets had known the two brothers for thirty years, and he appealed to them when he found that the club could not finish the stadium unless more funds were forthcoming. The McKeevers furnished the needed capital, superintended the completion of the job, and each of them became a vice president of the club.

They loved baseball, but trotting and pacing horses were their greatest enthusiasm. For years their famous horses were among the prime attractions at the Brooklyn Speedway. There is something very engaging about the Mc-Keevers, hearty sportlovers who yet had so great a part in the building of the city.

It is significant of the Irish that they could be found on all levels of Brooklyn industry, from iron-muscled worker to brilliant executive. At the eve of the Second World War few manufacturing regions the world around could equal Brooklyn's great industrial rim. Factories were also scattered widely in other areas. One hundred and sixty thousand men and women prepared foods and chemicals; worked in the garment industries; helped to manufacture leather goods, glassware, and wood, paper, and metal products; were employed in machine shops and other industries. Brooklyn's huge war industries increased the number of workers by a hundred thousand. And the waterfront, greatly expanded and modernized since the 1890s, was a subject to which only superlatives could do justice. In peacetime it was the nation's leading center of foreign trade. At 187 piers seventy-five shipping companies berthed as many as seven hundred steamships, which sailed all the seven seas, visiting on regular trips two hundred of the world's ports. All this, in addition to a large domestic commerce. Brooklyn's geographical advantages were the explanation of this tremendous development—its shoreline from Newtown Creek along East River, and its great bay frontage, and in addition the small waterways and canals which penetrated deep into industrial centers. In wartime, of course, Brooklyn's waterfront activities were multiplied. No other strip of coastline in the country approached it in importance. Thousands, toiling at twenty private shipyards, supplemented the tremendously expanded operations at the Navy Yard. And while the war shipping came and went and the workers bent their backs to achieve victory, approximately three hundred thousand of the borough's young men and women were in uniform, scattered far and wide in the global war. None of them were more genuine, dyed-in-the-wool Brooklynites than the boys and girls who bore Irish names.

From the time, a century ago, that Dr. John Byrne of Brooklyn won international fame for his pioneering achievements in cancer surgery, the Irish played an ever-expanding role in science and education. College professors, laboratory workers, schoolteachers, priests, intellectuals of many stripes, had immensely important parts to play in these matters. So also in the arts and general culture. An unbroken line of journalists succeeded McCloskey and Kinsella, some of them sensitive and gifted men, such as John A. Heffernan of the *Eagle's* staff. Mark Murphy, native of South Dakota, a contributor to the *New Yorker*, the *Saturday Evening Post,* and other magazines, was one of the brilliant younger writers who came to the Heights in the 1940s.

There were times, entirely apart from St. Patrick's Day, when the Celtic nature had a chance for untrammeled expression. Rich and poor hailed Eamon de Valera when he came to Brooklyn, a hunted fugitive, in 1919. Brooklyn gave him a demonstrative welcome such as no one before him had had. It was an emotional release, a wild and generous outburst of devotion to the old country. But the Friends of Irish Freedom of that day were also the passionately loyal Americans of '17 and '41. After Ireland became free in fact there was no need to champion her cause, and so one of the strong bonds which Irish people of all sorts had felt began to lose its power. Many, however, continued to cherish a cultural tie with Ireland, just as many Scots hold fast to their Scottish heritage.

The generalization that Brooklyn's complexity has been reflected by the Irish more perfectly than by any others suggests that one looking for a typical Brooklynite would have to search among the Irish. Probably there never was a typical Brooklynite, but certainly the Brooklyn Irishman who became mayor of Greater New York after the war ended was truly representative of the modern city. His training for the job was thorough, if a bit unusual. He had been a bright boy in high school back in Ireland, and his schoolteacher mother wanted him to prepare for the priesthood. So he went to Spain in order to qualify for a career in the church at the University of Salamanca. But it happened that his own ambition lay in quite another direction. In 1910 he took his fate in his own hands and sailed for America.

His decision led to the fulfillment of boyhood dreams, but at first it meant hard labor on the docks, and other jobs

that were just as strenuous. For a time he tended bar at the
Vanderbilt Hotel. Then he walked a beat along the Brooklyn waterfront. The man who finally graduated, in 1933,
from Fordham Law School, had had quite a bit of experience. He knew the secluded life of the student and he knew
how it felt to be a worker holding a union card. More important, perhaps, than either, he had acquired firsthand
knowledge of New York's police force.

He had been practicing law for a number of years when
Mayor Joseph V. McKee made him a city magistrate. But it
was not until 1939, after he had become a county judge,
that his name came prominently before the public in newspaper headlines. Brooklyn had been brought most unpleas-
antly into the notice of the whole country by the operations of a gang of criminals known as Murder, Inc. Judge
O'Dwyer consented to run for district attorney, and after
his election the chief killers were sent on their way to the
chair.

Such cool-headed competence meant political availa-
bility. New York had a habit of putting successful district
attorneys into high executive posts. The Brooklyn Irishman was nominated for mayor in 1941, but he could not
defeat Mayor LaGuardia, then running for a third term.
However, the war gave him a chance to undertake other
big responsibilities. He did valuable duty as a noncom-
batant officer in the army, becoming a brigadier general,
and in 1944 he went on a vitally important mission to Italy
as head of the Economic Section of the Allied Control
Commission. In 1945 he was elected mayor, and in 1949
he was re-elected.

We shall let the Irish story end with him. But it is a fast-
moving story, with a great future in Brooklyn.

The Versatile Italians

Early in January in the year 1835 Signor Ravaglia, "primo tenore" of the Italian Opera, crossed the river to the newly-fledged city of Brooklyn. At a concert given at Eames and Putnam's Classical Hall he sang some Rossini arias. Besides being connected with the Italian Opera which had been performing at the Richmond Hill Theater in New York, Ravaglia, according to the advertisement in the *Star,* was "composer to the Theater Royal, Covent Garden, and English Opera House, and Member of the Royal Academy of Music." The little city of Brooklyn was not then accustomed to such approved talent. It was not, in fact, accustomed to Italian music. And yet this Latin note, this lilting, soaring strain, having once been sounded, was never again wholly strange to the ears of Brooklynites.

Within a century it was to be one of the dominant notes in Brooklyn. In the year 1935 hundreds of thousands of Italians lived in the borough. They were a people to whom music was a natural form of expression. Suddenly, in the dusty street, in the midst of traffic and commerce, one's spirit would be lifted and one's ear enchanted by the spontaneous singing of a young baritone or a free-throated soprano. The story is told of one natural genius, a bricklayer, who in a recent year stopped traffic on Fulton Street at the noon hour, and was afterwards snatched from his scaffold high above the street to become a concert singer. But thousands in Brooklyn sang or hummed a bit of opera while they toiled, with no thought of good fortune, just as their cousins were doing in the Sicilian hills and on the Campanian plains.

It was toward the end of the nineteenth century that Italians began to come in large numbers. The great migration to Brooklyn began in the 1870s and continued in a swelling flood until the eve of the First World War. After that war, and before the Second World War broke out, Brooklyn's Italian population, by migration and by natural increase, went beyond the half-million mark. Like Brooklyn's Jews, the Borough's Italians, if set apart, would constitute a great city—an industrious hive with all social classes represented as well as all degrees of wealth, from poor, struggling workers to millionaire manufacturers and contractors.

The first migration was largely one of laborers who came over without their families. They came from southern Italy and Sicily, in the main. Their homeland was impoverished, but it was beautiful. They were deeply attached to it, and a large proportion of them came over to get a better living for a few years, to save some money, and then to return to Italy.

It was only dire necessity, in fact, which drove them from their homes, for they belonged to a static society. Normally, generation followed generation in the same valley, in the same village, in the same occupation, following the same customs and repeating the same bits of proverbial wisdom. But exploitation and oppressive taxation induced landless peasants to seek temporary employment far from home. Workers got in the habit of going for several months each year to Germany and France. With the growth of steamship lines and cheap transportation many crossed over to South America. So, when the flow of migration set in strongly to the United States, the process was not a new one.

At first, the magnetic power of the native villages exerted an irresistible attraction across the North Atlantic. No matter how they earned their living, the Italians were still peasants of Palermo or Trapani or Salerno or Avellino or Molfetta. But gradually the pull of America overcame that of the homeland. The transient workers remained longer in the United States thah they had been accustomed to remain elsewhere. Five years in the "States" was the rule. More and more frequently this changed to permanent residence. Then wives were sent for, and families were raised in the New World. On the other hand, there were periods of depression when great return migrations to Italy set in, such as after 1893 and 1907. But these periods were temporary. America won the tug of war with the great host of permanent settlers because the country was rich, and growing richer, because there were jobs and opportunities, and because of the freedom and lack of restrictions in America compared with the social rigidity in Italy.

It is true that many of the newcomers found it hard to adapt themselves to American conditions. They often found themselves victims of exploitation. The harshness of the American scene, the bleak unloveliness of the city streets, oppressed them. They were frequently crowded tier on tier in congested tenement districts from which every semblance of beauty had been rooted out and excluded. They remembered the beauty of their homeland, and sometimes forgot that there, too, they had been exploited.

One of the motives for the movement to Brooklyn in the eighties was to escape overcrowding in Manhattan. Those who first came settled in the vicinity of the Hamilton Ferry, along Union and President streets. Here, in Red Hook, near Buttermilk Channel and the old India wharf, was Brooklyn's Little Italy. The pioneer settlers were joined by many families from New York's Mulberry Bend, one of the most densely populated districts in Manhattan. Afterwards, Italian colonies spread in all directions—into the Navy Yard district, Gravesend, East New York, Williamsburg, Greenpoint, Ridgewood.

The tenacity of Old-World culture was never better illustrated by any people. Amid natural conditions as un-Italian as imagination could devise, the Sicilian or Campanian or Calabrian village persisted. Each street in which Italians settled became a community of old Italy in a literal sense, filled with transplanted neighbors and kinfolk. No streets in Brooklyn were so given over to unrestrained life. None were so exuberant, and none so spontaneous. The first generation Italians lived as they had been accustomed to live under the azure Italian skies, where much of the day's functions and the intimate affairs of life were carried on in the open village piazzas. Little Italy was natural and unashamed.

On fine summer days young mothers sat on doorsteps, babies at their breasts; children swarmed the streets; neighbors sought the sunshine and exchanged confidences. Everything possible was done out-of-doors and in the companionship of neighbors and friends. When letters from Italy came, they were often read aloud by a neighboring savant—Giuseppe the barber, perhaps—where they could be shared and discussed by all.

There were shops where Italian delicacies could be bought—black and white olives, raisins, currants, prickly pears, greens of various sorts, brightly-colored pastries, long loaves of bread, macaroni twisted in amazing shapes, cheeses in varied forms, huge cans of imported olive oil. There were butcher shops where hung the gory heads of steers, and where entrails could be bought for the stock pot. There were fish markets where, in addition to a variety of fish pleasing to the Italian palate, one could buy a great slice of "tonno"—tunny, or horse-mackerel, which we now purchase in small tins under its euphemistic disguise as "tuna."

One could find plenty of evidences of poverty in Little Italy. As the influx into Brooklyn increased, living conditions in many areas approached those in New York's lower East Side. There were some sections where it was especially hard for the sanguine Italian spirit to rise above outward circumstances. This was true of parts of that neglected region of ill-paved streets which lay between Brooklyn Bridge and the Navy Yard, a region in which Calabrian peasants crowded small wooden tenements and crumbling brick dwellings—some of them erected a century before by Yankees. These houses had been handed down from one generation of newly-arrived immigrants to another, becoming ever more dilapidated in the process. A section of the district was the Irishtown described in the last chapter, but now Irish only in name. The Italians were there by the thousands in the years before the First World War, their horizons hemmed in by factories to the northward and warehouses to the south. But in the poorest home one might find bright bits of color, shrubs or plants growing in carefully tended pots or tubs, chromos of Italian royalty, and holy pictures, including a treasured likeness of the patron saint of the Italian village whence the family and their neighbors on the same street had come.

In the Navy Yard district, in Red Hook, Greenpoint, and elsewhere, Old World and New World traditions and ideas were mingled. As time went on, and a measure of prosperity came to some of the homes, Antonio or Salvatore or Guiseppe went to college, and came home a sophisticated young American engineer, pharmacist, or lawyer. He might still wear a charm to protect himself from *mal-occhio* (the evil eye). He would wear it as a matter of sentiment, because it had long ago been given him by someone for whom he cared. And yet he would half believe in it. His cousin Angelina, a quick-witted, warm-hearted girl who had not had his advantages, might believe implicitly in the ritual handed down by word of mouth from generation to generation, a potent formula which could cure one lying sick from the effects of the malign glance of some ill-wisher. Perhaps she herself, like the "hex-doctors" of the Pennsylvania Dutch, had received the ritual from a knowing old grandmother, and had practiced its incantation when a neighbor's baby would not stop crying, or the neighbor herself had a headache. Salvatore, the young pharmacist, was sure to see that the baby got the right remedies if there was real need for it.

No people were more blessed with that élan, that exuberant vitality which overcomes adverse circumstances, than were the Italians. A note of gaiety, sometimes subdued, and sometimes boisterous, pervaded the teeming life of Little Italy. Even the poorest were always ready to forget care if the means for enjoyment were at hand. There were inexpensive amusements long before the days of motion pictures. For instance, one could pay a few cents to see a good show at a marionette theater on Union Street. But Union Street, like other streets in Italian Brooklyn, reached its fullest expression of Old World enthusiasm at the times of the religious festivals. For all the people of Little Italy there were two of them—the feast of the patron saint, and on August 14 that of the Assumption of Our Lady (*Festa dell' Assunzione della Vergine*, or, colloquially, *l'Assunzione*).

They were carnivals of piety. Slender arches strung with thousands of electric bulbs turned night into day. There was a religious procession, and the saint's statue was carried aloft. At night, everyone from the youngest to the oldest devoted himself to the business of having a good time. Finally came the fireworks—rockets well primed with powder which produced an ascending scale of noise until the loudest crashing explosion of all ended the celebration.

Staid residents of the Heights, who saw the rockets against the night sky and heard the explosions wondered what it was all about. If it had been explained to them, they would have found the *festa* hard to understand, for their inheritance was North European. They could not share the untrammeled emotions of the Mediterranean peoples.

Some of the Italian community leaders looked askance at these celebrations, but when attempts were made to tone them down those to whom the old Italian custom was dear rallied to its defense. Difficulties of understanding also developed between those of the old generation whose hearts were still in Italy and many of the younger people who were no longer bound by Italian ideas. The boys and girls went to school, learned English, and picked up the street vernacular. They became knowing in the ways of Brooklyn. Some of them, estranged from the old people before they were oriented in the new society, became loose and restless. Fortunately, there were correctives and ameliorating influences, including the democracy of the public schools, the libraries, the athletic fields, and the bathing beeches.

The church, of course, was always a restraining and guiding force. From their earliest days in Brooklyn it bound the Italian people together. It would be impossible to overestimate its importance as a social influence. It meant much more to them than religion in a formal sense. It made them feel safe in a strange land. They could always seek its protection. The simple, illiterate masses turned to the priest for advice in all affairs of life. He was the all-wise man, the man who knew, who could help them. The first generation of immigrants leaned on him as a small child on its parent. They even entrusted their savings to him before they acquired the habit of taking them to a bank. The hold of the church was strikingly illustrated by the fact that when radical anticlericals wanted to harangue the people they had to go to the church to do it, for that is where they would be sure to find them. So harangue them they did, within the holy walls, and gave little thought to the incongruity of the act.

The church symbolized permanence and security. It upheld all the deepest values of Italian life. Its closest ally was the family group. In the case of many families solidarity and stability were maintained by the strong force of transplanted habit. The habit, for instance, of visiting the house of the oldest member of the family on Sundays and anniversary occasions. It was done in the old home in Italy, and it was continued in Brooklyn. Thus, families were bound closely by the strongest of cements, a cement made up of a little wine, much talk, and much laughter. In ways like this the essentials of Italian life—the deep understanding, the link with the past—continued through generations.

For most of the Italians the steps up from extreme poverty and illiteracy were slow and laborious. The first generation, for the most part, did the hardest of day labor. Gradually a few who had a little capital began to pull themselves up by opening fruit stores or by importing olive oil and wines and other foods which Italians craved. Others started small private banks. The first business enterprises were all small ventures, and they all operated within the Italian community. Most of them met the real needs of the people.

Some of the banks, however, were run by sharp practitioners who were ready to take advantage of the trusting majority. Organized ostensibly to send the depositors' money home to needy relatives in Italy, they were really contrivances for robbing the simple. These blood-sucking institutions were finally curbed by the state banking laws.

Not all the private banks were of that sort. One of them, the Banca Sessa, was managed so well that the Italians who timidly entrusted their savings to it saw them mount steadily, with accruing interest. Moreover, they were given good counsel in the management of their affairs by the shrewd and far-seeing Mr. Sessa. The Banca Sessa was a very small business to begin with, but it grew to great size on the savings of the thrifty people of Brooklyn's Little Italy. When Antonio Sessa died, his son, Joseph, succeeded to its management. Joseph was one of Brooklyn's outstanding bankers and one of its very wealthy citizens, with a great mansion on Ridge Boulevard. After going through a series of mergers his bank became a branch of the National City Bank of New York.

The careers of the Sessas illustrate one of the notable chararacteristics of Brooklyn's Italian people—their business acumen. Not all the Italians who engaged in business pursuits could get rich. Most of them had to be content with hard work and comparatively few returns. But a great many did go into business, and even the moderately successful were able to live on a scale that would have caused great wonder in their native villages.

Some of the small business enterprises spread beyond the Italian neighborhoods in time, and found customers in a wider field. Fruit businesses and contracting, especially, touched the larger community. Sicilian and Genoese fruit vendors went about the streets or opened small stores throughout the borough. In Red Hook an Italian pushcart market lined Union Street. Some of the stores, in favored locations, became large retailing establishments. A substantial majority of the traders in Wallabout Market were

Italian, and a few of them acquired considerable wealth. Some of those who went into contracting and building also made fortunes, like the Irish a half century or more before them. They found their workers among their own countrymen. Angelo Paino, for instance, went to East New York, Red Hook, Coney Island, the Navy Yard district, Williamsburg, and Greenpoint for men to work on his sewer construction contracts. In like manner Carmelo Pellegrino and Salvatore Sabbatino, who made fortunes on the waterside, hired Italians as stevedores. Among the big building contractors of Brooklyn were James and Louis Camardella and Frank Scavullo. Bartholomew Turecamo, the "sand baron," had a huge asphalt plant in Gravesend Bay and a fine residence on Ridge Boulevard. John Daurio, builder of houses, schools, and factories, was a native of Somma Vesuviana, in the province of Naples.

One of the first and best known of the Italian contractors was Charles Bennett, who came from Salerno in 1894, at the age of seventeen. After an early career in politics, he secured contracts for such great projects as Nassau Boulevard, Far Rockaway Boulevard, and the Saw Mill River Parkway in Westchester County. Vincent Giffuni, a native of Potenza, came over in 1904, and built up a large business in Brooklyn as a contractor, builder, and real estate operator.

Better known, perhaps, than most of the Italian businessmen of Brooklyn, was Joe Balzarini. He came to the borough soon after the turn of the century, with only a few dollars in his pocket. Within a score of years he and his associates were very rich. His three "Joe's Restaurants" were famous, and his real estate holdings were extensive.

Italians also became a big factor in Brooklyn's huge garment industry, as workers, as managers, and as owners. The nature of the industry made it possible for comparatively small enterprises to get started and grow. For example, Albert Figuccio, Ernesto Gallo, and Louis Isabella —all three of them natives of Italy who came to the United States about 1910—employed from fifty to one hundred men each, in the manufacture of coats, suits, and dresses. Daniel de Vita, general manager of the Naval Clothing Depot in Brooklyn, and designer of uniforms for the United States Navy, was a second generation Italian, born in Newark, New Jersey.

As the twentieth century advanced Brooklyn Italians got definitely into politics, and progressed from a state of political innocence to comparative sophistication. The prodding of practical politicians of Italian blood accelerated the rate of naturalization. The racial boss was more or less common to all groups, but Italian bosses were among the craftiest of the genus.

The first powerful Italian leader appeared very early in the century. His name was Francis L. Corrao. Corrao's power was in large part exerted through his presidency of the Italo-American Political Union, to which the various Italian Democratic political clubs sent delegates. After Corrao came a succession of politicians and bosses—Michael T. Laura, Judge Sylvester Sabbatino, Anthony F. Mayo, Gasper Liota, Jerome G. Ambro, and others.

Some of the organization workers and officeholders were figures of significance in the gradual adjustment of the Italian people to New World conditions. One of those whose career is worth citing as an example was Vincent d'Agrosa, president of the Columbus Political Club of the Fifth and Eleventh wards, at Bridge and High streets. Mr. d'Agrosa was born in Italy, received part of his education in France, and came to Brooklyn alone when a boy of sixteen. He got a job with Chapel Frères et Cie, Brooklyn furriers. He studied English and other subjects at the night school in old Public School 1, at Concord and Adams streets. In 1888, at the age of twenty-one, he became an American citizen. His opportunity in Brooklyn arose from his unusual facility as a linguist. For many years he was interpreter of Italian and French in the Kings County Supreme Court, a post which required a very particular talent, when one considers the great number of local dialects and the bewildering colloquialisms of Italians from widely separated provinces.

As the Italian vote grew, the names of Italians began to appear on party tickets. Matthew T. Abruzzo, a native of Brooklyn, became a Federal district court judge. Francis X. Giacone, who had been an assemblyman, an assistant district attorney, and Deputy Fire Commissioner of New York City, was made a city magistrate. Henry Ughetta was elected to the state Supreme Court. In recent years a number of Brooklynites of Italian blood have achieved unusual distinction, but no one of them has been more conspicuous than Juvenal Marchisio, judge of the Domestic Relations Court, who during the Second World War became national president of American Relief for Italy.

Politically, Brooklyn Italians were distributed from the extreme left to the extreme right. Economic interest, as with most groups, was a powerful factor in political preference. Many of the more prosperous were Republicans. Nicholas Selvaggi, president of the Italian Country Club, was Republican leader. The Republican party organization was geographically complete. Each assembly district had its club, and these were bound into a manageable union in 1919 by Mr. Selvaggi, when he organized the Kings County League of Italian-American Republican Clubs.

But it was not only in business and in politics that the versatile Italians were doing significant things; they were busy in medicine, education, the fine arts, and other fields. Many years ago the Italian doctors of Brooklyn formed their own medical society. In 1948 their position was underscored by the election of Dr. A. W. Martin Marino to the presidency of the Kings County Medical Society, which was then one hundred and twenty-six years old. The Italian Teachers' Association, organized in 1915, was headed for many years by Dr. Mario E. Cosenza, a distinguished classicist and archaeologist. Hundreds of Italian men and women have taught in the public schools and colleges of the borough. In 1948 Dr. Dominick F. Maurillo, of Brooklyn, became a member of the State Board of Regents, New York's highest educational tribunal.

Intelligently appreciative Italian listeners for years have been conspicuous in concert audiences, whether in the Academy of Music or elsewhere. Conspicuous among the artists in the field of music was Professor Salvatore Avitable, teacher of Marion Talley, who came from Naples many years ago, and made his home in the Park Slope district.

The rich culture of the church and of the homeland was kept alive for many Italians by priests educated in Italy, such as the Reverend Arsenio Caprio and the Reverend Eliodoro Capobianco—who was born in Buenos Aires of parents who had emigrated from the Italian province of Avellino. Father Capobianco's parochial school at the Church of Our Lady of Loreto, where hundreds of children were given instruction in the Italian language, was one of many centers where Italian traditions were cultivated.

Mutual benefit clubs, beginning in Red Hook, were in time located throughout the borough. The Italian Benevolent Society for the benefit of the sick and the helpless, at 35 President Street, was organized and supported by the United Italian Societies of Brooklyn. Social clubs, organ-

ized at an early period in the Red Hook district, were also
spread widely, and there were charities supported by
the entire Italian community of Brooklyn, such as the
Brooklyn branch of the Italian Welfare League.

Long before the Second World War Italian society in
Brooklyn had become exceedingly complex. Italians were
in every walk of life and in nearly every conceivable occupation; from the socially prominent to the relatively obscure, they functioned in a great variety of organizations.
Among them were fraternal lodges, such as the Sons of
Italy; the Etna, Roma, Leonardo da Vinci, and Caesar
Masonic lodges; lodges of the Order of the Eastern Star;
lodges of the Foresters of America. At the social apex was
the Italian Country Club at 1305 86th Street, surrounded
by residences of wealthy Italians.

The reason that there were Italians of prominence and
ability in nearly every field of activity in Brooklyn was
plain enough. It was not simply that the Italians were a
versatile people; it was because there were so many of
them. In the 1930s and '40s the great majority were still
poor, and life for them was relatively hard. But if we were
to compare their condition with that of their relatives in
Italian villages, their progress would seem considerable.
To their Italian kinfolk they were rich Americans. Those
who crossed the ocean to pay visits took an understandable
pride in the impression they made. The Italians had more
than the average love of gadgets, which is said to be an
American characteristic. They boasted to their cousins in
Italy of their refrigerators, their radios, and their automobiles, and they scoffed at the primitive conditions in the
homeland, at donkey carts and simple village ways. The
boasts were usually well-founded, no matter what their
economic condition, for there were many who would own

a big Buick even if it were necessary to live in poverty otherwise.

When Mussolini and his Blackshirts seized power in Italy in 1922, Italian people in Brooklyn read the news with interest and with some excitement. There were differences of opinion about this new leader, but no one thought that his rise to dominance could ever mean anything to Americans. At first, public opinion in general in the United States was not markedly unfavorable to him. The Italian homeland had been rent by strife since the close of the war. The Fascists restored order. They achieved reforms by compulsion. The Italian people and Italian industry were thoroughly regimented, and great public works were started. All this meant the end of chaos and the promise of achievement. Mussolini was the symbol of a resurgent Italy.

It was the most natural thing in the world for thousands of Brooklyn's Italians to be elated over the revival of Italy, and to applaud the leader who brought it about. American democratic principles did not seem to be involved. Few gave a thought to conflicting loyalties. European developments were something apart, not to be connected with American policy or political doctrine. The dictator's scowling visage was cheered in news reels because he promised Italy a great role in the world, not because the majority in the audience took any particular stock in fascism.

As time went on both fascism and the German nazism which was patterned on it had their subsidized exponents in American cities, Brooklyn included. This paid fascist propaganda was subtly calculated to mislead the unsophisticated majority of Brooklyn's Italian community. Many did not comprehend the direction in which they were being led. Those who gave money to the cause—and a great many were induced to do so—were, for the time, basking in the reflected glory of Mussolini's glittering regime and the dictator's promise of empire. They appropriated it as their own as a compensation for their own relative illiteracy and poverty and deprivation—their own consciousness of being "little people" in the midst of the opulent American civilization. Thus Italy's sudden rise to apparent greatness gave them a new importance in their own eyes. But there was also counterpropaganda, especially by labor organizations. And so the tensions and emotions of Italy's domestic struggle flared for a moment in Brooklyn's streets.

Little Italy rang with shouts of *Viva l'Italia! Abbiamo vinto la guerra!* when, in May of 1936, the news of the fall of Addis Ababa reached Brooklyn. The victory not only canceled the defeat suffered at Adowa in 1896, it seemed to mean that Italy was moving into the ranks of the greater colonial powers. But to the great majority who shouted happily it was simply victory, and victory was always good.

The point to bear in mind is that this reaction implied no lack of essential Americanism. In 1939 Brooklynites of all races poured through the gates of the World's Fair at Flushing Meadows—a gaudy exposition which hopefully pointed to a "World of Tomorrow." There was a "Court of Peace" at the Fair, and adjacent to it stood Italy's pavilion, one of the largest national exhibits, surmounted by a huge tower from which a cascade of water descended a great flight of steps. Here, in a lavish display, Italy's renaissance was revealed. No informed person could doubt the genuineness of the renaissance. For Brooklynites the lesson of this exhibit was that a part of Italy's great cultural treasure was deposited permanently in the borough, in the memories and skills and genius of its Italian citizens.

Before the summer was over the brightness of the Court of Peace was dimmed by the shadow of war. And in the spring of 1940—after the fair dedicated to peace had opened bravely for a second season—the shadow had become a thick pall. On the 10th of June Mussolini declared war on the Allies. There was no cheering in Brooklyn's Little Italy on that day. People listened to the familiar tones of the Fascist leader, shrugged their shoulders, and turned away dazed and saddened. The enthusiasm which paid fascist propaganda had so cunningly stimulated was now followed by a deep revulsion. "We're not Fascists. We're Americans. We don't want war," Italians were saying to each other with fervor in every Italian neighborhood in Brooklyn.

Pearl Harbor completed the disillusionment; but it also aroused a keen awareness of American citizenship. Many thousands of Italian boys—and girls—from all parts of Brooklyn were soon in the uniforms of their country. Italian political leaders, businessmen, and labor leaders now came forward to support the war effort by every means in their power. The Italian clubs and organizations did their part. Frank Serri, a Brooklyn lawyer who was active in the Mazzini Society, became chairman of the Fight for Freedom Committee.

The older people who remembered the homes they had left many years before could not be expected to be happy over the turn of events, but they maintained stoic fronts. When American troops landed in Sicily, they said, "Let's get it over with fast." Mussolini, the idol whose clay feet were now apparent to everyone, was ousted from power in July. In September the Italian government made terms with the Allies, and in October joined them as a cobelligerent.

For Italy it was now a war of liberation. It is not our business here to review the long-drawn-out fight of the Allied forces to oust the occupying German army from Italy's mountains and valleys, one of the toughest phases of the war. American boys of Italian blood were there, of course, many of them from Brooklyn. Democracy had made many blunders, and was to make more, but the American servicemen in Italy who bore Italian names and who could speak in Italian to peasants and townspeople were probably as good ambassadors as it has ever had.

Those who came back to Brooklyn after the war were sure of their Americanism. They were ready to be active in the great democratic society of the borough. It is evident that the Italians will play a tremendously important role in Brooklyn's future, not only because there are so many of them, but because of their great energy and their qualities as a people. Their talents, their gentle manners, their sensitiveness to beauty of color, form, and sound, their buoyancy of spirit and their zest for living, have been felt throughout Brooklyn's society. No racial group in Brooklyn, from the Dutch down, has exhibited greater versatility. No group has accomplished more within a brief period.

Three Centuries of Colored Brooklyn

Everybody knows of the great migration which made New York's Harlem the Negro capital of the world. Brooklyn's Stuyvesant Heights-Bedford district, as everybody should know, simultaneously became one of America's truly important centers of colored life. The tidal wave also rolled into Chicago, Detroit, and other industrial cities. All this occurred in the period of the First World War and the years following it. Few migrations or social movements in the history of the United States have been so dramatic or of such far-reaching importance. The vast trek has been described and interpreted by brilliant writers, both colored and white. A colored artist, Jacob Lawrence, of Brooklyn, has put it on canvas in a series of magnificent paintings—a moving and unforgettable historical record.

Not many, even in Brooklyn, know that a mature, full-orbed Negro society existed in Kings County long before this twentieth-century phenomenon took place. It was a deeply-rooted society, for the Negroes were, of course, one of the colonial peoples of Brooklyn. Only the Dutch could claim a longer descent. The colored people had grown steadily, but not spectacularly, in numbers from the seventeenth century to the early twentieth. In the 1890s there were families sufficiently well-to-do to afford to buy large houses and to furnish them lavishly. They could drive in expensive carriages, employ servants, and go abroad on annual trips. More in keeping with Brooklyn's characteristic rhythm of life were the considerable number of Negro commuters who went daily to New York offices and, like others, preferred Brooklyn to Manhattan as a place of residence, because one could get more living space and comfort there for his money. Strictly in line with Brooklyn's temper and tone, also, was the importance of the churches as the social basis of Negro community life.

This Negro society—from the humble unskilled worker to the man of means, from the comparatively unlearned to the eager, inquiring scholar—was the product, like the white society around it, of heredity and environment, of Brooklyn's particular history, and of the social and economic forces that created the great port. It was as indigenously American as any society in Brooklyn. Its story from colonial days was a vital, indispensable part of Brooklyn's story.

Francisco the Negro was a pioneer of Brooklyn. He was one of the original patentees of Boswyck, as the colonial records of the year 1660 witness. He was therefore a man of property and peer of his Dutch neighbors. In 1633 he was listed in the roll of officers and soldiers of Boswyck, and in that roll there appeared also the name of "Antoon the Negro."

The records give us little knowledge of these dark-skinned New Netherlanders of Peter Stuyvesant's time. But we can be reasonably sure that Francisco the landholder was not the only Negro in the province to occupy a position of independent dignity among his fellow colonists.

The great majority were slaves. But if the colonial picture is to be kept in focus it must be remembered that not only Negroes were held in bondage. Indians were enslaved, and thousands of Englishmen and other Europeans, in the seventeenth and eighteenth centuries, were bound in the fetters of indentures, some of them unwilling workers, kidnapped and brought forcibly to the New World.

It was a brutal and heartless business; but in the treatment of bondmen the early Dutch record in New Netherland was comparatively good. The first Negroes brought to the colony for forced labor arrived in 1626. Eighteen years later, on their own petition, they were freed and granted land in the part of Manhattan now called Greenwich Village.

The Dutch boers of Brooklyn had never asked for slaves; but the West India Company, always eager for profits, introduced the system and tried to encourage it. When the English took over, in 1664, conditions gradually became worse. The slave trade from Africa was a flourishing and infamous business in the latter seventeenth and early eighteenth centuries, and the slave codes in America were increasingly harsh. The Brooklyn Negro slave—relatively well-treated as he was on the Dutch farms of Breukelen and Midwout and New Utrecht—felt the pressure of the new laws. He was bound hard and fast in the fetters of chattel slavery. The fact that Englishmen and other Europeans were offered publicly for sale on the New York auction block did not make his lot easier. It only meant that those who did much of the basic hard labor in the planting of colonial America, whether colored or white, had little freedom of action and scant control over their own destinies.

Nevertheless, the Brooklyn Negro bondman frequently had ways of easing his condition. He could sometimes bargain for more satisfactory working conditions or arrange a sale to a new master. Sometimes the relationship between the master and mistress and the bondman and bondwoman was close and friendly. They often worked side by side in the fields or labored together at household tasks.

Like apprentices and indentured servants, Brooklyn slaves were taught many trades and skills. Eighteenth-century newspaper advertisements give a clue to their social and economic importance. From such sources we learn of Negroes who were acquainted with several languages, who were able to carry on "all sorts of business in city and country," of ship carpenters and other artisans. Such items, of course, furnish partial and incomplete evidence of the role played by the Negro people in colonial Brooklyn and of their influence in modifying the culture of the community.*

Although most people in the American colonies took slavery for granted, a few voices were raised against it early in the eighteenth century. Samuel Sewell, the Puritan judge, was one protester. Elihu Coleman, a Nantucket Quaker, was another. In the mid-century, a New Jersey Friend, John Woolman, went about the colonies preaching against it. But the majority were unmoved, and in the province of New York and the villages and farms of Kings County apathy was deep.

The most somnolent, however, were due for a shaking up. In the 1760s the winds of Revolutionary doctrine began to blow through the colonies, winds that became a hurricane in the next decade. Phrases that stirred the blood passed from mouth to mouth. There was much talk about the "rights of man." The word "liberty" took on a wide significance. In 1776, in the midst of war, Jefferson, a reluctant slaveowner, declared that all men are created equal. This doctrine became part of the creed of the new nation. Those who subscribed wholeheartedly to such ideas could not help recognizing the inconsistency of holding slaves.

There were, of course, other factors, chiefly economic, which made for the overthrow of the system in the Middle and Eastern States. For whatever reason or combination of reasons, after the Revolution it had few apologists in

* Henry R. Stiles, *A History of the City of Brooklyn*, I, 215 ff.

Brooklyn or in New York. Successive acts of the Legislature gradually brought it to an end in the state, a process which—supplemented by manumission on the part of masters—began in 1785 and ended in 1827. But most of Brooklyn's Negro people were free citizens long before the final year of emancipation, and under the state Constitution of 1821 their right to vote had been confirmed.

They and their brethren in other parts of the state had certainly earned the right by faithful service to the Republic. Colored patriots had died in its defense in many a battle on sea and land. And apart from actual combat, they had performed many services for the nation. In Brooklyn more than a thousand Negro men and boys were among the "patriotic diggers" who constructed entrenchments under General Joseph G. Swift's direction during the War of 1812. They were not all Brooklynites. Many hundreds of those historic "diggers"—whether Negro, Dutch, Yankee, Irish, or what not—came from over the East River.

Brooklyn Ferry, it will be remembered, was still a small village at that time. The census of 1820 credited the entire township with 7,175 people. Of these, 657 were listed as free Negroes and 190 as slaves. The population of the incorporated village of Brooklyn in that year was 5,210.

Probably about one in ten of the villagers was then a Negro. Brooklyn's most unfortunate minority group, most of them found shelter in the narrow alleys east of Fulton Street and along Gold Street and the far ends of Nassau and Concord streets, near the ropewalk. The youngest had never known slavery, but poverty they knew well enough. For a generation and more Negroes released from the comparatively mild bondage of Dutch farms had gravitated to the ferry settlement. The more resourceful found employment as coachmen and gardeners, cooks and housewives. There were some, however, who could not find a secure place for themselves. These unfortunates caused much annoyance to the majority of their own race as well as to the white householders of Brooklyn village. Barred from many occupations, skilled and unskilled, they were forced to beg or scrape up a living in a haphazard fashion; they caught oysters and crabs and peddled them about town on Sundays; they got drunk to forget their misery and found themselves in Judge Garrison's court of rough-and-ready justice, charged with being vagabonds.

Comfortably-placed villagers judged them and condemned them in their own parlors, forgetting that the responsibility for their condition rested with the community. They often extended the condemnation to Negroes in general. All the evidence, however, shows that most of the village Negroes lived as good citizens. Their culture, of course, was the culture of the people around them. White customs and institutions they freely copied or travestied, sometimes improved upon. Contemporary observers—newspaper editors and essayists—noticed, sometimes sympathetically, their gay abandon under tragic handicaps, their spontaneous humor, and their odd originality in song and melody. Yet their serious and constructive achievements escaped all but the more observant.

This little group within a pushing, expanding society faced serious, almost disheartening obstacles. Freedom meant a bitter, competitive struggle—the odds heavily against them—with aggressive immigrant workers. The influx of Yankees from every quarter and of Irish and German immigrants gave them a steadily smaller proportion of the total population. In 1825 there were 875 listed in the census. Ten years later the township, now become the city of Brooklyn, had about 25,000 inhabitants all told, but the colored population had increased only slightly. At the eve of the Civil War they numbered about five thousand in a total city population of 270,000.

Although many remained on Kings County farms and continued on a wage basis the familiar pattern of colonial days, maintaining a close relationship with the leading Dutch and Yankee families as domestics, seamstresses, and farm workers, occupations gradually became more diverse. Seamen, craftsmen, and workers in various fields charted new courses.

Cultural interests and art expressions undoubtedly touched the Brooklyn Negroes at a very early period. No people were more naturally receptive to the arts. Over the river, in 1821, Negro players opened a theater called the African Grove, which must have drawn some of its patronage from Brooklyn.

Active leaders organized mutual aid societies and independent Negro churches. These institutions were basic. They were the Negro's very own. However small at first, they were historically important because they were permanent and, in fact, indispensable. The New York African Society for Mutual Relief was founded in 1787, and was chartered by the state in 1810. Early in the nineteenth century, leaders in the Brooklyn Negro community started a similar organization for mutual aid called the Brooklyn African Woolman Benevolent Society. In 1819 Negro Methodists came down from the gallery of the Sands Street Methodist Church and began to worship in their own way in their own chapel under the pastoral care of a colored minister of the newly established African Methodist Episcopal Church.

It happened that the pastor of the Sands Street church at that time—Alexander McCaine, a native of Tipperary, Ireland—was proslavery in sympathy. He afterwards went to Virginia, and there he wrote a treatise entitled "Slavery Defended from Scripture." The Brooklyn Negroes were certainly not in sympathy with such a preacher; but they would have broken off at about that time in any case. The first step in the birth of a separate Negro denomination had been taken in Philadelphia three years earlier, and the new Brooklyn chapel was thus part of a larger movement.

This first Brooklyn Negro church and others which followed it were the chief centers of Negro community life. They were centers, too, of antislavery propaganda and part of the great Underground Railroad system which cared for the fugitive slave, protected and sheltered him by day, and helped him on the road to freedom by night. Long before Leavitt and Tappan and Elizur Wright organized the Brooklyn Anti-slavery Society, in 1835, Brooklyn Negroes—Henry C. Thompson, James Pennington, George Woods, George Hogarth, and others—had been speaking the language of abolitionism. *Freedom's Journal,* the organ of their movement, had been started in New York four years before Garrison started his *Liberator.* It was edited by a young Negro journalist, John B. Russwurm, a native of Jamaica, who had been graduated from Bowdoin College in 1825.

It was both morally and practically necessary for Negro leaders to join with others in working against slavery in the South. It was not merely a matter of sympathy with the oppressed. So long as Negro slavery existed under the Stars and Stripes their own citizenship was compromised. Whenever possible they took pains to signalize the fact of freedom with appropriate ceremonies. For instance, in 1827, when the last vestige of slavery was brought to an end in New York State, the New York and Brooklyn benevolent societies met together in Brooklyn and demonstrated publicly with a spectacular parade, "bands of music," and speeches.

A less spectacular, but more serious, demonstration took place a few years later. It resulted in a strong assertion of American citizenship. A number of Brooklyn's literate colored citizens, on a June evening of 1831, gathered in a small wooden building on Nassau Street near the ropewalk, a building which bore over its entrance the sign African Hall. Here in the candlelight they discussed the practical problems facing all colored people in Brooklyn, the handicaps which Negroes suffered in employment and occupations generally, and the limited chance that their children had for training in any skilled trade or in any profession. They were facing these issues because the colonization of American Negroes in Africa was being actively promoted at that time by the zealous philanthropists of the Brooklyn chapter of the American Colonization Society. The promise of a commonwealth under colored management was attractive to some Negroes, but the African Hall assembly strongly opposed the whole idea. They issued a statement which was a patriotic assertion of their citizenship, a warning to Brooklyn Negroes to shun the movement, and an appeal to Brooklynites to treat their colored neighbors more equitably.

It was published in the Brooklyn papers, and it contained an earnest declaration that the United States, not Africa, was the native land of the Negro people of Brooklyn, who were "brothers, countrymen, and fellow-citizens" of their white neighbors. "This is our country," the address continued. "We were born here. We know of no other country we can justly claim, or demand our rights as citizens, whether civil or political, but in these United States of America, our native soil." * Those were moving

* *Long Island Star,* June 8, 15, 1831.

phrases, but not convincing to some. Even Russwurm, erstwhile abolitionist editor, changed his mind and went to Liberia.

But most of Brooklyn's able Negro leaders persisted in their course as Americans, and tried to build Negro life in Brooklyn on the American pattern around them. They pushed educational and literary projects, formed political organizations, and engaged in antislavery activities. When the African Tompkins Society, in 1833, put on a demonstration in the form of a parade through the principal streets, it was noticed by editor Alden Spooner of the *Star*. Significantly he wrote of the marchers as "the abolitionists of Brooklyn, composing the greater portion of the colored male population." Apparently it was not until a couple of years later that the term "abolitionist" became biracial in Brooklyn, and white citizens publicly attached themselves to the radical antislavery movement.

Until the late 1820s Negro children had been taught in District School Number 1 on Adams Street. At that time a separate school under Negro auspices was started, supported in part by public funds. An evening school for adults was opened in the '30s. In the early '40s books were collected for a library, and a school for children was started in the village of Williamsburg. A rather bizarre development of the '30s, which soon petered out, was the "infant school" movement. It was a Utopian educational project inspired by a group of Brooklyn Yankee enthusiasts who took their cue from the English social experimenter Robert Owen. The purpose was to start the babies—both colored and white—along the path of wisdom early in life by teaching them the "elements of natural science." That generation was littered with the wreckage of such high-minded, vaguely-conceived enterprises. It was a day of tentative beginnings. But most of these institutions, whether colored or white, were forerunners of larger, community-wide institutions of succeeding decades.

By the mid-century the policy of educating children in public schools had won fairly general support. Segregation, however, had prevailed in Brooklyn's schools for a generation, and it was now fixed in the city's system, one of the fourteen schools in 1850 being reserved for colored children. This school was, nevertheless, a first step of importance. It led eventually to participation, on the part of Negro educators, in public education in Brooklyn on all levels, from the primary to the collegiate.

The Civil War, the Emancipation Proclamation, and the Constitutional Amendments that were adopted as a result of the war held immediate implications for Brooklyn's Negro people, and even deeper implications that only time would demonstrate. Some of them, in fact, have only recently begun to be realized in such advances as New York's fair employment law. They were certainly not fully grasped in the generation following the war. Nevertheless, the basis of civil rights was laid in Federal law. What did happen in that generation—and it was an important historic advance—was the gradual growth of that many-sided Negro society which flowered around the turn of the century.

That society was a demonstration of the Negro's Americanism, a demonstration almost lost in Brooklyn's immensity, but none the less a demonstration. The abilities and achievements of the outstanding Negroes of Brooklyn in the period between 1880 and 1914 were the abilities and achievements characteristic of Brooklyn's teeming people at large. These leading colored citizens were businessmen, lawyers, public officials, doctors, dentists, druggists, journalists, educators, clergymen. The best way to get an insight into the scope of their interests, perhaps, is to pick a few individuals almost at random, and briefly to notice their records.

That, for instance, of Samuel R. Scottron, an inventor-manufacturer, who had the practical kind of inventive genius that is sometimes claimed as a Yankee trait. He produced such devices as "Scottron's Adjustable Mirror" for barbers and hairdressers, an extension cornice, and an extension curtain-rod. These were all displayed at the New Orleans World's Fair, the Cotton Centennial of 1884–85. In 1894 Scottron discovered a method of making, from glass, an imitation onyx which, in the shape of lamp bases and candlesticks, brought him handsome profits. He had the same sort of instinct that guided Edison and Ford, and many another lesser American, producing what was needed and wanted by the public. Mayor Schieren appointed Scottron to the Brooklyn Board of Education, and in 1898 he was reappointed by Mayor Van Wyck to serve on the Education Board of the newly consolidated city of Greater New York.

An enterpriser of another sort was Peter W. Ray, who reached his seventy-fifth year at the turn of the century. Dr. Ray had functioned as a surgeon in the Civil War, and for a half century he was in the drug business at South Second and Hooker streets. He was associated with the beginnings of the Kings County Pharmaceutical Society and the Brooklyn College of Pharmacy, now a department of Long Island University, and he was treasurer of both institutions.

Another prominent colored Brooklynite of that day was Lewis H. Latimer. He, too, had served in the Civil War, as a landsman aboard the U.S.S. *Massasoit*. He was born in Massachusetts and was educated in Boston. His association with both Alexander Graham Bell and Thomas

A. Edison in their early experiments gave him an unusual education in his profession of electrical engineering. He was a man with scholarly tastes and a genuine gift for verse. As Latimer, Ray, and Scottron were passing from the scene, their logical successors were appearing—modern-minded businessmen whose outlook was toward the twentieth century.

Fred R. Moore was such a man, a resident of Brooklyn, but really a citizen of the metropolis. He was one of the ablest and most aggressive Negro leaders of his generation. For years he did a large business in mortgages and real estate, and in 1893 joined with others in organizing the Afro-American Building and Loan Company. But it was as the editor of the New York *Age*, a crusading Negro journal, that he was known to the larger public. Another prominent Brooklynite, Jerome B. Peterson, was coeditor and co-owner of the *Age*.

The careers of many others could be cited to show the versatility of colored Brooklynites—those of public school principals such as Charles A. Dorsey and Dr. William L. Buckley; those of D. Macon Webster, maritime lawyer, and Sumner Lark, the first Negro to be appointed Assistant District Attorney of Kings County; those of the political leaders Perry Wilson, John Syphax, Wesley Young, Edward Horne, grandfather of Lena Horne, the actress, and Jerome Peterson, co-owner of the *Age*, who was United States Consul to Venezuela and served in the Internal Revenue Service, both in Puerto Rico and in New York.

Negro women, also, demonstrated their resourcefulness and talents. Among them were scores of teachers. One of the outstanding women of Brooklyn was a colored practicing physician, Dr. Verina Morton Jones. Mrs. Jones was born in Cleveland in 1865, and was graduated from the Woman's Medical College of Pennsylvania in 1888.

She was not only a trail-blazer for the women of the colored race, she was one of those who have helped to cut paths for countless women of all races. For years an active social worker, she was connected with many civic enterprises, and served as commissioner of the Brooklyn Bureau of Charities. Her career bridged the old and the new centuries, but she really belonged to the twentieth.

So, also, did Arthur Alfonso Schomburg, one of the most distinguished of American antiquarians. Schomburg began to collect materials relating to Negroes while still a boy in his native Puerto Rico. He came to New York in 1897, at the age of twenty-three, and later became a resident of Brooklyn. In 1911 he and others organized the Negro Society for Historical Research, and Schomburg was made its librarian. His zeal in the collection and preservation of all things of value by and about Negroes resulted in the building up of a remarkable library, containing many thousands of books, manuscripts, etchings, and pamphlets relating to Negro life and history. In 1926 it became the property of the New York Public Library, and from 1932 until his death in 1938 Schomburg was its curator.

This was one of the newest Negro cultural institutions. The oldest Negro organization in the country—the New York African Society for Mutual Relief, Incorporated, founded in 1787—was mentioned earlier in this chapter. Its president in recent years was a Brooklyn man whose professional career began near the turn of the century, Dr. Walter N. Beekman. Dr. Beekman was the first Negro to be graduated from the New York Dental School, and the first to be licensed to practice dentistry in New York State. A widely traveled man, witty and accomplished, his high position in Brooklyn was recognized by Mayor Walker, who appointed him to the city's Tercentenary

Commission; and more recently by Governor Dewey, who made him a member of the Committee on Discrimination in Employment in the State.

Dr. Beekman and others of his generation had seen the changing events of fifty years. They had witnessed the successive waves of migration which swept up from the South during and after the First World War and flooded into industrial cities all across the Northern states. There was something to excite awe in the immense and sweeping trek from the stricken cotton fields of the South, from the semi-serfdom of tenant farming and share cropping, from the boll weevil and the Ku Klux Klan. Harlem, in upper Manhattan, became the largest Negro center in the world, and the Negro people moved into a major position in Brooklyn.

Some interpreters of the migration have asserted that while the opportunities held out by large-scale Northern industry were contributory factors in inducing it, the great movement was fundamentally a mass reaching out for a share in the American promise of democracy, so frequently and glibly expressed, so often denied. The migrant, they have said, had become aware of a chance for the improvement of all the conditions of life. In taking this momentous step he was passing—like the Eastern European Jews before him—from mediaeval conditions to modern times; but unlike any immigrant, he was making the passage within the country of his ancestry through many generations. He was an American, determined to claim the American birthright.

Not many of the migrants would have expressed it in such terms. A great many would have said something like this: Mr. Potter, the storekeeper, took a chattel mortgage on the migrant's mule when he borrowed money for seeds and food; the migrant had had a bad year and couldn't

pay his debt; and the storekeeper took his mule away from
him. How could he farm without a mule? He came North
so that he could earn some money, enough to live on, and
not get deeper and deeper in debt.

Many of the younger generation could see the trend of
things and were anxious to make a break. A South Carolina Negro who left his home in 1917, when he was seventeen years old, told his own story in these words:

> I figured it this way. I just wanted to travel. I could work and
> dig all day on the Island (St. Helena Island, South Carolina)
> and best I could would be to make $100 and take a chance on
> making nothin'. Well, I figured I could make 'roun' thirty or
> thirty-five dollars every week and at that rate save possibly
> $100 every two months. 'Cos I was single then. Couldn't save
> that much married. So I decided I'd be a fool to stay there n' dig
> all my life at that rate. Pay-day, little as it was, would come once
> a season. In public work you get paid every week.
>
> First place I went to was Savannah. Went there because that's
> the seventy-five cent stop. Most people who leave the Island
> stop there first. Thought I'd soon save up enough to travel up
> North. I began writing my brothers who were up here. They
> said, "Yes, jobs are good up here."
>
> In 1923 some of my friends I was working with and I decided
> to catch the boat and travel up to Philly. We stopped there,
> worked one month. Didn't like it. Came on over to my brothers
> in Brooklyn.*

Thousands upon thousands of such stories could be
told by migrants, differing in detail, but much alike in
general tenor. Very human stories they would be, and very
American. They came North to find a better life; they
would agree to that statement, which is only another way
of saying that they came to claim their birthright, which
seemed to be denied in many parts of the South.

* Clyde Vernon Kiser, *Sea Island to City*, New York, 1932, p. 126.

Negroes flocked to Harlem from other parts of the world as well. It became an intellectual and cultural focal point for Negroes of all nations. Brooklyn's Negro community could not help feeling the impact of the new forces. The concentration into small geographical areas in the two boroughs, of the city bred and the country bred, of the native American and the foreign-born; of laborers, industrial workers, business and professional men, and intellectuals of all types; of the conservatively minded and the radical; of politicians and labor leaders—of all possible elements in a complex restless society—gave the people of both areas a sense of community never before experienced. There were articulate leaders who could express this sense. A new spirit was born, an independence that was neither truculent nor apologetic. It has been expressed in the term "the New Negro." It survived the shock of many disappointments and was inherited by the generation born after the First World War.

The wave of migration in Brooklyn spread through Stuyvesant Heights and Bedford and into other districts. There was an especially dense concentration along the main streets of the Bedford-Stuyvesant districts—Fulton, Myrtle, Sumner, and Gates. In the first years of the inflow the newcomers for the most part found employment, but the problem of housing was grim indeed. Both problems became acute when post-war prosperity was succeeded by prolonged economic collapse.

For many thousands of Brooklyn Negroes then and since, living conditions have been far below the standards of decency. High rates for small, dilapidated apartments in many store-front buildings and old residences levied a tremendous toll on wages. During the depression Negro workers in Brooklyn as elsewhere were more often than not "the first to be fired," and when conditions began to

improve they were too frequently "the last to be hired."
There was plenty of hardship in other sections of Brooklyn during the bleak years that followed the collapse of
1929, but misery laid its hand more unrelentingly over
this district than over any other.

Prominent among those who grappled with the issues
of employment and housing and social welfare were the
leaders of the National Urban League, which had been
established in 1910. They furthered the interests of Negro
workers in all fields, and worked effectively to lift Union barriers against Negroes. In the depression winter
of 1929–30 the New York and Brooklyn branches of the
League were active in the drive to unionize the ladies' dress
industry. The International Ladies' Garment Workers'
Union, which conducted the drive, was in full sympathy
with Negro labor and worked to obliterate the color line
in industry.

Robert Elzy, head of the League, a Brooklyn resident, developed the work of the Brooklyn branch along
many lines. Its trained social workers operated on many
levels of helpfulness, in the fields of vocational guidance,
welfare, recreation, youth problems, and so forth. The
League's widely circulated magazine, *Opportunity*, was
sold on news stands throughout the city, and was a most
impressive witness in itself to the New Negro of the advancing century.

The vast army of newcomers found guides in politics
among the seasoned Negro politicians of Brooklyn, the
men who had come to the front long before the migration.
George E. Wibecan was the Republican leader. His career
stretched from the quiet times at the beginning of the
century to the turbulent 1940s. He built up a Negro Republican organization and attended most of the party con-
ventions, state and national, between 1910 and 1940. But

Wibecan was much more than a party worker and race politician. He had an active part in the beginnings of the National Association for the Advancement of Colored People. Brooklyn knew him for his tireless zeal, his fearlessness, and his wide sympathies. He was founder or head of many community organizations, including the Federation of Colored Organizations of Brooklyn and Long Island, and he gave his support to the cause of Irish freedom, and a free India, and to political emancipation generally.

Wibecan was a Republican, but the Brooklyn Negroes of the 1920s and after found and followed leaders in other parties as well, and cast their votes from the right to the left. One of the newer types of officeholder was Clarence Wilson, Assistant District Attorney, able and quiet-spoken, a native of Antigua, British West Indies, and a graduate of Brooklyn Law School. An unmistakable sign of the new political significance of Negroes in Brooklyn was the election to the state Assembly in 1948 of Bertram L. Baker, nominee of the Democratic and American Labor Parties, the first Negro to be elected to office in Brooklyn.

The Brooklyn Negro community of 1948 was very different from that of the 1900s, but the basic institutions of the past remained. The churches were still fundamental in colored society. Baptists and Methodists led in numbers of communicants and the value of church property; but there were now many other religious divisions, including Protestant Episcopalians, Presbyterians, a growing Roman Catholic membership, Adventists, Nazarenes, Pentecostals, and African Orthodox. Affiliated with the churches were scores of social clubs, Boy and Girl Scout troops, dramatic clubs, benevolent aid societies, and health services. Co-ordinated organizations—the Carlton Branch of the Y.M.C.A. and the Ashland Place Branch of the

Y.W.C.A.—had been pioneered a generation before by the Reverend and Mrs. A. J. Henry. Herbert Miller, an energetic modern executive, was now secretary of the Carlton Branch.

The mid-twentieth century was fully reflected in the tone of the periodical literature read widely in the borough. *Ebony*, a brilliantly edited weekly, was the Negro counterpart of *Life*. This new, fully awakened press found a number of staff writers in Brooklyn, such as Thomas Watkins, editor of the Brooklyn section of the *Amsterdam News*.

New doors were opening. Brooklyn College, like many other colleges and universities throughout the North and West, invited Negro scholars to join its faculty—Dr. Marian Starling to the English Department and Dr. Marian Cuthbert to teach anthropology and sociology. A brilliant scholar who resided in Brooklyn, Dr. Lawrence Dunbar Reddick, well-known contributor to national magazines who succeeded Schomburg as curator of the Schomburg Collection, and joined the history faculty of New York City College, became librarian of Atlanta University in 1948.

The New Negro was opening doors on his own part. Lena Horne, stage and screen star, born in Brooklyn, was the first girl of her race to be idolized by the whole American public as a beautiful American girl. Theodore Ward, of Brooklyn, won a Broadway success as a playwright with "Our Lan'." From the studios of Brooklyn painters such as Jacob Lawrence and Donald Reid there went to New York exhibitions canvases which made an important contribution to the richness and variety of American contemporary art.

An athlete, James Roosevelt (Jackie) Robinson of the Dodgers, made baseball history as the first colored player on a major league team. The spectacular success of this college-bred young man brought other Negroes into the game, in the Brooklyn club and elsewhere. But the cheers of baseball fans did not turn Robinson's head or cause him to lose a sense of reality. He knew well enough that the problem of racial discrimination was not solved by the admission of a few men of his race to a sport hitherto denied to them.

In the summer of 1949 he made a statement to the Un-American Activities Committee of the House of Representatives, in Washington, as simple and sincere a statement as that body had ever heard, in all probability, from the lips of any citizen. "You can put me down," he said, "as an expert on being a colored American, with thirty years of experience at it. And just like any other colored person with sense enough to look around him and understand what he sees, I know that life in these United States can be mighty tough for people who are a little different from the majority—in their skin, color, or the way they worship their God, or the way they spell their names." *

He spoke in the accents of the New Negro, addressing the committee courteously, but with the assurance of an American proud of his citizenship and determined to claim for his people their full share of the privileges and duties of democracy.

Uncle Tom, if he ever lived, died long ago. There are those, however, some of them in Brooklyn, who still see the caricature and not the actual man, when they look at the Negro. The Americans of Brooklyn whose eyes are wide open to the future, however, are seeing the Negro people for what they are—a many-sided, many-talented people who will have a vastly greater part in the unfolding drama of Brooklyn's democratic life than they have yet had an opportunity to play.

* New York *Times,* July 19, 1949.

The World's Biggest Jewish Community

THAT BROOKLYN has people in abundance—all kinds of people—the poor, the rich, the struggling, the well satisfied, the discontented, the learned, and the unlearned—could be well attested by pointing only to Brooklyn's Jewish masses. A thriving city, and a large one, could be constituted by them alone.

It would be a city of more than a million. There would be lights and shades in it—a high degree of culture, a warm and friendly family life, and, it must be admitted, instances in some quarters of depravity and social decay. Is there a city in this country of a quarter of a million without such dark spots? Its average wealth would not be great, for only a few, relatively, of Brooklyn's Jews are wealthy.

No one could doubt that it would be a busy, well-run town, with prosperous business enterprises growing more prosperous as time went on. Outstanding, however, would be its educational institutions and its charities.

There has been a growing consciousness of unity among Jews, and of dignity and standing as citizens of the borough, the city, the state, and the nation. And along with it has come that subtle change that America has given to all its people. The sons and daughters of immigrants have become, in time, neither Eastern nor Western Europeans, but Americans.

Anyone could see that a Jewish kid with a baseball, in a sand lot in the south of Brooklyn, was American, as surely as were his Irish and Yankee playmates. So, also, were the brilliant Jewish lawyer in his office in downtown Brooklyn, the Jewish judge on the bench, the Jewish Congressman or Assemblyman, and the rabbi who learned how to bring the truths of his ancient faith to a generation of young people keenly alive to the thousand influences and ideas of the street, the campus, the theater, the radio, the newspaper, and the flood of literature pouring from our presses.

The mental alertness with which the rabbi had to reckon was no accident. It came from an instinctive drive for knowledge. The age-long struggles of the Jewish people against discrimination, restriction, and persecution made them deep respecters of knowledge. But persecution alone does not account for it. There are other peoples in the course of history who have responded differently to such pressures. The real basis of Jewish respect for education is found in Rabbinic Judaism itself, in which study of the Hebrew Bible and the law as elaborated in the Talmud is central. This, with persecution as a spur, has implanted deep within the people a passionate urge for improvement.

Many an immigrant father of Brooklyn has bent for long hours over an exacting factory task, expecting no real reward but the realization that his children would have that which he had had no chance to acquire. No labor was too exacting, no drudgery was too hard to achieve that great goal—a better life for a rising family. Jewish children, of course, could have the benefit of Brooklyn's free school system. Orthodox congregations established their parochial schools—Talmud Torahs and Yeshivahs—in all the Jewish neighborhoods of Brooklyn. And the campuses of Brooklyn's colleges were thronged with Jewish youth. Their racing pencils filled notebooks, and their keen questions challenged the instructors.

Many Jewish young people were striving for two almost incompatible ends: for educational, artistic, and scientific achievements; and for material prosperity. They were not the only young people in Brooklyn who sought these goals, but it was, perhaps, more characteristic of Jewish youths than of others to combine the two aims.

They were often practical and this-worldly and at the same time idealistic. There were those, of course, who were achieving harmony in the search. In time some of them would also achieve distinction. But even though the dual aims might often fail of attainment, the fact that an appreciation of immaterial values was characteristic of Jewish youth, many of whom would go to a concert rather than to a ball game, was a fact of importance for Brooklyn's culture. These young people could very well understand why Abraham Cahan, the novelist, put in the mouth of the successful manufacturer, David Levinsky, those words of frustration: "I love music to madness. I yearn for the world of great singers, violinists, pianists."

But there were conspicuous examples of the sought-for harmony in the borough. Brooklyn's Jewish youth could find inspiration in the careers of men of wealth who did a great deal in one way or another for the general welfare. Abraham Abraham, the merchant, was such a man. And there were two brothers, Nathan and Ralph Jonas, known to all Jews and to all the other peoples of Brooklyn, who were the very patterns of practical, public-spirited idealists. It will be worth while to notice in some detail the careers of these brothers. Such an examination will tell us something about the Brooklyn Jews as a people and about their creative contributions to society.

The Jonas brothers, like most of the Jewish leaders in Brooklyn before the First World War, were children of the Western European migration. Both of their parents were

German-born. The elder Jonases were cultured people, members of the German migration of 1848, which brought so much talent and high idealism to this country. They settled in Montgomery, Alabama, and when the Civil War broke out, Jacob Jonas served in the Confederate Army.

In 1869, however, he brought his wife and his year-old son Nathan to Williamsburg. There he struggled for years with only partial success, as a small cigar manufacturer. In common with others, the Jonas family felt the pressure of that wave of migration into Williamsburg which was to become such a resistless tide in succeeding decades. So, in the late '70s, they moved to Gates Avenue and Quincy Street, near Broadway. Their new home was in a section then thinly settled, and young Nathan went to Public School No. 26 in a comparatively rural part of Brooklyn. When he was thirteen his schooling came to an end, and he went to work.

Nathan got a job as an errand boy for a firm located at the corner of Broadway and Liberty Street in Manhattan. His pay was three dollars a week. Of this he kept a dollar and turned two dollars over to his mother. There were eight children, and his earnings were needed. He was a tall, thin lad, but there was no question about his physical endurance. His working hours were from seven in the morning until six in the evening. Every day, according to his own account, he walked four miles to work and four miles homeward, and for several nights a week attended Wright's Business College in Williamsburg in order to learn bookkeeping and other business subjects.

Add to the boy's willingness to work unremittingly the fact that he possessed a mind that was keen, analytical, and always constructive, and a buoyant, sympathetic nature. It was a sure formula for extraordinary business success in an expanding society. In his case "willingness to work" is perhaps too weak an expression. Nathan Jonas was driven by a dynamic *necessity* to succeed which sharpened all his faculties. Always attending strictly to the business in hand, but being gracious and even humorous about it, he rose through various jobs to be a salesman, an insurance broker, a bank president, and one of the richest men in Brooklyn.

But while he was climbing the ladder he did a great deal more than to attend to business and grow rich. While still a young man he became an unusually active member of the New York City Board of Education. Mayor Seth Low appointed him to the board in 1902, and in 1905 he was reappointed for a five-year term by Mayor George B. McClellan. He was made a member of the committee on supplies, and when he found irregularities, he corrected them; he even forced the resignation of the executive who had charge of school supplies.

He gained a working knowledge of many fields, including politics, public service, and philanthropy. He was on friendly terms with the Democratic political leader of Brooklyn, John H. McCooey, and in later years with his successor, Frank V. Kelly. Prominent Jews in politics and public service were his intimate, life-long friends. By the time he had reached early middle age he was one of the central, commanding figures of Brooklyn's great Jewish community.

He had a deep sense of the social obligation of the "strong for the weak," and expressed his feeling in memorable words.

The man who loves only his own immediate family [he wrote] has made some advance away from self. The man who loves his *neighborhood* and *community* has widened his soul still more. The man whose heart can beat for his own *race* has again moved forward in his humanity. But it is not a great step from there to the really fully matured heart, which has compassion and real interest in the welfare of *all* races.*

The drive for knowledge and for material success which Nathan Jonas' career so brilliantly illustrated was thus linked with a strong humanitarianism. It was not an isolated, purely personal characteristic. In his case it was consciously disciplined and developed, but it arose from an instinctive tendency common among Jews, related to the tribulations of the Jewish people through the ages—the tendency to care for the sick and the unfortunate.

Nathan Jonas was responsible for a practical expression of this age-long urge when he started the movement for the Jewish Hospital of Brooklyn. It was at the turn of the century, when he was young and comparatively unknown, that he broached the idea of a hospital to the skeptical old merchant, Abraham Abraham, secured his conditional pledge of $10,000, raised $90,000 additional within a year, and made the institution a substantial fact in five years' time.

The Jewish Hospital became a great metropolitan institution, one of the finest in Brooklyn, but when it was first opened it was unsatisfactory in one respect to the orthodox Jews who were then coming into the borough in such great numbers. It did not have a kosher kitchen. So Beth Moses Hospital was erected at Stuyvesant Avenue and Hart Street to supply that lack. Other hospitals with kosher kitchens were established in later years—Israel Zion, in Borough Park, and Beth-El, in Brownsville.

As the years went on, the Jewish charitable enterprise became one of the most impressive features of the borough's institutional life. There were dispensaries, sanitariums, homes, schools, one orphan asylum, Young Men's

* Nathan S. Jonas, *Through the Years; an Autobiography*, New York, 1940, p. 180.

Hebrew Association organizations, and numerous ladies'
auxiliaries of the hospitals and other institutions. Charity
was certainly not an exclusive concern of the Jews, but it
loomed larger in their community life than in that of other
groups.

And in Brooklyn, more than elsewhere, charity organization has had historic significance, for Brooklyn is the birth-
place of federated charities. Through the Brooklyn Federation of Jewish Charities the idea that has since blossomed
into community chests all over the nation was first worked
out in practical detail.

Nathan Jonas conceived the plan. As chief founder of
the Brooklyn Jewish Hospital he had had full experience
of inefficient soliciting and conflicting drives for worthy
causes. At that time some nine or ten institutions were com-
peting for the benevolent attention of Brooklyn's Jews at
various times during the year. Their officers and supporters
were harassed by projects for selling tickets, for giving
dances, for strawberry festivals and bazaars and for conducting drives for funds.

Jonas persuaded the chief Jewish charities to unite in
a project which would make it possible for one collecting
agency to do the whole job at one time each year. The Federation was launched in 1909, and as Jewish charities multiplied in Brooklyn, they were taken under its wing. Its annual dinner became one of the biggest social events staged
by Brooklyn Jews. The plan was so successful that it was
copied by the Jews of Manhattan.

There it succeeded, also, and as realization grew that efficiency would be served by a combination of the two organizations, they were finally merged as the Federation of
Jewish Philanthropies. It was not only a great constructive
achievement and a model to be copied throughout the
nation; it was a strong force for unity in Brooklyn. Jews

who differed in matters of religion and politics were associated in happy harmony in the great charitable enterprise.

Ralph Jonas gave a million dollars to inaugurate the merger. He was ten years younger than his energetic, resourceful brother. His impact on Brooklyn was fully as great. Educated in the law, he gained a large fortune, and became a principal creator and supporter of great public institutions whose influence reached far beyond the Jewish community—such institutions as the Brooklyn Chamber of Commerce, the New York City Board of Higher Education, and Brooklyn College.

The mere recital of the foregoing facts shows that the passion for improvement which burned within Nathan and Ralph Jonas, the two sons of the poor, but high-minded, immigrant of 1848, brought immeasurable benefits to their city. Few others did so much, but many who were associated with the federation were also deeply involved in the forward-looking concerns of Brooklyn. They were interested in the general welfare, and some of them had distinguished public careers.

Justice Mitchell May, for instance, who was president of the Brooklyn Jewish Charities Federation in the mid-twenties, also served as a member of the city Board of Education. He was a native of Brooklyn, and served as a Congressman, as Secretary of State of New York State, as county judge, and as New York Supreme Court justice. Justice Edward Lazansky's career was very similar. Only two years younger than May, he, also, was born in Brooklyn. He, too, was Secretary of State of New York, a member of the city Board of Education, a justice of the Supreme Court, and finally presiding justice of the Appellate Division. And he served both the Charities Federation and the Jewish Hospital as director.

Justice Harry E. Lewis, who rose to be presiding justice

of the Appellate Division of the state Supreme Court, was active in the Charities Federation, the Jewish Hospital, and in many other enterprises. At one time he was president of the Hebrew Educational Society, which established a charitable center in Brownsville. Its chief function when it was started in 1897 was the Americanization of immigrants. Jews newly arrived from Russia and from New York's East Side were given instruction in American history and the English language. In 1911 Judge Lewis led an expansion program, and a large building was erected at the corner of Hopkinson and Sutter avenues. It became a most significant institution in that neighborhood, alive with social, educational, musical, and religious activities.

Judge Lewis was district attorney of Kings County for several years before going to the Supreme Court bench. He won a reputation as a vigorous and fearless prosecutor. But he did something more noteworthy than to convict the notorious bandits Chapman and Hanby. As chairman of the Bill of Rights Committee of the New York Constitutional Convention of 1937, he put through the following amendment, now a part of the state's fundamental law:

No person shall be denied the equal protection of the law of this state or any subdivision thereof. No person shall, because of race, color or religion be subjected to any discrimination in his civil rights by any other person or by any firm, corporation, or institution, or by the state or any agency or subdivision of the state.*

Brooklyn's Jewish leaders also gave attention to general cultural interests. Edward C. Blum, Abraham Abraham's son-in-law, who had a long career as a merchant, was pre-eminent among the Jews in this field. He was a man of wide experience and of cosmopolitan tastes. This Jewish

* Article I, Section II, Bill of Rights, New York State Constitution.

citizen of mellow wisdom served his city generously as trustee of the Brooklyn Institute of Arts and Sciences and as vice-president of the Brooklyn Museum.

The list of notable Brooklyn Jews might be indefinitely extended. It would include Congressmen, such as Lester Volk and Emanuel Celler, lawyers and judges, such as Herman S. Bachrach, Meier Steinbrink, Algernon Nova, and the late Grover M. Moscowitz; educators, such as Dean Adele Bildersee, of Brooklyn College.

A small proportion only, of Brooklyn's Jewish people, became very wealthy. A somewhat larger percentage, if not rich in the usually accepted meaning of the term, became well-to-do. One of the chief evidences of this advancing prosperity was the development of the Eastern Parkway community. In the heart of this community there was born an institution which became an expression of Jewish culture at its finest, and at the same time a focus of liberal opinion.

The community and the institution were a Jewish expression of the sort of civilization which Dr. Charles Cuthbert Hall had so lovingly attributed to Brooklyn Heights a generation before. Here one might find, not the blending of the New England and European traditions which Dr. Hall found in the Heights, but a blending of cultures, nevertheless—the ancient Hebrew and the very modern, both American and European. And here was a forum in the great Brooklyn succession, following the historic precedent set by Beecher at Plymouth Church.

This new institution was the Brooklyn Jewish Center. Its fine, impressive building arose on the Parkway in the years following the First World War. Its first sponsors were Louis Cohen, Moses Ginsberg, and Samuel Rottenberg. They wished to set up a religious organization which would reproduce in a modern setting the various functions of the ancient synagogue. The synagogue of old, they believed, was not only a place of worship but also a place of study and of fellowship. So the building which they planned was a social center, not an ecclesiastical structure.

It was the second Synagogue-Center to be established in the United States, the first one having been built in Manhattan one or two years earlier. Israel H. Levinthal, the young rabbi of Temple Petach Tikvah, was called to its leadership. He was a scholar, but he was a firm leader, eloquent, gentle, persuasive, and he guided it successfully from its small beginnings to its position of outstanding importance.

As the Center developed, it came to include a synagogue, a gymnasium, an afternoon Hebrew School for children, a progressive day school for Hebrew and secular instruction, an institute of Jewish studies for adults, and a weekly public forum. Early in its history an extension department was conducted at the Center under professors designated by Columbia University.

Notables in many fields appeared before crowded forum audiences or in special lecture courses, among them William Jennings Bryan, Clarence Darrow, Senator Borah, Alexander Kerensky, Rabbi Abba Hillel Silver, and Eleanor Roosevelt. The Hebrew poet Chaim Nachman Bialik addressed a Center audience. Sholom Asch was a speaker in a series of Yiddish lectures by writers in the field of Yiddish literature. Exhibits of Jewish art included paintings and art objects from Palestine. It would be hard to imagine subjects more various or points of view more diverse than those expressed before Center audiences.

The Center members included the young and the old and persons of various origins and outlooks. Many were Americans by birth and habits of thought, and others were recent arrivals in this country. Religious attitudes were as various.

It was felt that it was necessary to engage a social director to break down barriers and to bring people together. Dinners, dramatics, and other social events were planned. For a brief period, Moss Hart, who was then unknown, was social director and coached the Center Dramatic Group. It is interesting to record that his improvised skits lampooning Center dignitaries led to a demand for censorship.

The Center building came to be the meetingplace for most of the important general Jewish interests in the borough. Mass meetings and banquets were held there to promote many objects. During the Second World War Red Cross activities and many other civilian war functions made it one of the busiest spots in Brooklyn.

A group of distinguished Americans gathered at the Center in December, 1934, to do honor to Albert Einstein and his friend Heinz Liepmann and to signalize the opening of a new library. Rabbi Levinthal spoke to the assembled guests, and others were heard, including Borough President Raymond V. Ingersoll, Will Durant, Rabbi Stephen S. Wise, Edwin Markham, the white-haired poet with his great flowing tie, Dr. S. Parkes Cadman, and Dr. Samuel Margoshes.

All of those present, Jews and Christians, shared one deep emotion. They felt a sense of outrage over the threat that had been made in Germany against the cultural heritage of the ages. They had come together at this dinner to bear witness to their faith in civilization in spite of the efforts which Adolf Hitler and his gangsters were currently making to break it down.

A year and a half earlier an event had occurred in Germany which symbolized worse events which were to follow. Young fellows influenced by Nazi doctrines had pillaged public and private libraries, stripping them of works by Jewish authors. In Berlin there had been a great bonfire of the books in front of the State Opera House, and Goebbels had made a speech. There was no moderation in this "purge." Great works of literature and of science were thrown into the flames along with books of lesser writers. It was an act of stupid malice, a revelation of the true nature of nazism. Meanwhile, Hitler's blood purge had given the world another startling and ominous demonstration of the meaning of Nazi dictatorship.

One of the writers whose works had fallen under the Nazi ban was the dinner guest, Heinz Liepmann. He had reached New York shortly before, after escaping from a concentration camp in Germany. Now he sat surrounded by friends, and he had the satisfaction of witnessing the opening of the Library of Nazi-Banned Books, in a special section of the Jewish Center Library. He had the satisfaction, also, of knowing that the books destroyed in Germany had been restored to mankind in England and in France, as well as in the Brooklyn collection. It was something to know that doors closed by fanatics could be opened so promptly and so determinedly by enlightened men. It was an event in the Brooklyn tradition. So, nearly a century before, in Plymouth Church, had Beecher opened a door to Wendell Phillips when freedom of speech was being challenged in New York.

During the darkening years of the '30s and the war years that followed them, when the Nazi fury was directed against the Jewish population of Europe and a fiendish program of extermination was set in motion, all Jews in Brooklyn were stirred by a poignant consciousness of the plight of their brethren overseas. After the war there was anxious concern about the fate of the surviving remnant. The hopes of Brooklyn's Jews for this remnant was bound up in the fate of the Jewish Palestine state.

There is no space in this chapter to give an account of

Zionism in Brooklyn. Only a few comments are possible. A generation ago Brooklyn's Zionists were a limited and select group. The events of the '30s and '40s made Zionists of the Jewish masses. It could hardly have been otherwise. There is an interesting parallel between Brooklyn's Jews of today and Brooklyn's Irish of yesterday. Both have been acutely conscious of wrongs suffered by their kindred overseas. Both have ardently supported the cause of a national state.

In Brooklyn's early days, as we have seen, funds were sent to Daniel O'Connell to aid Catholic emancipation. Down through the years until freedom was won and Eamon de Valera was head of an independent nation, the hearts of many Brooklynites were very much in Ireland. Yet no people in Brooklyn were more truly and more intensely American than were the Irish. And when their hopes for Ireland were realized, their preoccupation with the fate of Ireland and her people lessened. So it has been, and so in all likelihood it will be with Brooklyn's Jews now that the Jewish state in Palestine has been firmly established.

Zionism has functioned in Brooklyn through organizations of various sorts, national and international, and through committees and local groups scattered throughout the borough. As a consequence of the constant work of these devoted bodies it became a factor of immense consequence in Brooklyn's life, and the movement found in Brooklyn's Jewish community an important source of its strength.

The big dinners of the Charity Federation, Hadassah balls, and other large affairs were spectacular evidences of the social awareness of Brooklyn's Jews, who have always been friends of social reform. Deep in their consciousness there has remained the memory of their people's history, and it has been natural for them to identify themselves with the "forgotten man." But they have not taken an exclusive attitude. Their minority consciousness has made them friends of other minorities. They have sympathized with the share cropper, and they have been indignant over Jim Crow laws. Coupled with this social consciousness there has been a strong desire to mix and to share with others.

Institutionally they have always continued to grow, and have been constantly receptive to new ideas. In recent years their communal life has been unified through the active agency of the Brooklyn Jewish Community Council. New leadership began to emerge. Among the new men were such widely-known figures as Rabbi Alexander Alan Steinbach, author of "In Search of the Permanent," a master of expression, a psychologist, a poet, and a worker for a unified America.

The older leaders in Brooklyn were children of the western European migration. Most of the younger men were sons of the vast movement of the people of Israel from Russia and the other countries of eastern Europe. Such men were democratic by instinct, because they had a sense of identity with Jews *en masse* and with their struggles on both sides of the Atlantic. No one of them, perhaps, was more significant of the future than the brilliant young Rabbi Eugene Sack, of Temple Beth Elohim, in the Park Slope district, a second generation American—American, in fact, to the core—yet with a sense of the deep tragedy of his people in the present bloody century always in the balance to counter his natural American optimism and to temper his creative vision.

Nothing could be more bright with promise for Brooklyn than the robust democracy of the Jewish masses of the borough. The democratic city is their proper environment. They have loved its street crowds, its busy markets, its theaters. They have flocked happily wherever there was music to be enjoyed in company with others. They have known how to relax. They have done so by the hundred thousand at Coney's crowded beach and at the Rockaways on hot Sundays in midsummer. Those in a somewhat higher income bracket have driven over the smooth Long Island highways to the wider spaces of Jones Beach, and other resorts. Many young fellows and girls have gone out of town during their two weeks' vacation to enjoy the gregarious joys of camps up the Hudson or the Connecticut. They have had little genius for solitary pleasure. In great numbers, comfortable family groups, like their kindred from Manhattan and the Bronx, have gone to summer hotels in the Catskills and the shores of Adirondack lakes. They have sat in pleasant companionship on the wide verandas of the hotels along Saratoga's Broadway.

The wealthier have been able to enjoy more expensive pleasures, such as trips abroad or winters in Florida or Bermuda. In Brooklyn the leading families have established social institutions such as the Unity Club. But, whether wealthy or poor, Brooklyn's Jews have always known how to enjoy themselves. They have been distinguished for a pervading friendliness.

Who can estimate the contribution of such a people to the social, the political, the economic, and the cultural future of Brooklyn?

Brooklyn's Northland

Brooklyn's Northland lies to the southward. It fronts the Bay and stretches toward the Narrows. Here the tall, strong, handsome, easy-striding children of the Northern countries—the Swedish, Norwegian, and Danish peoples of Brooklyn, and their neighbors, the Finns—have made their homes in the spreading borough. It is natural for them to live where the sharp, briny air makes the nostrils tingle—and where, near at hand, stretches Brooklyn's tremendous shipping industry—for the sea has played a chief role in their racial background. The Norwegians, especially, have seen seafarers throughout their history.

Even those Norwegian farmers and town dwellers who did not get their living directly from the sea were as conscious of it, as a pervading presence in their lives, as they were of the towering Norse mountains, for its giant fingers reached deeply into the land, and grasped at the bases of the hills all along the western coastline.

The Norwegians are still seafarers today. No story of Brooklyn's vast outreach across the oceans which ignored them would be worth a second glance.

The Bay Ridge Norwegians look back to the arrival in the Narrows on Oct. 9, 1825, of the sloop *Restaurationen* as New England Yankees look back to the *Mayflower*. Their Swedish neighbors look back to an American colonial past along the shores of the Delaware. But the association with the New World goes farther back still, to the discovery of America by Leif Ericsson. The northern peoples did not come to Brooklyn as strangers. They came as the possessors of a prior lien on the land.

The *Restaurationen* was a tiny vessel of about thirty-nine tons, less than a fourth as large as the *Mayflower*. Its passengers, when it entered the Narrows, numbered forty-six, including a baby born at sea. There were only seven in its crew. It seemed to New Yorkers amazing that the Norwegians would dare to venture across the stormy North Atlantic in so small a craft.

Most of the passegers went into the interior of the country to be farmers. Their voyage marked the beginning of one of the major migrations to the New World. Only a few of the early comers remained in the East, and there was no sudden influx into Brooklyn. Permanent settlers, in fact, came very gradually as growing commerce brought Norwegian ships and seamen to New York harbor.

In the early years of the nineteenth century Norwegian vessels were old and small, and their range was limited. However, the little country was rich in seamen, and the most common dream of the boys in the coast towns of Norway was to take ship to America. They talked of the American ports and of their plans to reach them. Their dreams were to come true. About 1850 Norway's shipbuilding industry experienced a great revival, and Norway began to be a bigger factor in world trade.

It was then that the American clipper ship was writing a glorious chapter in the history of the sea. Two young Norwegians—Annanias Dekke and Rasmus O. Haerem—made up their minds to discover its secret. They came over to make a thorough study of it. When they went home to Bergen and Stavanger they applied the lessons they had learned to Norwegian ship construction.

Most of the Norwegian vessels, however, were smaller than the swift American clippers. From mid-century onwards, in growing numbers, they crossed the North Atlantic. By the 1880s as many as one thousand were coming annually to New York. Eventually, they came in such numbers that it was said that three hundred Norwegian brigs and barks might be seen in the harbor at one time. Little Norway had become one of the world's chief maritime nations.

Among the articles of commerce that helped to bring about this great upsurge of trade were Norwegian immigrants bound for the American West. On the return voyage grain from America filled the ships' holds.

After the American Civil War the migration curve from the Scandinavian countries went sharply upward. Hundreds of thousands from Sweden and Norway caught the "America fever." There were not sufficient Scandinavian ships to carry the growing human cargoes, and this surplus freight became one of the chief sources of income of the British lines. At first sight this mass movement seems hard to account for. The peoples of the Northern countries were not suffering from oppression. But the mounting pressure of population, as in other European countries, was causing agrarian discontent and social unrest. Norway tripled in numbers in the century and a quarter after 1800, in spite of the mighty outflow to the New World.

Tales from America of land for the landless and of opportunities for the restless and ambitious kindled the imaginations and stirred the hopes of a race that had inherited the spirit of adventure. The younger people, especially, were moved by the "America letters," as they were called—letters that poured in from relatives and neighbors who had made the Atlantic crossing and who could cite facts to back up their enthusiasm. Such letters were read over and over and passed from hand to hand. So also were books and other printed materials relating to the land of opportunity.

For years Ole Rynning's guide book "for the instruction and use of the peasants and common people," was studied line by line in many a Norwegian home. First published in Christiania in 1838, it was followed by many other such guides for prospective emigrants. As the migration increased, countless souvenirs of America became treasured possessions in the homes of peasants and villagers—photographs of American relatives and American scenes, of New York and Chicago and the plains and mountains, of Brooklyn Bridge and the Statue of Liberty, and knick-knacks innumerable. America became so familiar to the Northern peoples, it was so constantly in their thoughts, that crossing the North Atlantic seemed a natural, not an extraordinary, procedure. For many, in fact, the decision to cross was an easier one to make than would have been a decision to try to improve one's fortune at home.

Others were strongly attracted by American democratic principles. The belief that men lived on a plane of equality in America—that there one did not doff his hat to social superiors—made a strong appeal in nineteenth-century Scandinavia, where caste distinctions were still rigid. Religious freedom was an inducement to some. For the most part those attracted by the great American magnet were drawn to the upper Mississippi valley. They were peasants, and a prosperous farm was their goal.

But hundreds, and gradually thousands, for whom the wheat fields of the Northwest held no appeal, tarried at the great port and made their homes along the ridge overlooking the harbor.

Many immigrants properly equipped with passports came over with the intention of joining the American mer-

chant marine service. Thousands of sailors, however, didn't
bother about legal formalities. There were plenty of jobs
and good pay in New York and Brooklyn for those who
knew ships and shipping. So Scandinavian seamen, after
reaching the port, often deserted their ships and bargained
for better wages on American merchant ships. Others found
jobs on harbor craft or in East River shipyards.

The reasons that so many took service on American vessels are not far to seek. For one thing American shipmasters
valued the Scandinavians because they rated high as seamen who knew their jobs. For another, American pay was
often double or more than double the amount they received
in the Scandinavian service.

For one reason or another, thousands became permanent residents. For a time there was a Norwegian colony in
New York near the East River docks and shipyards, but by
the '70s and '80s the trend had set in strongly to Brooklyn.

In the '80s and '90s and during the first decade of this
century, Hamilton Avenue, near the Hamilton Ferry, was a
Norwegian street. Norwegian shipworkers lived in the
neighborhood, and Norwegian seamen from vessels moored
in the Atlantic and Erie basins thronged the avenue at
night. It was a lewd and lurid street then, filled with traps
to separate the sailor from his money. As time went on,
evil-smelling rackets grew up along the waterfront. Crimps
and boardinghouse keepers bled sailors and shipmasters
alike.

But there were protecting arms stretched out to save
the generous, unwary lads from the sirens and the swin-
dlers. The story of these protective measures is one of the
most characteristic features of the history of Brooklyn's
peoples. Its first chapter begins back in 1844, when the
famous Bethelship, a Methodist mission for Scandinavian
sailors, was first tied to Pier 11 on New York's West Side.

The Bethelship *John Wesley* was conducted by the Swedish immigrant clergyman, the Reverend Olof Gustav Hedström. He made it his business to help sailors and immigrants in every way possible, and was "a father to the Scandinavian people who came to New York." His brother Jonas went to Illinois as a missionary, and the two Hedströms were in part responsible for directing the stream of Swedish migration to that part of the West. The Bethelship continued as a Swedish mission for sailors until 1876, and the Swedish Immanuel Methodist Church of 422 Dean Street, in Brooklyn, is its direct successor. In 1876 the Norwegian Bethelship Congregation took charge of the mission. Under Norwegian auspices it cast its anchor at the foot of Harrison Street. Soon after this the old ship was sold, and the Bethelship congregation moved ashore. However, it long conducted a seaman's branch on Sullivan Street, which, with its lodginghouse and its shipping office, was in later years taken over by the Y.M.C.A.

Meanwhile, the Lutherans in Norway had become concerned about their wandering sons. In 1878, through their efforts, a Lutheran mission was started on Hamilton Avenue, near the ferry, by the Reverend Ole Bugge Asperheim. The following year the mission was moved to Pioneer Street, nearer the center of growth of the Norwegian population.

There it took over a large church building that had been thrown on the market, and it became known as the Norwegian Seamen's Church. The roll of its official members at about the turn of the century included ship captains, engineers, marine insurance agents, stevedores, ship chandlers, and other men of the sea. In the course of its history scores of thousands of seamen were aided in countless ways.*

* A. N. Rygg, "The Norwegian Seamen's Church," *Nordisk Tidende* (Brooklyn), Jan. 15, 22, 29, 1948; Feb. 5, 1948.

Another protective institution was the Scandinavian Sailors' Temperance Home, which was first opened in 1886. One of its features was an employment bureau to protect sailors from the predatory activities of the vicious gentry who preyed on them. However, the rackets which exploited all sailors, whether Scandinavian or any other breed, were not finally ended until Congress passed the Seamen's Act of 1915. This so-called Charter of Liberty for Seamen, sponsored in the Senate by the elder Bob La Follette, was the culmination of a long battle waged by the Norwegian-American president of the International Seamen's Union of America, Andrew Furuseth.

In the course of years Brooklyn—especially Bay Ridge—became a center of Norwegian-American life in all its phases, economic and professional and cultural. A very large percentage of the whole number of Brooklyn's Norwegians—perhaps a third—continued to supply their skills and their labor to the borough's great maritime business. The activities of the other two-thirds were as diverse as those of most Americans. A large proportion, like the Irish and others, went into various lines and levels of the building trades, as contractors, engineers, carpenters, bricklayers, or plumbers.

Others were mechanics. Many were in the professions, and a few did notable work in the arts. Ole Singstad, who built the Holland Tunnel, was a resident of Bay Ridge. So were Bernt Balchen, air pilot for Admiral Byrd, and Waldemar Grvinge, painter of cathedral murals and altar pictures.

Although they maintained many of the ways and customs of the homeland, from the first the Norwegians took their places in a quiet but assured way in Brooklyn's democratic society. To them democracy presented no riddles. It was a part of their inheritance. Like their Swedish and Danish neighbors, they were accustomed to breathe a free air. Since this was the case, visitors and newcomers from Norway felt perfectly at home in Brooklyn. In fact, they found in the borough many of the amenities of life, and some of the sights and sounds, to which they had always been accustomed. Brooklyn could not reproduce for them the fjords and the mountains of Norway, but it could show them a shoreline crowded with shipping and immense shipyards. They could dine at a Norwegian restaurant on 5th Avenue, Bay Ridge, and could look around them and see people reading Oslo and Bergen newspapers. And they could see in Brooklyn a statue of Grieg carved by Sigvald Asbjörnsen, of Chicago.

The *Nordisk Tidende,* a Brooklyn paper—of which Sigurd J. Arnesen, one of the leaders of the Norwegian community, was publisher—would give them an introduction to life and thought in the New World. Familiar Norwegian foods were on sale in countless Bay Ridge delicatessens and bakeries, and Norwegian books could be bought at Hansen's book store. Norwegian Lutheran churches were scattered throughout the district. There was a Norwegian hospital on 5th Avenue, and there were homes for old people and children.

Around the churches and fraternal lodges a vigorous social life revolved. No people in Brooklyn had a greater love for good food and good times. They kept their love for the Norwegian drama and went to Dongan Hall, 76th Street and 4th Avenue, to enjoy the plays of Strindberg, Björnson, and Ibsen as given by the Intime Group. The Borgnyhammer Players presented modern Norwegian plays at the same place. They cultivated the folk dances of Norway, and through the Norwegian Turn Society they promoted sports.

During the Second World War there came to Brooklyn

seamen of Norway's merchant fleet who were completely
cut off from their own land. They were members of the
crews of those vessels which, on the afternoon of April 9,
1940, ignored the instructions broadcast by the Quislings
and steamed "with all possible speed to British or Allied
ports." All the vessels not then in Nazi-occupied ports got
away—80 percent of Norway's merchant marine, 4,000,000
tons of shipping representing one of the finest merchant
fleets in the world, and the fourth largest.

In the years that followed, this fleet of an exiled democratic government was a big factor in the battle of the Atlantic, when Nazi submarines were sinking or capturing
Allied vessels at an alarming rate. During all those years
many members of the crews knew nothing of the fate of
families left behind in Norway. So, when the chances of
war brought them to Brooklyn, they were not looked on as
ordinary visitors. They had been engaged in a critical task
in democracy's fight for survival. Their fleet was a decisive
factor in the fight. They were homesick men, thinking of
their families, with memories of years of service in sub-
marine-infested seas.

It is indicative of the importance of Brooklyn in this Norwegian war effort that the Norwegian Royal Government
in London, through its Social Welfare Committee for Norwegian Seamen in America, bought and equipped a large
seamen's home in Brooklyn. The Norwegian-Americans of
Bay Ridge had a part in furnishing the home—a thirteen-
story building on Hanson Place. They took more than an
ordinary interest in the enterprise. Some of them had kins-
men in the Norwegian fleet. The husbands and the sons
of many more were sailing in merchant ships under the
Stars and Stripes. And in the shipyards of Brooklyn a host
of Bay Ridge Norwegians were giving their skills and their

muscular efforts in a ceaseless battle of construction and repair to beat the submarines.

In 1938 their Swedish neighbors in Brooklyn celebrated the three-hundredth anniversary of the colony that Gustavus Adolphus planted on the Delaware. In commemorating the part Sweden played in American colonial history they could not help but remember with pride Sweden's great role in the sixteenth, seventeenth, and eighteenth centuries. In later centuries the Swedish contribution to history may have been less spectacular. It has been the part, however, of a mature people, a people who understand the responsibilities of civilization.

The great Swedish migration to America, beginning a century ago, swelled into a tide of more than one million souls. It reached its peak in the late nineteenth century and gradually subsided in the early twentieth. Most of the Swedes, like the Norwegians, went to the Northwest, where they helped to establish an agricultural empire on the American continent such as Gustavus Adolphus had never dreamed of. There were many thousands, however, who resisted the lure of the Western lands and settled in Eastern cities and villages. So far as Brooklyn is concerned, the growth of the Swedish population paralleled that of the Norwegian, but with certain differences. There was not such an intimate relationship with ships and the shipping industry. There was, perhaps, a somewhat greater diversity of occupations and interests.

One great Swedish name, however, will always be associated with a famous vessel, although its association with Brooklyn is not so well known. Few are acquainted with the fact that John Ericsson's *Monitor* was built in Brooklyn. It was from a Greenpoint shipyard that it steamed to Hampton Roads in March, 1862, to do battle with the *Mer-*

rimac, or *Virginia,* as the Confederates called the unwieldy, iron-plated ship which had been systematically destroying some of the finest sailing vessels of the old Navy. The strange little craft from Greenpoint, as the whole world soon knew, ended the career of the *Virginia* and inaugurated a new era in sea warfare.

When Brooklyn was a very young city, its people were alive to Swedish talent and Swedish culture. Brooklynites crowded into Castle Garden to hear Jenny Lind. While the beautiful singer was making her sensational conquest of the country, another famous Swedish woman was visiting in American cities and villages. She was the novelist, Frederika Bremer, and for a time she was in Brooklyn, as a guest in a Brooklyn home. Like Mrs. Trollope, mother of the novelist, Anthony Trollope, and like Charles Dickens and a host of others, she wrote a book about the Americans.* No subject seemed more interesting to Europeans in the mid-century.

A generation later Christine Nilsson repeated Lind's triumph. The great singer was so impressed in 1882 by Brooklyn's Swedish Glee Club that she invited its stars to go on a tour with her. It was only the beginning of the Glee Club's long and brilliant career. In 1921 it made a tour of the concert halls of Sweden. In recent years Brooklyn produced many notable Swedish musicians, such as Anna Balthy, the concert soprano; Oscar Lundberg, the basso, and the organists, Gustaf Lindgren, Arvid Samuelson, Tobias Westlin, and Viola Spongberg.

Viola Spongberg was one of the most prominent of Brooklyn's younger musicians of the Second World War period. She had long been well known in the musical world, for she made her debut as a child prodigy at Town Hall in

* *The Homes of the New World,* translated by Mary Howitt, New York, 1853, 2 vols. It was published in Stockholm, 1853–54, in three volumes.

New York, at the age of ten. She afterwards sang in opera as a prima donna, both in this country and in Europe. Her versatility was remarkable. Few of Brooklyn's musicians could match her record as organist, pianist, violinist, and composer, and fewer still could vie with her in the field of scholarship. She had studied at Hunter and Columbia and New York University, had emerged with a doctorate in the field of philosophy, and became a contributor to philosophical journals. But during the war it was the soldiers' welfare and morale that claimed her energies.

She won citation after citation for her work in canteens and hospitals and with the USO. As director of music at the Brooklyn State Hospital, she experimented in musical therapy for mental patients. But her deepest interest, perhaps, was in the Swedish cultural contribution to America. At the Women's International Exposition, held at Madison Square Garden and the Park Avenue Armory in New York, she was chairman of the programs for Sweden, and in 1947 she organized a Swedish cultural group which visited hundreds of schools and colleges. All these interests, apparently so diverse, were really closely related. The career of this attractive young woman of Brooklyn reveals in a brilliant flash the qualities and the competent maturity of the Swedish people.

The Swedish cultural deposit in Brooklyn was nurtured more or less actively by many institutions. Among its agencies, of course, were the Lutheran churches of the Augustana Synod. They were of fundamental importance to the Swedish people. The established church in the homeland was Lutheran, and churches of that faith were built in every Swedish neighborhood. They helped to preserve the Swedish language in the borough. Many of them, including two of the largest—Salem Church at 450 Sixty-seventh Street, and Bethlehem Church, at Pacific Street and Third Avenue—continued its regular use in the services.

As important, perhaps, from a social standpoint, as the founding of the churches was the establishment of Vasa, an all-inclusive benevolent and protective society that took into its membership men, women, and children. In 1900 there were two lodges of Vasa in Brooklyn and two in Manhattan, and that year the Vasa Grand Lodge was formed. Since then Vasa chapters have spread into Swedish neighborhoods throughout the country. In 1948 Brooklyn had nine lodges: Bjorn, Syskonkedjan, Stragnas, Harmony, Nordstjernan, Valkyrian, Sture, Nobel, and Liljan. Valkyrian, founded in 1902, was a woman's organization, the first Vasa ladies' club in the state. All but three of the lodges used the Swedish language in their meetings, the exceptions being Stragnas, North Star (Nordstjernan), and Harmony.

In Vasa's two buildings in Brooklyn—Vasa Club House, at 465 Dean Street, and Vasa Hall, on 52d Street—the old Swedish culture was actively fostered, and folk plays and musical comedies were given in Swedish. One of many Vasa projects to maintain strong ties between the old and the new lands took place in 1924, when forty-five Brooklyn children between the ages of seven and sixteen toured Sweden under the direction of Dr. Johannes Hoving. A strong link with the fatherland was also maintained by the Brooklyn branch of the Swedish Cultural Society, which brought before its audiences prominent scholars from Sweden.

The charitable feelings fostered by Vasa and the churches reached concrete form in such institutions as Kallman Orphanage and the large Swedish Hospital at Dean and Pacific streets. A Swedish academy was founded in Brooklyn more than a half century ago. It was conducted from 1894 to 1898 in St. Paul's Lutheran Church, and then this plant which was first nurtured in Brooklyn was transferred to New Jersey; it grew up to be Upsala College.

In spite of the close cultural and fraternal ties these institutions promoted, no Brooklynites were more confidently American than were the Swedes. They read the *Nordstjernan* (North Star), a weekly issued from Park Row, Manhattan, but their daily newspaper diet was exactly the same as that of the Irishman and the Yankee.

Some of them were prominent in the American engineering world. Eric A. Lof was celebrated for his work in the electrification of the Panama Canal. Emil F. Johnson was engineer for the chemical test laboratory of New York City. These men were members of the Swedish Engineers' Club, founded in Brooklyn sixty or seventy years ago, a club which in recent years moved to Manhattan. Other Brooklyn Swedes, such as Sig Cederstrom, the real estate expert, were business leaders. Judge Peter B. Hanson, a native of Sweden who grew up in Brooklyn, became prominent in the Democratic organization. Scores of others, men and women, were well known throughout the city.

There were Brooklyn Danes who were fully as well known. The name of one of them, perhaps, had been better known throughout the country at one time than any other Scandinavian in Brooklyn's history. This was Jacob A. Riis, the friend of Theodore Roosevelt and the champion of the city's slum-dwellers. He was born in Denmark in 1849. When he was 21 he came to New York. In his book *The Making of an American* he told his own story, which was in essence, if not in detail, the story of countless other immigrants.

But Jacob A. Riis was different in certain respects from most Americans, whether native or foreign-born. He was a practical idealist. He had caught a vision of a sound democratic society, and he hated injustice. Moreover, he knew how to write in simple, graphic English. In *How the Other Half Lives* and *Children of the Tenements* he brought home to a hitherto unawakened people the deep disgrace of New York's slums. Jacob A. Riis was a newspaper man. He wrote for the *Tribune* and the *Sun*, but he also edited a Brooklyn weekly he named the *South Brooklyn News*. His son, Edward Valdemar Riis, was for many years a reporter for the Brooklyn *Eagle*.

The Danish migration to Brooklyn was much smaller than were the Norwegian and the Swedish. The Danes were a friendly people, with urban tastes, and they found an outlet for their social instincts in clubs, fraternal orders, and benevolent societies. A benevolent order called Fremad (Forward) was established in 1888. Dania, Inc., a Brooklyn men's club, was started in 1886 and became famous for its big annual masked balls. Many other societies were formed, such as Dannevirke, Vort Land (Our Country) No. 200, a branch of the Danish Brotherhood of America, Enigheden (Friendly), a branch of the Danish Sisterhood of America, and Stella and Dagmar, both women's organizations.

All these clubs and societies and the Danish churches were tied together by a central committee that met every month at luncheon in convivial Danish fashion. Although many Danes made their homes in Bay Ridge, there was no tendency to herd in an exclusive colony. In fact, Brooklyn's Danish people were widely scattered, living in many neighborhoods throughout the borough.

The Finns of Brooklyn (or Suomalainen, as they call themselves in their own language) were more inclined to stick together. They came to this country in considerable numbers between 1880 and the First World War, when they were still subjects of the Russian tsars. They were an outdoor people, strong and rugged, and most of them settled in the same Northwest farm regions to which their Scandinavian neighbors were drawn.

The side-movement of the Finns to Brooklyn, like that of the Scandinavians, was, in part, a by-product of the great trek to the wheatlands. Even in the East the Finns avoided when they could the confinement of factories and indoor occupations. A large proportion of Brooklyn's Finns went into the building trades and the contracting business.

When they first came to Brooklyn, in the 1880s, they made their homes in East New York, well outside of the closely-built city. But Bay Ridge, and especially the Sunset Park neighborhood, was more to their liking. They started their colony in the Sunset Park district with a building society of sixteen members. In the course of the years this modest original enterprise expanded, until, before the Second World War, there were nearly thirty large co-operative apartment houses. The Finns were past masters of the co-operative technique, a system they had tested in meeting the rigorous conditions of life in their homeland. In their Brooklyn neighborhood they established co-operative restaurants, bakeries, groceries, and meat markets. Their Co-operative Trading Association was located at 43d Street and Eighth Avenue.

There were other habits besides co-operation that had been bred into this virile race. Nothing was more characteristic of them than athletics, and their athletic center was the Kaleva Club. Even those Finns who had no athletic ambition could enjoy the Spartan rigors of the Finnish Steam Bath on 41st Street—an institution of unique importance in their culture.

The Finnish people of Brooklyn have also expressed themselves in many other ways: in their churches, both Lutheran and Congregational, in Imatra, their social center;

in the arts and crafts, in the decorative pottery making of
William Soini, in music, in the professions. Above all, they
have expressed themselves as self-reliant American citizens.
They have demonstrated that they are an independent,
high-spirited people, a people who know how to live as
freemen.

Brooklyn has long been cultural headquarters for the
Finns and the Swedish Finlanders of the United States.
The Finnish language newspaper, *New Yorkin Uutiset,*
edited by Onni Syrjaniemi, circulated wherever Finnish
people lived throughout the continent. *Norden,* a weekly
edited by Otto Gullmes, was published in a neighboring
block on Eighth Avenue. The history of this organ of the
Swedish Finlanders covered the span of a half century and
more. Brooklyn's Swedish Finlanders were not a large
group, but they were proud of their Swedish blood, of their
culture, of the role of their ancestors in the history of Fin-
land, and of the literature which their people had given to
the world through such poets as Runeberg and Topelius.

All of these Northern peoples of Brooklyn share the independent, adventurous spirit of those who love the sea.
They share a love of liberty, and they have a natural aptitude for democracy. Although they have perfected co-
operative techniques, they are devoted to individualism,
to what Erik Gustaf Geiger, Swedish historian, called an
"energetic love of freedom."

In recent years all of them—Swedes, Norwegians,
Danes, Swedish Finlanders, and Finns—have had a deepened sense of their heritage and a deepened feeling for
their motherlands. The war has done this for them. But
it has also brought them a corresponding sense of their
essential Americanism.

Eastern Europe Moves In

He was a man of striking appearance. A mass of reddish-gray hair floated above his head like a halo. He had the face of a patrician, sensitive and unforgettable. He was an artist, acknowledged everywhere to be the world's greatest master of the piano. Over and over again through his long career, both in Manhattan and at Brooklyn's Academy of Music, succeeding generations of Brooklynites had crowded to see him and to fall captive to his marvelous interpretations.

But Ignace Jan Paderewski was also a patriot. During the First World War he was the very embodiment of Poland to all Americans. Under his active leadership the Polish people of Brooklyn and the country at large rallied with enthusiasm behind the cause of Polish freedom. They were stimulated by the thirteenth of President Wilson's celebrated fourteen points—the point which called for an independent Poland.

When the United States entered the war, no people in Brooklyn were more completely enlisted in the fight than were the Poles. And when President Wilson authorized the organization and equipment of a Polish army, Brooklyn's Polish Falcons took an active part in the movement, and a thousand Brooklyn boys were trained at Fort Niagara and went to France to take the field under Polish colors. Back of the enthusiasm of Polish-Americans for the Allied cause lay a deep and passionate devotion to freedom. But it was not only the exciting prospect of a free Poland that inspired them. They were very conscious

of the part which Poles had played in American history.
They could point to the presence of Polish colonists in
Dutch New Netherland. They remembered Kosciuszko
and Pulaski, and other Poles—some of them of Colonial
descent—who had fought in the American Revolution.
In Greenwood Cemetery there lay the body of General
Wladimir Krzyzanowski, Polish-American hero of the Civil
War.

Krzyzanowski had been inspired by the same devotion
to freedom as his predecessors of the Revolution. He was
one of the host of young Europeans who had been caught
up in the revolutionary movements of the 1840s and who
had had to flee from their homelands when the uprisings
collapsed. The son of a noble, a cousin of Frederic Chopin,
he was born in Roznow, in Prussian Poland. Like many
another high-born refugee in America, for a time after
his arrival he had to struggle for a living. However, he
managed to study civil engineering, he had a part in railroad construction in the West, and he finally became a
merchant in the city of Washington.

When war broke out in 1861, Krzyzanowski enlisted as
a private, but he rose rapidly in rank, becoming a brigadier general. He fought gallantly on the field of battle
throughout the war. He served with the Army of the
Potomac and later with the Army of the Cumberland, and
he had a conspicuous part in many of the bloodiest en-
gagements, including Second Bull Run, Chancellorsville,
and Gettysburg. The martial spirit which he exemplified
and the devotion to liberal ideals which he shared with
Kosciuszko and Pulaski were part of the Polish-American
heritage which was remembered and cherished by the
Polish people of Brooklyn. Recently, through the agency
of some of Brooklyn's Polish leaders, his body has been

reverently removed from Greenwood Cemetery and interred in the National Cemetery at Arlington.

Until after the Civil War, Polish immigrants to America were for the most part intellectuals and rebels against tyranny. The post-Civil War Polish migration was one of the incidents in that vast movement of European workers to the New World which continued in full flood until the First World War. It furnished industrial workers, market gardeners and farmers, and in the second generation it began to furnish recruits in business, the professions, and politics.

The progress of Polish settlement in Brooklyn can be charted by taking note of the location and the time of organization of the various Roman Catholic parishes. The first church, St. Casimir's, was a frame building at the southwest corner of Lawrence and Tillary streets. Mass was first celebrated there in December, 1875. But Poles were soon settling in considerable numbers in the Greene Avenue neighborhood. It happened, about a decade and a half after the dedication of St. Casimir's first building, that the Jews of Temple Israel, on Greene Avenue, near Adelphi, were looking for a new location in the Bedford district. So St. Casimir's purchased Temple Israel. It was renovated, two steeples were erected, and in due course it was dedicated by Bishop McDonnell. The second church, Our Lady of Czenstochowa, on 24th Street, near 4th Avenue, was organized in 1897. The Right Reverend Boleslaus Puchalski was its parish priest throughout its entire half century of existence. About fifty years ago, also, St. Stanislaus Kostka Church was erected in Greenpoint, on the corner of Driggs Avenue and Humboldt Street. It grew to be the largest Polish parish in Brooklyn.

When the Polish immigrants first came to Brooklyn, they found jobs in the Williamsburg sugar refineries. Later, they were drawn to Greenpoint in great numbers because of the jute mills and oil refineries in that industrial hive. They knew how to work hard, and they knew how to save their money. In time, a very large proportion owned their own homes, and the region was given the nickname Little Poland.

But the Poles did not confine themselves to two or three neighborhoods. They spread throughout the borough, especially in South Brooklyn, East New York, Bay Ridge, and Ozone Park. Wherever they concentrated in considerable numbers, they organized parish churches. Besides the seven Roman Catholic parishes, two Polish National churches were established, in which the services were conducted in the Polish language instead of Latin.

The parish church was a focus of community activities. Each one had its youth club, which fostered Polish culture and traditions. Each parish had its parochial school, which carried its children through the grammar grades. In 1898 the three original parishes—St. Casimir's, Our Lady of Czenstochowa, and St. Stanislaus Kostka—organized more than three hundred volunteers for the Spanish-American War. And in 1917 and 1941 all of the Polish churches made great efforts in behalf of the war.

No people in Brooklyn have had a greater genius for social organization than have the Poles. Parallel with the elaborate parish systems there developed an even more elaborate secular apparatus. Seven Polish National Homes, scattered throughout the borough wherever the Polish people lived in numbers, formed the basis of a many-sided community life. In these social halls the young and the old met for study and for play, for strenuous exercise and for mild amusement, to promote and foster the culture of the old country, and to enter with vigorous efficiency into the activities of the borough, the state, and the Nation. The various National Homes were equipped with meeting rooms, restaurants, and ballrooms. Here one could meet a cross-section of Brooklyn's Polish people.

The halls were the headquarters of the "Sokols," or Polish Falcons. The Falcons, as everyone should know, have produced a magnificent crop of athletes. To the Poles athletics are instinctive. The attainment of physical well-being is one of their basic expressions. But the Falcons had other goals than the development of good physiques. In training the young in the right and wise use of their bodies they did not neglect the larger aim of good American citizenship. They believed that the preservation of the Polish language and the traditions of the old country were consistent with Americanism. So Polish cultural schools were set up in each of the National Homes.

The Falcons developed track and field teams and swimming, basketball, and baseball squads. Women as well as men participated in gymnastics, tennis, and other sports. Groups of boys were trained in boxing, wrestling, tumbling, gymnastics, and military close-order drill. Girls took part in gymnastics, basketball, and folk dancing. One result of this stress on athletics was that relatively few Poles were rejected for physical reasons by the Selective Service boards.

Many other Polish societies and clubs met in these neighborhood halls. Binding them together in a type of federal union was the United Polish Society of Brooklyn, which was made up of delegates of the United Polish Societies of Greenpoint, of South Brooklyn, of East New York, and so forth. This elaborate social machinery was, in part, a guiding and protective device to help bridge over the immense transition in the lives of many tens of thousands of people who came to Brooklyn with no knowledge of the customs of its people. The parishes and the National Homes provided strong links with the old country, but they were also extremely important factors in the process of Americanization.

New organizations arose out of the experiences of the Poles as Americans. After the First World War, for instance, there appeared in South Brooklyn the Frank J. Dombrowski Post of the American Legion. More significant than that was the founding of the Polish Legion of American Veterans, whose posts were scattered throughout the borough. Like the Falcons, the Polish Legion undertook the task of training young people to be good Americans.

Long before the First World War the Polish National Alliance came into being. It was a fraternal order, with insurance and benevolent features. Its Brooklyn membership, including both men and women, ran up to many thousands. In 1904 the Alliance established a weekly paper called *Czas* (The Times), Brooklyn's only Polish newspaper. But all Poles in Brooklyn also read the New York Polish daily, *Nowy Swiat* (The Polish Morning World).

The progress of the Poles as Brooklynites was underscored by the rise of such bodies as the Polish Business Men's Association of Greenpoint and by the activities of political clubs throughout the borough. Outstanding among the charities was the Polish Day Nursery, a model institution promoted by *Nowy Swiat*.

Among the Polish leaders were Peter P. Yoelles, the managing editor of *Nowy Swiat*, Frank Januszewski, general secretary of the Polish-American Alliance, Frank A. Jurek, bank president, Assemblyman John Smolenski, of Greenpoint, Joseph Schlichta, president of Kings County

Polish Democratic Club, and Judge Kosicke, of Special Sessions. Poles became as intimate a part of Brooklyn's life as the representatives of any other group. They rose to prominence in manufacturing, finance, and in the professions. An instance of Polish enterprise sustained for half a century was the Polish-American Cooperative Savings and Loan Association, an institution which grew through the years and became in 1938 the Atlas Savings and Loan Association.

Some of the Polish leaders had gone through the schools and universities of Poland before coming to Brooklyn. Peter Yoelles, for instance, was a student at the University of Lwow, in his native land; but after coming to the United States he did graduate work at Columbia and also studied at the School of Journalism of New York University. More of the leaders were American-born, and graduates of American institutions. The education of Vincent J. Kowalski, a prominent Eastern District lawyer, was typical of many. Kowalski was born on New York's lower East Side, but grew up in Brooklyn and went to school as a boy to the Franciscan Brothers who conducted the parochial school at the Church of St. Vincent de Paul. From there he went on to high school and college. He attended Temple University, at Philadelphia, and afterwards was graduated from the Brooklyn Law School.

By the time of the outbreak of the Second World War Brooklyn's Polish people were keeping well in step with the community. In some respects they believed themselves ready to set the pace. This was especially true in their bent toward military training. The history of Poland —its tragic strangulation by surrounding powers in the eighteenth century—its precarious position between rival dictatorships in the twentieth—planted deep within the Poles a desire for security. This history, which they cannot forget, helps to account for their respect for military strength and their relative indifference to other measures for peace.

They were proud of their record in the American armed services in both World Wars. In 1941–45, 18,000 Poles were inducted into the army from Kings County. More than two thousand were wounded, and twelve hundred were killed in action. Many Polish officers from Brooklyn served with distinction, including Colonel Michael Fibich, who commanded a field artillery battalion; Colonel William Anuskiewicz, of the 6th Air Force, who served in the South Pacific; Lieutenant Colonels Henry Kucinski and Anthony Malinkowski, who commanded infantry battalions; Lieutenant Colonel Edward Nosek, who commanded a battalion of engineers in Africa and Normandy; and many others.

One of the most prominent of the Brooklyn Polish officers, Colonel Benjamin T. Anuskiewicz, commanded a chemical amphibious battalion. Colonel Anuskiewicz served in the D-Day operation in the North Pacific theater. He was twice wounded and received both American and French decorations. It was not his first experience as an American soldier. He had served in the First World War, and he had been a member of the expedition which followed Pershing into Mexico in pursuit of Pancho Villa. After the war, still suffering from the effects of his wounds, he was an outstanding leader in Brooklyn's civic life.

These officers were all sons of hard-working immigrant fathers. Kosciuszko and Pulaski fought for liberty and human rights as great ideals. They were not ideals to the Polish officers of the Second World War. They were facts of their own experience. That is what Brooklyn had done for them.

The Polish people of Brooklyn, spread out as they were

in various parts of the borough, took an increasingly prominent part in its affairs and made their influence felt in a very definite way. Politically they were a most important factor. Many of the freedom-loving Poles who had come to America before the Civil War—such liberals as General Krzyzanowski—had been drawn to the Republican party because of its antislavery stand. The Poles of the later migration to Brooklyn were so fired by President Wilson's enunciation of the Fourteen Points that their devotion to the Democratic party seemed eternally fixed. A Democratic President had promised freedom to Poland. But years went by, and differences of opinion gradually developed. Poles, like Yankees, Germans, Irishmen and Jews, had more than one point of view on points of policy. The Polish people of Brooklyn were thinking and acting as Brooklynites. A generation had come that was thoroughly American in its manner of living, in its restless ambition and in its plans for the future.

In the 1920s the Brooklyn readers of the *Novoye Russkoye Slovo* (The New Russian Word)—many of them garment workers in Brownsville and others employees of the great industries of Williamsburg and Greenpoint—were all talking excitedly about Igor Sikorsky. These thrifty workers were making up their minds how much money they could spare him. For it was their money, contributed in small amounts, and the money of other Russians in Manhattan which enabled the famous refugee to build his first planes in a Long Island chicken coop.

Sikorsky was one of that great company of Russians who fled from their country as a result of the Revolution of 1917. It was to a large extent a migration of intellectuals and aristocrats, of impecunious princes and officers of the Tsar's army, of doctors, lawyers, scientists, writers, artists, and musicians. They had had to leave most of their possessions behind them. Not many of them went to Brooklyn; Manhattan was more to their taste. But there were already Russians in Brooklyn who had lived there long enough to feel themselves a part of its teeming life.

These earlier Russian-Americans had begun to come to Brooklyn in the late years of the nineteenth century— poor peasants from western and southwestern Russia. Many had come with only the clothes on their backs and a few articles tied in a bundle. Most of them had been sufferers from the blind reaction of the Tsars. It was during the years of terror following the collapse of the revolutionary movement of 1905 that the greater number came.

The work to which these peasants turned their hands in Brooklyn was hard and unaccustomed work, but they made their way. In Brownsville they took up garment-making, the occupation for which that district was famous. There they developed co-operatives, as contractors and operators. In Greenpoint they worked for the Standard Oil Company. Superficially, their social organization in the borough seemed much like that of the Poles. But actually there were great differences. Compared with the Poles, they were few in numbers, amounting to about ten thousand on the eve of the Second World War. Their churches—Holy Trinity, in Brownsville, and the Church of the Transfiguration, in Williamsburg—were Russian Orthodox. In their homes, on religious feast days, they burned candles before icons.

In the vastness of the great borough, amid the teeming masses who were strange to them, they strove to preserve their Russian heritage. A Russian community house was erected in Brownsville in 1920, at 120 Glenmore Avenue. It was called the Russian People's Home. Here met societies for the study and appreciation of Russian literature, art, and music. In its auditorium Chekhov plays were given.

In its social halls blending notes of balalaikas carried the older people back to the steppes. There were lectures in Russian. The young were carefully instructed in the Russian language, history, culture, and traditions.

In the preservation of a culture, food is no small item. The Italian's spaghetti and the Virginian's fried chicken are more than food; they are sacred symbols; they carry with them a deep emotional content. One can feel a deeper security, a heightened self-assurance, when one can find far from the old home the flavors and the aromas which sustained life and gave satisfaction there. Russian housewives found the means to this kind of security in food stores along Pitkin Avenue, between Saratoga and Pennsylvania—delicatessens, grocery stores, and meat markets.

The passage of time, however, and a thousand influences in streets and schools and shops tended to promote the integration of Brooklyn's Russian Slavs with the mass of the borough's people. Such Russian leaders as Michael Zwariko, treasurer of the Russian division of the Liberty Loan Fund during the First World War, formed a link with the larger American world. In the 1920s their desire to reject all association with Communism led to a great rush for naturalization papers. Russian young people began to attend college in Brooklyn and elsewhere. This tendency was encouraged by a student loan fund inaugurated in 1921 by Alexis Wiren. And when war came in 1941, Russian youth from Brooklyn became more fully aware of their Americanism. As with others, their association and fellowship with the great host of young Brooklynites who served in the armed forces magnified likenesses and caused differences to fade. There was something very American about the Russian youth, in physique, in manner, in easy-going friendliness, in energy.

They were genuine Brooklynites, these young people of

Russian blood, and so were the young Lithuanians from Brooklyn who served their country during the war.

The Lithuanian migration to America had got under way in the late 1870s and '80s. A non-Slavic Baltic people, the Lithuanians were ruled and oppressed by the autocratic Russian regime of Tsar Alexander III. In their homeland most of them cultivated the soil, but the majority of Lithuanian immigrants in the United States found work in industrial centers, in the textile mills of New England, in Pennsylvania steel and coal industries, and in the great mills and factories of the Middle West. A considerable number, however, like the Poles, found their way to the countryside, both in the Middle West and in the East, and took over the farms of Yankees and others who had drifted citywards.

In Brooklyn, the garment industry gave a large proportion of them an economic footing. For many years both men and women worked as contracting tailors on men's clothing. A large proportion of the men who were not thus engaged worked in the sugar and oil industries or in other factories of Williamsburg and Greenpoint. Time and increasing prosperity took many into business, the professions, journalism, and other activities.

Probably no people in Brooklyn in proportion to their numbers were so active in the various phases of journalism. *Laisve* (Freedom), their daily newspaper—which circulated wherever the Lithuanian language was read in North America—was issued from 46 Ten Eyck Street. Besides this daily, no fewer than four monthlies and weeklies were published in the borough. Brooklyn thus became an important center of Lithuanian culture. This, however, was a gradual development, for *Laisve*, founded in 1901, had been published in Boston until 1917; and as early as 1879 a Lithuanian newspaper had been printed in Shamokin, Pennsylvania, sent overseas, and smuggled into the homeland.

For the Lithuanians the preservation of language and literature has had a special significance. Most immigrant peoples in America could find in their respective mother countries the sources of their culture. But during the regimes of Tsar Alexander III and his son Nicholas II the Lithuanians and other non-Russian peoples of the Empire were subjected to a process of "Russification." This meant that all the Tsar's subjects were to speak and read Russian. Lithuanian—a euphonious tongue closer to the parent Sanskrit than any other European language—was banned by law.

So Lithuanians in the United States became the custodians and preservers of the Lithuanian language. Books and papers printed in this country helped to defeat the tyrannous policy of the tsars and kept the language very much alive here. It is not to be wondered at that Lithuanians in Brooklyn, as elsewhere, retained a strong feeling of attachment to their homeland, that they longed for its freedom, and that many hoped someday to return to it. But the desire to return faded as a thoroughly Americanized younger generation grew up and as economic interests and political sympathies identified the people generally with Brooklyn's democratic society.

When they first came to Brooklyn, the Lithuanians faced the same housing problem that has unfortunately been thrust upon many immigrant groups, before and since. Large numbers of them had to live in ramshackle houses cast off by preceding generations of occupants. But they were a thrifty people, and as time passed many of them were able to save sufficient money to own their homes. A Lithuanian building and loan association eventually helped in this process. Classes in English and American citizenship overcame their isolation in the community and promoted naturalization. Union locals tied up their interests with those of other American workers. Business activities had the same effect with a growing number. Americanization was also fostered by social relationships, by the schools and colleges of the borough, by intermarriage with other groups, and by a thousand other influences.

In addition to such factors there were agencies which sought consciously to promote Americanization and good citizenship while endeavoring at the same time to preserve Lithuanian culture. Among them were the Lithuanian-American Citizens Club, the Lithuanian Athletic Club, and various fraternal organizations and literary societies. The same objectives were sought by several workers' organizations. No group in Brooklyn was more labor-conscious, and no group combined the labor interest more closely with the cultural interest. The Lithuanian Workers' Literary Society of America, which published and distributed periodicals and books was one of the agencies which illustrated this tie-up.

The strong and active cultural movement was continued in these and other ways, paralleling the Americanization process. A contributory force in Brooklyn was St. George's Church on York Street, where services were conducted in Lithuanian. Another was the Aida Chorus of young men and women, an agency through which Lithuanian songs were kept alive and popular in the community. Family customs and traditions, habits of life carefully maintained, were not unimportant. The groceries and delicatessens and butcher shops along Grand and Lorimer streets, where *kilbasas* (a sausage) and *kopusta* (cabbage soup) and other Lithuanian delicacies could be bought, did their part.

A concession was made to the Americanized Lithuanian young people when *Laisve* started a Youth Section in the English language as well as the Lithuanian. Perhaps this was a portent of things to come. A generation that had worn the uniform and mingled with other young Americans in camp, in canteens, on the march, and in battle would, perhaps, not be as interested in the maintenance of Lithuanian culture as its predecessors had been.

The Smaller Groups

IN ADDITION TO the larger groups which have already been reviewed there were numerous smaller ones which had a part in the diverse unity of the borough. Their cultures were widely dissimilar, and they differed widely in the extent to which they were incorporated into Brooklyn's general society. Among them were people from every country in Europe, from the Near East and the Far East, and from Latin America and the South Seas. Rumanians, Bulgarians, Turks, people from Spain, Portugal, the Azores, French and English-speaking Canadians, Cubans and other West Indians—these and others lived in Brooklyn's vast reaches.

If a search were made, it would be possible to find in some quiet neighborhood, working and living without ostentation, men and women whose genius the world acknowledged—such, for instance, as the Chinese artists, Dong Kingman, Ssu-tu Chaio, and Ssu-tu's talented wife, Amy Ssu-tu. Brooklyn had, also, many temporary residents who were glad to get away from Manhattan's garish and expensive hotels. Much might be said about the floating population. However, our concern in this chapter is with the smaller groups which had got, or promised to get, a permanent footing in Brooklyn.

Most Brooklynites were unaware that thousands from the Ukraine, often classified statistically as Russians, had brought to the borough their own distinct culture. Their chief social centers were two large Catholic parishes, one church being located at 160 North Fifth Street, and the other at Nineteenth Street, between Fifth and Sixth avenues.

The peoples of the old Austro-Hungarian Empire have been coming to Brooklyn since the last decades of the nineteenth century. Hungarians, largely laborers, settled in widely scattered neighborhoods, especially in Bensonhurst, Bath Beach and Coney Island. Czechs also settled widely throughout the borough. As a rule the thrifty, steady-going Czechs owned their own homes. Better educated than most newcomers of the last half century, they were distributed in many occupations and trades, from factory worker to the professions. Their Sokol at 210 Franklin St. has long been a center for sports, gymnastics, and Czech culture.

For many years the peoples of the troubled Balkans have lived in harmony in Brooklyn. Like the Hungarians and Czechs, they, also, in varying numbers, have spread out into many districts. The Rumanians did not establish any definite colony, but settled in practically every neighborhood. The Greeks led in numbers in the Balkan migration. Thousands of them poured into Brooklyn and in a few decades became thoroughly integrated in its business, political, and professional life.

One of their best-known leaders was Nicholas Psaki. Mr. Psaki was brought to the United States as a boy, at about the turn of the century. He rose to a high position in the Brooklyn Democratic party and in the legal profession. Brooklyn Greeks have an especial aptitude for business. Many of them became wholesalers and retailers of candy. Others became florists, proprietors of restaurants, and owners and operators of moving picture theaters. They are a self-reliant, enterprising, home-owning people.

In religion they have adhered to the Eastern, or Greek

Orthodox church. St. Constantine's, at 64 Schermerhorn
Street, was their first church in Brooklyn. In an effort to
keep their children loyal to the ideals and customs of the
homeland, they sent them, after regular school hours, to
special schools for instruction in religion and the Greek
language. Every Greek neighborhood established its institution of this type. Outstanding among their benevolent
societies was the Order of Ahepa, the letters of the word
being the initials of the full name of the organization—the
American Hellenic Educational Progressive Association.

Unlike the Balkan peoples, the Syrians established a
definite colony in Brooklyn. Atlantic Avenue from Court
Street to South Ferry was its Main Street, but it pushed
deeply into the Heights. It was a little city of the Near
East tucked within the borough. It wore a very peaceful
aspect, and no one passing through it casually would guess
that one might sample within its borders many, if not
most, of the bewildering religious complexities of the
Levant.

The first Syrians came to the United States sixty or
seventy years ago as peddlers of linen goods, laces, and
souvenirs of the Holy Land. As more came over, they
opened shops in Manhattan or engaged in the needlework,
art embroidery, or rug trades. Soon after the turn of the
century Brooklyn's Syrian colony began to grow into a
substantial center of population. There were keen businessmen in the colony. Some of them rose to great wealth.
Others went into industry, engineering, science, and the
professions. A few turned to journalism and literature.

Among the Syrian migrants were college-trained men
who had felt a strong tie with the United States before
they came over, graduates of the American University
at Beirut, an institution founded by American missionaries
in 1863. One of them was Rabbi Josef H. Hakim, who be-

came a leader of Brooklyn's Syrian Jews. Some thousands of the Jewish Syrians settled in Bensonhurst and Mapleton Park. Their chief colony stretched along 22d Avenue, between 62d and 75th streets.

Most of the Syrian Christians remained within the South Ferry and Brooklyn Heights districts, although a few established their homes in other neighborhoods, such as Bay Ridge and Park Slope. They worshiped in Eastern Orthodox, Roman Catholic, and Protestant churches. Within these groups there were interesting and sharply marked divisions. Two Catholic rites were represented. In 1944 the Reverend Mansour Stephen, pastor of the Maronite rite Church of Our Lady of Lebanon, which had been located on Hicks Street near the corner of Joralemon, negotiated the purchase of one of the historic Congregational churches of the Heights—the Church of the Pilgrims, whose members had united with Plymouth on Orange Street to form the Plymouth Church of the Pilgrims. Non-Lebanese Catholic Syrians worshiped according to the Latin rite in the Virgin Mary Church, at the corner of Clinton and Amity streets.

A large proportion of the Syrian colony was attached to several Eastern Orthodox churches on State and Clinton streets. There was a Syrian Presbyterian congregation at Pacific and Clinton streets, and there were also Moslems and Druses among the Brooklyn Syrians. Certainly no other people in Brooklyn displayed so complex a pattern of faiths. Nor does this complete the record of division. There was a split among the Eastern Syrian Christians when Bishop Ufeish purchased the former Protestant Episcopal Church of St. Peter on State Street and attempted to use it to promote a movement for an independent American Orthodox Church.

In fact, the whole Syrian picture was a very complicated

one, and it deserves a much more complete study than is possible in the present chapter. Among the many Syrian social institutions apart from churches and synagogues was the Damascus Lodge, 867, of the Free and Accepted Masons. Another one of especial importance was the American-Syrian Federation. This institution was especially devoted to the preservation of Syrian culture. One of its principal members was George Dagher, who was also prominent in the First Assembly District as leader of the Syrian Republicans.

Other Syrian leaders in Brooklyn included N. G. Hadran, editor of the *Syrian Eagle,* George J. Faour, a New York banker and broker, and Dr. Najib Barbour, of 154 Clinton Street, who practiced medicine in Brooklyn for many years. Dr. Barbour was one of those Brooklyn Syrians who had studied as a young man at the American University at Beirut.

Another graduate of that famous school who made his home in Brooklyn was H. I. Katibah, the well-known writer, author of "Other Arabian Nights" and "Arabian Romances and Folk Tales." After coming to this country, Mr. Katibah studied at Harvard. He contributed many articles on the Near East to the Brooklyn *Eagle.*

The Syrians, it is evident, were among the most versatile of Brooklyn's peoples. There were a number of other groups who have long held their own place in Brooklyn's life. Sometimes, because of their small numbers and the location of their settlements, they have been little in the public eye. The chief Spanish neighborhood lay under the shadow of Brooklyn Bridge. Many of their men worked as stevedores and stokers, in the great industries that lined the waterside, and in the tobacco trade.

In the Bridge neighborhood, also, a colony of Filipinos

lived an unobtrusive life in the borough. They were engaged in a variety of occupations. Some were artisans of various sorts, some were small businessmen, others were service men in navy or army uniforms. In the Filipino restaurant at 47 Sands Street they could order tropical fruits and familiar dishes of their far-off islands, such as *sinigang isda* or *sinigang visaya* (fish soups), *mixta* (beans and rice), or *adabong gaboy* (pork fried in soy sauce and garlic).

Far away from this neighborhood, at 2216 E. 21st Street, a company of Brooklyn Indians and others met on Sunday nights to worship the pagan gods of ancient Yucatan. There were other American Indians in Brooklyn, who were quite conventional Christians. They may almost be said to have been camping out in the borough, for the home country of most of them was a Mohawk reservation in Canada. A closer inspection, however, shows that the little band, which first came to Brooklyn around 1930, really became a part of the great community.

In coming to Brooklyn they were invading the domain of their ancient enemies, the Algonquins. The Long Island tribes, which the earliest Dutch and English settlers found in possession of the soil, lived in great fear of the war-like Mohawks, to whom they paid tribute. Today's Mohawks have been collecting tribute from New York and Brooklyn in the shape of good wages for work faithfully and skillfully accomplished.

They rented apartments in the quiet streets of South Brooklyn. Their children went to public school, wearing the conventional togs of American school kids. The boys played ball in the streets, and the girls skipped rope. Father and mother and children, on Sundays, looking exactly like other Brooklyn church-goers, attended St. Paul's Roman Catholic Church on Congress Street, or the Cuyler Pres-

byterian Church on Pacific Street, where they listened to
sermons preached in the Mohawk tongue. One of their
young ladies sang in the Presbyterian Church choir.

Politically, the status of the Mohawks was different from
that of any other Brooklynites. They were wards of the
Canadian Government, although by treaty they were al-
lowed to live anywhere in North America. It was at the
Caughnawaga reservation, on the St. Lawrence River, that
the braves learned their trade as structural steel workers.
After the First World War, when a St. Lawrence span was
projected, it happened that the best site for the Canadian
bridgehead was at Caughnawaga. The Mohawk tribesmen
were quick to seize their opportunity. They stipulated that
a number of their young men should be employed as ap-
prentice workers. It was a line of work as well suited to
these keen-eyed, sure-footed braves as were the hunting
trail and war path to their ancestors. After the bridge was
completed, they came to Brooklyn to live, and between
the wars they worked on many Manhattan skyscrapers, including the Empire State and Rockefeller Center buildings.

During the war the men were employed on ship construction. Many of the women had jobs in war factories, and the
youth volunteered to serve overseas. Like other groups,
they cherished their native culture, but they brought forth
feathered head-dresses and tribal costumes only for ceremonial and festive occasions. In almost all respects they
were like any other Brooklynites, although more than a
little proud that they were the first Americans.

Few in numbers, too, were the French, who made their
social contribution to Brooklyn as individuals, rather than
as a distinct group. But they made a decided and lasting
contribution, especially in the early years of the nineteenth
century, when Brooklyn was young and gawky and much
in need of refinement.

Refugees from the West Indies and revolutionary France came over to Philadelphia and New York during the Terror and the Napoleonic age, and little Brooklyn, like some other small suburban towns, benefited from the visits and the services of some of these people.

After the War of 1812 French dancing masters began to come over the river to Brooklyn. In summer their "public balls" were often held at the establishment of one J. F. L. Duflon, a Frenchman of gracious manners who was a very prominent figure in Brooklyn's early social system. His Military Garden was at the outskirts of the village, about where the Kings County Courthouse is now situated.

The teachers of the art of the cotillion who came over in the winter months used the "Long Rooms" of taverns nearer the ferry, such as Benjamin King's or Mrs. Chester's Coffee House. Sometimes they were attached to a young ladies' school. In 1811 Miss Gervais and L. Sansay taught at Miss Wiley's academy. For decades the politely phrased advertising "cards" of Chevalier, Berault, Guigon, and many others enlivened the columns of the newspapers.

French language teachers bore a substantial part of the burden of polishing young Brooklyn. French was an "accomplishment" taught in all the young ladies' seminaries, and Brooklyn was full of seminaries. Peter Chazotte, who in 1829 took up his residence on Cranberry Street, was one of those who had a special sense of mission to bring good breeding to the barbarians. Other Brooklyn Frenchmen, such as Aimé Barbarin, who opened a French evening school for boys in 1820, were less evangelistic.

The Scots, also, have been an influential factor in Brooklyn from an early period. It is not easy to appraise their contributions, because they never formed a distinct group, and they were at least as versatile as the Yankees. Indeed, our loose definition of the Yankee as a Britisher from overseas, from New England, and elsewhere made a Yankee of the Brooklyn Scot. Many of them, like the men from Salem, were sea captains.

One of the smaller groups of Brooklynites may soon attain major status. The Puerto Rican post-war migration has been in some respects like that of the great Negro migration from the Southern states; in other respects quite dissimilar. The Puerto Ricans, like the Southern Negroes, are American citizens and they have come to Brooklyn to better themselves. They have been settling in considerable numbers in the area between Hicks Street and the waterfront and scattering into Red Hook, Gowanus, Greenpoint, Williamsburg, and Stuyvesant Heights. The oldest settlement of Puerto Ricans in Greater New York was in the Navy Yard district, but the stepped-up migration during the Second World War and the still larger influx of more recent years penetrated into many new neighborhoods.

The post-war migration was called an air invasion, because so many came by plane. It tended toward Manhattan and the Bronx rather than toward Brooklyn. Nevertheless, Brooklyn's Puerto Ricans, who numbered about eight thousand in 1930 and about nine thousand in 1940, increased in a few years to thirty or forty thousand. Estimates of the number vary widely. It was by far the largest population group to move into Brooklyn in the 1940s.

The Puerto Ricans have many things in common—the Spanish tongue, the island culture derived from Spain, their Roman Catholic religious heritage—but they are not uniform in race. Probably a large majority of the early migrants to Brooklyn were white. In the recent influx the proportion of Negroes and mulattoes has increased. In addition to these there is a mixed group known as "grifo" and "indio."

It was the shipping along South Brooklyn's shoreline

which first attracted Puerto Ricans to that district. Many worked as stevedores, and their families lived along Columbia Avenue and in neighboring streets. They tended to scatter thinly in many areas, few neighborhoods becoming predominantly Puerto Rican. As their numbers increased, groceries and other stores operated by Puerto Ricans multiplied. One of the largest concentrations of the islanders in the borough was around the intersection of Flatbush Avenue and Broadway in the Stuyvesant Heights district.

The majority came to Brooklyn to get better jobs and higher wages. They found them not only along the waterfront but also in Brooklyn's manufacturing industries and other fields. A large proportion of the women who engaged in factory work were employed in the garment industry. Both men and women went into the service occupations, as busboys, waiters, and domestic servants. The majority were employed as hand-workers—unskilled, semi-skilled, and skilled. A growing number, however, were in "white-collar" work of various sorts, and Brooklyn began to be conscious of its Puerto Rican men of business, especially in wholesale and retail lines.

A lively, friendly people—these Spanish-speaking Americans—they have had no strong community consciousness to hold them together as a group. The family has always been the important unit with them, and here the ties remained very close. In Puerto Rico dancing was, perhaps, their favorite pastime. Baseball they loved as ardently as any other Americans, and on coming to Brooklyn they quite naturally adopted the Dodgers as their own and were able to enter into the borough-wide emotion which that fabulous outfit evoked. Brooklyn's beaches have also tended to identify them with the larger community of the borough, for the beaches of their home island had accustomed them to that form of relaxation. Unfortunately, Puerto Rican

Negroes have felt the sting of prejudice and have had to face some of the identical barriers and handicaps that have beset Negro Americans of continental United States.

The next generation—that brought up in Brooklyn and educated in its schools and colleges—will tell the tale of Puerto Rican accomplishment in Brooklyn, what it is to be in terms of citizenship and culture.

E Pluribus Unum

As we walk the streets of Brooklyn we rub elbows with people whose roots run back into diverse soils. We give little heed to the fact. To us Ole—or Karl, or Jim, or Abe, or Salvatore—are all Brooklynites. When we stop for a moment's conversation, we talk about our common interests, and these are many. If some one mentions that the friend with whom we had just been chatting came over from Italy twenty or thirty years back, we nod absent-mindedly. It is an interesting fact, but not so engrossing as the facts that his boy has just entered Yale in the same class as our boy, that we have planned to go on a fishing trip together, and that we shall probably conclude a business deal on that trip that will be to the advantage of both.

For, after all, Brooklyn is one and not many, notwithstanding the impression of separateness inevitably conveyed by the preceding chapters of this commentary. The thousand ties—business, political, cultural, social—which bind each group to the whole society are matters of day-by-day experience. As time passes, they become more intimate. There is no deliberate plan to promote unity. It is a democratic process which began in this western tip of Long Island three hundred years ago and has continued with the growth of Brooklyn from its Dutch infancy to its present giant stature.

It began with the Dutch, this give and take between peoples which has produced, not an ideal democracy, indeed, but at least a democracy that works. Even within their tiny pioneer settlements accommodation and adjustment were necessary, for colonial Brooklyn was not a simple homogeneous community, with one racial stock and a common language. We have seen that the term "Dutch" applied to the early colonists has to be stretched to include French-speaking Walloons; that Englishmen, under Dutch rule, colonized a part of the region; and that one of the original landholders of Boswyck was a Negro. There were still other non-Dutch settlers, including families of Italian and Scandinavian blood; and Asser Levy, the Jewish pioneer, although probably never a resident, owned property across the East River from Manhattan.

All these peoples brought something of their own special inheritance to Brooklyn, their own peculiar skills, the gifts of their own clans and races. So it has been through the centuries. The many groups, the great migrations have deposited in Brooklyn what their peoples were capable of bringing of the cultures of their homelands. After becoming part of Brooklyn's general community they have kept what they could or desired to keep of these cultures. Often, through practical necessity or indifference, certain aspects of a particular culture were dropped and certain features of another culture were adopted. Certain usages that the new environment encouraged, in time started the formation of a new common culture.

Thus, we have in Brooklyn tendencies toward diversity and tendencies toward conformity, which should result— if the society grows in a healthy way—in a rich and fruitful diversity in unity, a society which moves and acts together in all matters of common concern, at the same time preserving the best of its many-sided heritage. But social growth is never as healthy in practice as in theory. The rubbing of people against people in a small area cannot help producing some conflict, whether in the form of minor irritations or in more serious forms. The story of Brooklyn's peoples is not the story of a social miracle. In each case it is the story of the coming of a culture from overseas; of more or less conflict with other cultures; of adjustment sometimes complete, sometimes partial; and finally of the people's particular contributions to Brooklyn and America.

The cultural treasures of old Europe were brought to Brooklyn in a fragmentary way. In no case were they brought over intact and installed in full force to carry on as in the old land overseas. The ancient lady who welcomed Danckaerts and Sluyter to her fireside in 1679 was a woman of the frontier, strangely different from anyone in the homeland. Perhaps the chief cultural link with the society of her youth which she still retained was her native tongue, the French speech of the Walloons, and she undoubtedly spoke that with a colonial accent. She and the other early colonists had to get along without most of the things which made for comfort and dignity and good living.

Jacques Cortelyou brought his Cartesian philosophy to old Brooklyn, but he could share it with few or no sympathizers. His son—and his guests—had to sleep on straw in the barn, surrounded by the livestock. He had, we are told, some knowledge of medicine. But, although there were surgeons in the colony, medicine as a science had not been transplanted. Nor had any other science, nor learning in general. In sickness, home remedies were the chief reliance, many of them part of the imported cultural heritage, some of them remedies acquired from the Indians. If a Brooklynite wanted much more than the three R's and a little religious instruction, he had to go back home to get it.

The skills and the institutions that were brought overseas in the first half-century of Brooklyn's existence were few and simple. The *boer* (farmer) brought his inherited knowledge of farming; the *keuter* (mechanic) brought his simple craftsmanship; the domine and the schoolmaster their theology and Latin and Greek. The Dutch church was firmly planted. Architectural forms were adapted to New World materials. The Flemish cottage, with its gracefully curved roofline and its deep overhanging eaves, became the standard type for Hollanders as well as Walloons. As time went on furniture and materials from Holland brought refinements in living conditions.

Brooklyn was Dutch, indeed, but it was Dutch in its own way. Its currency was the Indian *seawant,* its drink West Indian rum, or "kill-devil," its food included the maize and the fish and oysters of the New World and the fruit which Brooklyn's soil produced in such lush abundance. Its labor force included Indian and Negro slaves. It grew and exported tobacco. Its people were toughened in fiber by frontier living conditions, and many were mixed in blood through intermarriage with non-Dutch families.

The Dutch were first in the field, but what has been said about them can be said about all the peoples who followed them. All cultures were brought over in part only, and all of them were changed in greater or less degree after being transplanted. With the English conquest of New Netherland, the general pattern that we have suggested is more fully apparent. Conflicts between the two cultures occurred, followed by gradual adjustment. The Dutch language, which long held out in the services of the church and within many households, finally succumbed completely to English. But before it gave way entirely there was a curious mingling of the two speeches, and in the end numerous Dutch words were incorporated into English as it was spoken in Brooklyn and elsewhere in America—such as "cranky" for the colloquial *krankie,* meaning querulous; "stoop" from *stoup,* meaning porch or door-step; and *dorp,* meaning village or the center of town.

After the American Revolution the Yankee flood swept

into Brooklyn. There were temperamental differences, difficulties caused by the clash between "Dutch tenacity" and "Yankee innovation." Brooklyn Yankee writers enjoyed spoofing the Dutch, in imitation of Washington Irving. In the end, although the Dutch were absorbed by the prevailing civilization, they made an impression upon Brooklyn out of proportion to their numbers, and the old Dutch families, more truly than any others, represented blue blood in Brooklyn.

The Yankee culture which became and remained dominant was widely different from that of the British motherland. Although language, literature, folk customs, government, law, and religion were all derived from Britain, they had been given an American pattern by the selective processes of colonizing and of nation-building. The Revolution had provided both ideology and an heroic age, and an American literature was in the making.

The Yankees brought to Brooklyn the ethical ideas, the moral movements, the reform impulses, and the intellectual currents of New England. They brought new churches derived from Anglican and Puritan parent stems—Protestant Episcopal, Methodist, Presbyterian, Baptist, Congregational, Unitarian. The enthusiasms that swept in from Connecticut and Massachusetts were balanced by the hard, practical business sense of Yankee merchants and enterprisers. It was on this amalgam of the utilitarian and the idealistic, the practical and the adventurous, that modern Brooklyn's foundations were laid in the mid-nineteenth century.

No people, perhaps, were ever more confident of their destiny than the Yankees of the generation after the War of 1812. Progress to them was axiomatic. The dazzling success of the young nation and its apparently unlimited opportunity for growth and prosperity made them boastful.

Many visiting writers from Europe paid their respects to
Yankee braggadocio. Charles Dickens was not guilty of
much exaggeration in his accounts of it in the *American
Notes* and *Martin Chuzzlewit*. The newspapers of the time
were full of this sort of exuberance. Brooklyn's General
Joseph G. Swift illustrated the propensity to boast by what
seemed, in the year 1825, a very natural performance. He
favored the guests at a public dinner with a song, composed, so it was said, on Brooklyn Heights by a visiting Englishman who was more moved by what he saw than most
of his countrymen professed to be.

> There is not in the wide world a land so complete
> As this land in whose bosom the bright waters meet;
> Oh! the last rays of feeling and life must depart
> Ere this day of proud triumph shall fade from my heart.
>
> Yet it is not that Nature has spread o'er the scene,
> Her purest of chrystal and brightest of green;
> It is not the sweet magic of streamlet or rill,—
> Oh no! it is something more exquisite still.
>
> 'Tis that Liberty chose this blest spot for her own,
> Where Seas, Lakes and Rivers unite now in one;
> And where Freedom, and Commerce and Industry prove,
> That the Gods are protecting the land of their love.

It was a Brooklyn version of "Hail Columbia"; an echo
of Joseph Rodman Drake's "American Flag." Fourth of
July bombast was at its glorious height in this period. But
it was not an unhealthy cockiness. It was youthful, assured,
evangelistic. The Yankees had something to give to the
world—successful republicanism—and many Europeans,
impressed by the achievement, were looking westward with
hope.

Although Brooklyn's Yankee civilization of the mid-
century had a decidedly New England character, it was

also strongly influenced by its neighbor city and by Brooklyn's old Dutch culture. In the later years of the century it was increasingly modified by contacts with the Irish, Germans, and others. In the process much of the typically Yankee culture was transmitted to the newer peoples and became the principal factor in the connective tissue which binds together Brooklyn's democratic society.

The Irish and the Germans came over in considerable numbers in the early nineteenth century, because—among other strong reasons—Yankee republicanism appealed to them. The name of Brooklyn's Vinegar Hill commemorated resistance to tyranny to the Irish refugees who lived there. They and the German liberals of '48 added strength to democracy in Brooklyn. But so did the mass of Irish immigrants who crossed the Atlantic, not because of politics, but solely to better their condition. They brought over a natural predilection for popular government and lined up with the Jacksonians. A large proportion of the Germans who came at the height of the excitement over slavery and free soil were led as naturally to take their stand with the new Republican party, which promised to halt the spread of slavery.

Both Germans and Irish found themselves, for a time, in an unwelcome conflict of cultures, precipitated by a wave of antiforeignism. Each had brought to Brooklyn certain features that were new to its society. The Roman Catholic Church, to which most of the Irish and many of the Germans adhered, was one. The foreign tongue which the Germans wished to preserve in their new home, was another. The church put down permanent roots, and in time Brooklynites of all faiths came to accept religious liberty, not as a principle only, but as a necessity in a democratic community. For many years the German language held on stubbornly. Dutchtown in Williamsburg was thoroughly

German, and Irishtown between lower Fulton Street and
the Navy Yard was "a little bit of Ireland."

Long before the end of the century both peoples had
found a solid and assured place in Brooklyn. For a much
longer period individual Irishmen, such as Cornelius
Heeney and Henry Cruse Murphy, had been powerful factors in Brooklyn's life. The Irish made vigorous use of the
democratic institutions which the Yankees had planted, and
came fully into their own as political leaders. The Brooklyn
soil was as favorable to their growth in other respects, and
the twentieth century saw them occupying many of the
prominent posts Yankees had held in the nineteenth.
Among them were gifted, urbane, socially-minded men—
men like Judge Gaynor, Judge Cullen, and Mayor O'Dwyer.
The English language was as native to them as to the
Yankees. Like the Yankees, they were the heirs of its literature and its cultural associations, and they could use it with
supple skill.

Many Germans surmounted the language barrier and
other obstacles to complete adjustment so successfully
that they were thought of as Brooklynites first and as Germans only in a secondary sense, if at all. Many others, however, were tenacious of their Germanism and chose to remain in predominantly German neighborhoods and to hold
to a German way of life so far as possible. Between them,
the Irish and the Germans did much to modify the general
tone of life in Brooklyn. They took on some Yankee colora-
tion, but they also lent some of their pigmentation to the
Yankees. The Brooklyn of the nineties was mellower, more
easygoing than it was a generation earlier. New England
austerity was in retreat, though by no means entirely
routed.

The great migrations of the Jews, the Italians, the Scandinavians, the Slavs, and the Negroes and the lesser migra-

tions of other peoples made the borough of the twentieth century one of the most heterogeneous centers on the planet. The Irish and—to a somewhat lesser degree—the Germans, were akin to the Dutch and the Yankees of Brooklyn in many ways. They shared with them the West European cultural heritage and were closely allied in race. Most of the more recent migrants did not have these advantages. The Negroes, of course, shared the culture, and many of them were Brooklynites through many generations of descent; but all Negroes felt the weight of discrimination because of color. All the others felt the language barrier, and all but the Scandinavians and the Western European Jews felt the strangeness of an essentially alien culture. And yet some of these groups made astonishingly rapid adjustments in Brooklyn. Most astonishing of all, perhaps, was that made by the Jews.

The Jews of the first migration brought with them the cultures of Germany, Austria, Alsace, and other countries of the West, as well as their common Jewish culture. The great migration from Eastern Europe which followed brought a people who had been so restricted in occupation and residence and so harshly discriminated against that they had absorbed less of the culture surrounding them. The treatment that they had endured had tended to preserve and reinforce their Jewish orthodoxy.

Western European Jews began to come to Brooklyn more than a century ago. At first their growth was slow. From time to time, a few families trickled into the community. They established one temple and then another as religious and social centers. Few came empty-handed. They worked hard and established small business enterprises. Toward the end of the century business and political leadership emerged. A genius for practical affairs and for idealism was exemplified in the careers of such men as Abraham Abra-

ham, Edward C. Blum, and the Jonas brothers. The union
of the practical and the ideal had been a Yankee quality,
but there was a difference in its Jewish application. The
Yankees had driven forward with a brash confidence that
the gods were on their side. The Jews were not so naïve,
but they possessed the same driving power. Their wits were
sharpened by the experiences of their fathers during long
ages, and they made full use of their opportunities in the
democratic city, building on the solid foundation the Yankees had laid.

A new temper and outlook came to Brooklyn with the
Jews—an Old-World quality, a mellow cosmopolitanism,
and a passion for the arts. Their easy sophistication made
it possible for them to move gradually into Brooklyn's
larger affairs and to form a sort of working partnership with
the powerful Irish leaders of the borough. In this way the
cultural transition was eased, and a practical adjustment
was effected.

The later mass migration of Jews from Eastern Europe
brought to Brooklyn in a generation the largest single element in its population. The newcomers were much more
self-consciously Jewish, and they made Brooklyn the largest Jewish center in the world. By an overwhelming majority they were humble, industrious workers, with a driving urge for self-improvement.

When this Jewish proletariat moved into Brooklyn, a
similar mass invasion of Italians had already got under
way. Simultaneously there was an influx of Slavic peoples.
Scandinavians had long been coming into Bay Ridge in
large numbers. Although some of these movements date
well back into the nineteenth century, their real impact
came early in the twentieth. Peoples from Latin America,
from practically every country in Europe, and from the
Near East made their homes in the swiftly growing bor-

ough. During the First World War and its aftermath a Brooklyn Harlem spread through the Bedford-Stuyvesant Heights district. The migration from Puerto Rico, which had been going on for more than a generation, became an important movement after the Second World War.

Each of these peoples brought more or less of their native cultures to Brooklyn. Some were highly self-conscious about their language, literature, religion, and folk customs, and took elaborate measures to preserve them. Some were comparatively indifferent. The literate, of course, brought more than the illiterate. On the other hand, the literate often had a greater desire to acquire the American culture.

The American society which they found in Brooklyn was, as we have seen, a Yankee-Irish-German society, Protestant and Roman Catholic in religion and ethics, highly literate, energetic, and resourceful. It was a society which gave "foreigners" opportunities, but which also, often unconsciously, put impediments in their way. The newcomer had to face and overcome a vague dislike of those who were "different," who spoke with an accent, who wore strange-looking clothes. There was sometimes outright race prejudice, systematically fostered by demagogic leaders. These were typical American attitudes, not peculiar to Brooklyn, attitudes which ran completely counter to American principles of equality. They were the twentieth-century counterparts of the antiforeignism of the mid-nineteenth century. Fortunately, they were condemned by public opinion generally in Brooklyn. More important in the long run was the fact that the immigrant found in Brooklyn a freedom of movement which he had not known before. He could rise in the world, and his children could get a good education.

The conflict between the old and the new cultures was not merely a matter of irritations between "natives" and

"foreigners." It took many forms. "Americanized" children
rejected the customs which parents wished to preserve,
and congregations disagreed over the use of the old language in the church service. Often there was no definite
conflict, but a gradual transition from the foreign to the
American. The shift in the colloquial speech was an illustration of this. As in the case of the Dutch, so in the case
of many later groups, the old and the new tongues were
mixed in many curious ways. In the end the American language was enriched by scores of expressive words, *kibitzer*
being one of many taken from the Yiddish. For a time
dialects were in use that would have been unintelligible
anywhere outside of the neighborhoods in which they were
spoken. The American-Italian dialect of Little Italy twisted
standard Italian words to suit its own purposes, and coined
its own equivalents of many English words, as the following
list shows.*

Italian Word	*Standard English Equivalent*	*Italian-American Equivalent*
carro	cart	car
costeemi	suit, habit	customers
cotto	cooked	coat
fornitura	supplies	furniture
stima	esteem	steam
genitore	father	janitor
pena	punishment	pain
checca		cake
ragnaia·		raincoat
stecca		steak
botto		boat
livetta		elevated

While the immigrant generation was still using the
American-Italian dialect, the children of that generation

* This word list was prepared by Mrs. Arnold Cassuto.

were already in full possession of Brooklyn's colloquial English. They acquired the language easily on the street, at play, and more systematically in public or parochial schools. Some of them went beyond this and gained a full mastery of English in college and university. They were Brooklynites rather than "foreigners."

Americanization classes helped many adults over the difficult language barrier. Parents and even grandparents went to school to catch up with the younger generation and to overcome a feeling of inferiority. Such classes were held under various auspices. They have not always been welcomed, but when intelligently and sympathetically conducted they have been important factors in the process of turning bewildered "foreigners" into happy and confident citizens of the borough. A sixty-nine year old woman, asked why she was studying English, replied: "Well, I like it. I like to know. When I go somewhere I am ashamed because I cannot talk. In old country I talk Russian, here Jewish and English, but not so good." *

Adjustment was not solely a matter of language. There were many who found a satisfactory economic adjustment without actually mastering English. The possession of money made it possible to have the American articles which all newcomers craved—refrigerators, automobiles, and everything else that contributed to the American standard of living. Department stores and beauty shops were glittering enticements. It would be difficult to overestimate the importance of the Fulton Street retail district as a social force in Brooklyn. It made Brooklynites—or a large proportion of them—uniformly smart in appearance. It did a good deal for Brooklyn's collective self-respect.

There were, in fact, all sorts of bridges to Brooklyn's common life—churches, fraternal orders, "national homes,"

* Sam Kaufman, Brooklyn *Eagle*, March 21, 1948.

sokols, military organizations, baseball from the sandlots to
the Dodgers, the bathing beaches, community-welfare organizations, political clubs, political organization activities, city jobs, police courts and other contacts with the
law as it is administered in Brooklyn, movies, the radio and
television, newspapers and magazines, both general and
those published for a particular group, hospitals and baby
clinics, parent-teacher associations, social agencies (such
as the Urban League), playgrounds, neighborhood stores,
soda fountains, barber shops, and the park benches.

In a thousand ways people were drawn into the great
network of the borough's society. The obstacles and irritations that separated peoples could retard this process, but
they could not prevent it. Day by day association in common enterprises did much to overcome race and religious
prejudice. The state interposed with a fair employment
law and a law which guarded against discrimination in
college admissions. Every day the free mingling of workers
in factories, shops, and offices and the association of students on the borough's campuses were overcoming prejudice and making it possible for Brooklynites to know each
other as fellow workers and fellow students.

There was danger that the agencies making for uniformity would crowd out values worth preserving. Fortunately, many of the churches, community centers, fraternal orders, military organizations, and other groups were
engaged in a dual enterprise: the promotion of good citizenship and the preservation of great cultural treasures.
The role of music has been a big one in this conservation
of culture in Brooklyn. One would have to make a tour of
the many social halls to understand its scope. Organizations such as the Swedish Glee Club have had a long history
stretching back for many decades. The Brooklyn Academy
of Music has had a part in the general appreciation of

such societies—as, for example, when the Maniusko Singing Society gave a Polish operetta there, "Night in Venice." Much of the musical heritage of the various peoples has, of course, been appropriated as a common treasure. Chopin and Sibelius belong to all who have ears to hear them.

When plays of Chekhov have been given at the Russian People's Home, and Polish movies have been shown in neighborhood theaters, and similar offerings given to others, the aim has been to serve group purposes, not to spread the culture to all. Such, also, has been the purpose in promoting foreign-language newspapers and foreign-language literature of all descriptions and also the very important periodical literature of the Negroes. On the other hand, some Brooklynites, deeply concerned for the preservation of the particular cultures of their people, have wished to share them with Americans in general. They have felt that they have something to put into America's common store that has not yet been fully appreciated. Sometimes their sense of mission has carried them outside Brooklyn, as when Viola Spongberg toured schools and colleges at the head of a Swedish cultural group.

Many of these activities have been aimed to prevent—and to cure—the rootlessness and consequent aimlessness of a society that is cut off from its native soil. They have been in harmony with the thesis of Rolvaag, the Norwegian-American novelist, that the truest Americanization can be found only in preserving a "cultural solidarity" with the past. Their promoters have shared the view that a people with roots running back into its own past and new roots striking into America's soil could find stability and satisfactions not otherwise obtainable and could make rich contributions to America's life and culture.

A glimpse of the future may be seen in the achievements of a few Brooklyn creative workers—writers, painters, sculptors, composers. Elie Siegmeister, for instance, has found his inspiration in American life. His symphonic poem, "Sunday in Brooklyn," may, perhaps be as good a symbol as any of the hope that Brooklyn holds out for democracy.

The story of Brooklyn's peoples becomes more and more complex with each passing decade. It is important that it should never become too simple. Brooklyn's peoples would be infinitely poorer if they all conformed to a single American pattern.

Each group grows to adult stature in the great democratic community as its members acquire the capacity to appreciate the cultural gifts of the other groups. Brooklyn, in its progress, has always found leaders who knew the necessity of practical co-operation and tolerance. Tolerance, of course, is not universally practiced in the borough. But there are enough people practicing it to make it work. There is a hint in this, perhaps, that Brooklyn can pass on to the apprehensive peoples of the world.

Bibliography

N<small>O BIBLIOGRAPHY</small> can give a complete picture of the sources consulted by the author in the preparation of this work, for the book is, in part, the result of many conversations with representatives of the various groups in Brooklyn. But the tangible items are listed below.

MANUSCRIPTS

Kings County Court records and records of the towns of Kings County, 17th and 18th centuries. In the office of the Commissioner of Records, Brooklyn.

Florent, Lyonel C., "Negro Migration, 1860–1940." Revised draft of a memorandum prepared for the Carnegie Corporation's Study of the Negro in America. Typed manuscript in Schomburg Collection, New York.

Spooner, Alden, "Brief Sketch of the Life of Alden Spooner." Typed copy of manuscript in Library of the Long Island Historical Society, Brooklyn.

NEWSPAPERS

Brooklyn Eagle
Brooklyn Times-Union
Long Island Patriot
Long Island Star
Nordisk Tidende

LOCAL HISTORIES

Callender, James H., Yesterdays on Brooklyn Heights. New York, 1927.

Furman, Gabriel, Notes, Geographical and Historical, Relating to the Town of Brooklyn on Long Island. Brooklyn, 1825.

Historic Brooklyn. A series of illustrated booklets covering the histories of Brooklyn's six original villages, prepared by the Brooklyn *Eagle*, 1946.

Howard, Henry W. B., ed., The Eagle and Brooklyn, 2 vols. Brooklyn, 1893.

Moore, Samuel B., "One Hundred Years of Brooklyn," *Brooklyn Life*, LIII (March 25, 1916), 35–132.

Prime, Nathaniel S., A History of Long Island, from Its First Settlement by Europeans to the Year 1845. New York, 1845.

Stiles, Henry R., A History of the City of Brooklyn. 3 vols. Brooklyn, 1867, 1869, 1870.

Stiles, Henry R., ed., The Civil, Political, Professional and Ecclesiastical History and Commercial and Industrial Record of the County of Kings and the City of Brooklyn, N.Y., from 1683 to 1884. 2 vols. New York, 1884.

Strong, Thomas Morris, The History of the Town of Flatbush. New York, 1842.

Syrett, Harold Coffin, The City of Brooklyn, 1865–1898. New York, 1944.

Thompson, Benjamin F., A History of Long Island. New York, 1839, 1843, 1918.

Vanderbilt, Gertrude Lefferts, The Social History of Flatbush. New York, 1881.

Weld, Ralph Foster, Brooklyn Village, 1816–1834. New York, 1938.

OTHER SOURCES

Abelow, Samuel Philip, History of Brooklyn Jewry. Brooklyn, 1937.

Adams, Alice Dana, The Neglected Period of Antislavery in America (1808–1831). Boston, 1908. Radcliff College Monographs No. 14.

Albion, Robert Greenhalgh, The Rise of New York Port, 1815–1860. New York, 1939.

Babcock, Kendric Charles, The Scandinavian Element in the

United States. Urbana, 1914. University of Illinois Studies in the Social Sciences, Vol. III, No. 3.

Bennett, William Harper, "Cornelius Heeney, 1754–1848," *American Irish Historical Society Journal,* XVII, 215–223.

Bernheimer, Charles Seligman, The Russian Jew in the United States. Philadelphia, 1905.

Blake, W. D., articles on various groups, Brooklyn *Times-Union,* 1937.

Blegen, Theodore C., Norwegian Migration to America, 1825–1860. Northfield, Minn., 1931.

—— Norwegian Migration to America; the American Transition. Northfield, Minn., 1940.

Brawley, Benjamin, The Negro in Literature and Art in the United States. New York, 1918.

Brockett, L. P., "The Commerce of Brooklyn," in Stiles, *Kings County,* II, 633–67.

Cahan, Abraham, The Rise of David Levinsky. New York, 1917.

Danckaerts, Jaspar, and Peter Sluyter, "Journal of a Voyage to New York, and a Tour in Several of the American Colonies in 1679–80," translated and edited by Henry Cruse Murphy. Memoirs of the Long Island Historical Society (Brooklyn, 1867), Vol. I.

Davis, Jerome, The Russian Immigrant. New York, 1922.

Gunther, John, Inside U.S.A. New York, 1947.

Haiman, Miecislaus, Polish Past in America. Chicago, 1939.

Halstead, Murat, "The City of Brooklyn," *The Cosmopolitan,* Vol. XV, No. 2, 131–44.

Hansen, Marcus Lee, The Atlantic Migration, 1607–1860. Cambridge, Mass., 1940.

—— The Immigrant in American History. Cambridge, 1940.

Heffernan, John A., "The Mazzini Society and Frank Serri," Brooklyn *Eagle,* April 11, 1942.

Hinten, Edward M., "Patrick Henry McCarren," in Dictionary of American Biography, XI, 568.

Hirsch, Leo H., Jr., "New York and the Negro, from 1783 to 1865," *The Journal of Negro History,* XVI, 382–473.

Hooper, Lucy, Poetical Remains of the Late Lucy Hooper, with a Memoir by John Keese. New York, 1842.

Hobart, George H., "The Negro Churches of Brooklyn, N.Y." Brooklyn, 1931. Mimeographed.

Whitman, Walt, I Sit and Look Out, edited by Emory Holloway and Vernolian Schwarz. New York, 1932.

Holmes, Oliver W., "Henry Cruse Murphy," in Dictionary of American Biography, XIII, 350.

Howe, Elizabeth Leavitt, My Early and Later Days. Auburn, N.Y., 1898.

James, Edward J., and others, The Emigrant Jew in America. New York, 1907.

Jonas, Nathan S., Through the Years; an Autobiography. New York, 1940.

Joseph, Samuel, Jewish Immigration to the United States from 1881 to 1910. New York, 1914.

Kiser, Clyde Vernon, Sea Island to City; a Study of St. Helena Islanders in Harlem and Other Urban Centers. New York, 1932.

Knott, H. W. Howard, "Gorden Lester Ford," in Dictionary of American Biography, VI, 514.

Levinthal, Israel H., "Brooklyn," in The Universal Jewish Encyclopedia, II, 544–57.

Lindberg, John S., The Background of Swedish Emigration to the United States. Minneapolis, 1930.

Locke, Alain, ed., The New Negro; an Interpretation. New York, 1925.

—— The Negro in America. Chicago, 1933.

Low, Benjamin R. C., Seth Low. New York, 1925.

McLoughlin, Maurice E., articles on various groups, Brooklyn *Eagle*, 1932.

Martyn, Carlos, Wendell Phillips; the Agitator. New York, 1890.

Meehan, Thomas F., Old St. James Churchyard. 1900.

—— "A Self-Effaced Philanthropist; Cornelius Heeney, 1754–1848," *Catholic Historical Review*, IV (April, 1918), 3–17.

Mills, C. Wright, Clarence Senior, and Rose Goldsen Kohn, The

Puerto Rican Journey, a Report to the Puerto Rican Government on Puerto Rican Migrants in New York City. New York, Bureau of Applied Social Research, Columbia University, 1948.

Mordell, Albert, Quaker Militant: John Greenleaf Whittier. Boston, 1933.

Morris, Richard B., "William Jay Gaynor," in Dictionary of American Biography, VII, 200.

Morrison, John H., History of New York Ship Yards. New York, 1909.

Mulrenan, Patrick, A Brief Historical Sketch of the Catholic Church on Long Island. New York, 1871.

Myrdal, Gunnar, An American Dilemma. New York, 1944.

Nevins, Allen, "Paul Leiscester Ford," in Dictionary of American Biography, VI, 518.

New York City Guide (Federal Writers' Project). New York, 1939.

New York Panorama (Federal Writers' Project). New York, 1938.

Ottley, Roi, New World a-Coming: Inside Black America. New York, 1943.

Pannunzio, Constantine M., The Soul of an Immigrant. New York, 1921.

Pickard, Samuel T., Life and Letters of John Greenleaf Whittier. 2 vols. Boston, 1894.

Piper, Jean, articles on various groups, Brooklyn *Eagle,* 1926.

Purcell, Richard J., "Immigration to the Canal Era," in History of the State of New York, edited by Alexander C. Flick (New York, 1935), VII, 1–27.

—— "Immigration from the Canal Era to the Civil War," in *ibid.,* pp. 31–58.

Raesly, Ellis Lawrence, Portrait of New Netherland. New York, 1945.

Ralph, Julian, "The City of Brooklyn," *Harper's New Monthly Magazine,* LXXXVI (April, 1893), 651–71.

Roberts, Edward F., Ireland in America. New York, 1931.

Rygg, A. N., "The Norwegian Seaman's Church," *Nordisk Tidende,* Brooklyn, Jan. 15, 22, 29, Feb. 5, 1948.

Saveth, Edward N., "New York City," in The Universal Jewish Encyclopedia, VIII, 175–95.

Spero, Sterling D., and Abram L. Harris, The Black Worker; the Negro and the Labor Movement. New York, 1931.

Steinman, D. B., The Builders of the Bridge; the Story of John Roebling and His Son. New York, 1945.

Steiner, Edward, On the Trail of the Immigrant. New York, 1906.

Stephenson, G. M., The Religious Aspects of Swedish Immigration. Minneapolis, 1932.

Stewart, Maxwell S., The Negro in America. New York, 1944. Public Affairs pamphlet No. 95. A summary of Myrdal's *An American Dilemma.*

Stuart, Sally, "Folklore in Brooklyn," Brooklyn *Eagle Magazine,* Dec. 14, 1930.

Weaver, Robert C., Negro Labor. New York, 1946.

Welch, Maude Stewart, Vrouw Knickerbocker. Philadelphia, 1926.

Weld, Ralph Foster, A Tower on the Heights. New York, 1946.

Wertenbaker, Thomas Jefferson, The Founding of American Civilization, The Middle Colonies. New York, 1938.

Wilson, Rufus Rockwell, Historic Long Island. New York, 1902.

Zink, Harold, City Bosses in the United States. Durham, N.C., 1930.

Index

Abbey, Edwin A., 84
Abend Zeitung, New York, 90
Abraham, Abraham, 106 f., 176, 182, 242
Abruzzo, Matthew T., 146
Academy of Music, 14, 74, 82, 96, 147, 207, 246
Adams, Charles Francis, 82
Adams, John, 34
African Grove, 159
African Hall, 161
African Methodist Episcopal Church, 159
African Society for Mutual Relief, New York, 159, 166
African Tompkins Society, 162
African Woolman Benevolent Society, 159
Afro-American Building and Loan Company, 165
Age, New York, 165
Ahepa, 224
Alexander III, 218 f.
Ambro, Jerome G., 145
American Antislavery Society, 44, 68, 161
American Colonization Society, Brooklyn branch of, 40, 43
American-Italian dialect, 244
Americanization classes, 245
American Legion, Frank J. Dombrowski Post of, 212
American Orthodox Church, 225
American-Syrian Federation, 226
Amersfoort, 22, 25
Amsterdam News, 172
Antislavery movement, 43-47; at Plymouth Church, 67-69
Antoon the Negro, 154
Anuskiewicz, Benjamin T., 214

Anuskiewicz, William, 214
Apprentices' Library, 53, 59
Arion Society, 98
Arnesen, Sigurd J., 197
Art Association, 82
Asbjörnsen, Sigvald, 197
Asch, Sholom, 184
"Ascot Heath," 26
Asperheim, Ole Bugge, 195
Astor, John Jacob, 40, 58
Astronomical Society, 71
Athenaeum, 71, 74 f.
Atlantic Basin, 13, 64, 76, 78, 194
Atlas Savings and Loan Association, 213
Avitable, Salvatore, 147

Bachrach, Herman S., 183
Baird, William, 58
Baker, Bertram L., 171
Balchen, Bernt, 196
Balthy, Anna, 200
Balzarini, Joe, 144
Banca Sessa, 143
Barbarin, Aimé, 229
Barbour, Najib, 226
Bath Beach, 8; Jews in, 112, 114
Bay Ridge, 8; Scandinavians in, 12, 190; Norwegians in, 196 ff.; Finns in, 205; Poles in, 210
Beauvois, Carel de, 23-24
Bedford, 8, 11, 27
Beecher, Henry Ward, 9, 40, 64, 66 ff., 75, 186
Beecher, Lyman, 40
"Beecher's Bibles," 69
Beekman, Walter N., 166-67
Bell, Alexander Graham, 164
Bennett, Charles, 144
Benson family, 35

Bensonhurst, 8, 10; Syrian Jews in, 225
Berault, Mr., 229
Bergen family, 27
Beth-El Hospital, 179
Beth Elohim, Temple, 188
Bethelship, 194 f.
Bethelship Congregation, Norwegian, 195
Bethlehem Church, 201
Beth Moses Hospital, 179
Blum, Edward C., 182-83
Burgoyne, John, 26
Bialik, Chaim Nachman, 184
Bildersee, Adele, 183
Björnson, Björnstjerne, 197
Black, Robert, 33
Blaine, James G., 81
Blum, Edward C., 242
Blumenau, Levi, 102
Borah, William E., 184
Borough Park, 8, 10, 179; Jews in, 112, 114
Bossert, Louis, 91
Bostwick, Mrs. Emma Gillingham, 74
Boswyck, 18, 25, 154
Bourne, George, 57
Bout, Jan Evertszen, 18
Bremer, Frederika, 200
Breukelen, 15, 18, 21 ff.; Negro slaves of, 155
Brooklyn: general description of, 4-14; evolution of name, 25
Brooklyn, Borough of, 118-21; its industries, 131-32
Brooklyn, City of: its commercial enterprise and industries, 62 ff., 76 f., 81; general description of, in 1855, 65-67; cultural activities, 64, 71-75; industries in 1870, 76; in 1890 and after, 77
Brooklyn, village of, 35 ff.; its growth, 36; Yankee and Dutch elements, 36-37, 38-40; industries, 37 f.
Brooklyn *Advocate*, 60
Brooklyn Antislavery Society, 160
Brooklyn Benevolent Society, 59

Brooklyn Bridge, 3-4, 77, 92-94, 123
Brooklyn Chamber of Commerce, 181
Brooklyn College, 172, 181
Brooklyn College of Pharmacy, 164
Brooklyn *Eagle*, 60
Brooklyn Federation of Jewish Charities, 180
Brooklyn Ferry, 26, 32, 157; its industries, 33 ff.
Brooklyn Heights, 8-9, 13, 34-35, 37, 62, 66 f., 71, 76, 79-80; characterized by Charles Cuthbert Hall, 79
Brooklyn Institute of Arts and Sciences, 71, 72, 75, 183
Brooklyn Jewish Center, 183-86
Brooklyn Lyceum, 42-43
Brooklyn Museum, 10
Brooklyn Museum (theater), 75
Brooklyn Polytechnic Institute, 75
Brooklyn Public Library, 10, 82
Brooklyn Speedway, 131
Brooklyn Temperance Society, 39 ff.
Brooklyn Young Men's Temperance Society, 41
Brown, John, 69
Brownlee, W. C., 57
Brownsville, 8, 10, 179, 182; Jews in, 110-11, 112, 114; Russians in, 216
Bryan, William Jennings, 184
Buchanan, James, 122 f.
Buckley, William L., 165
Buckley family, 58
Bull, Ole, 74
Burke, Charles, 75
Burnham, George, 63
Bush Terminal district, 8, 12
Bushwick, 5, 8, 65; evolution of name, 25; Germans in, 99
Butler, Andrew Pickens, 67
Byrd, Richard Evelyn, 196
Byrne, John, 132

Cadman, S. Parkes, 185
Cahan, Abraham, 176

Callaghan family, 58
Camardella, James, 144
Camardella, Louis, 144
Canarsie, 8
Capobianco, Eliodoro, 147
Caprio, Arsenio, 147
Carey, James F., 130
Cass, Lewis, 122
Cederstrom, Sig, 203
Celler, Emanuel, 183
Chanfrau, Francis, 75
Chazotte, Peter, 229
Chekhov, Anton Pavlovich, 216, 247
Chester, Mrs., Coffee House, 229
Chevalier, Mr., 229
Chinese, 222
Chopin, Frederic, 208, 247
Clark, Isadora, 74
Cleveland, Grover, 81, 124 f.
Clinton, De Witt, 54
Clipper ships, 62
Cohen, Abraham, 102
Cohen, Coleman, 104
Cohen, Jacob, 111
Cohen, Louis, 183
Coleman, Elihu, 156
Collins, James, 58
Columbian, New York, 36
Columbia University, 81-82
Columbus Political Club, 145
Coney Island, 8; Italians in, 144
Connolly, John, 52
Constable, William, 35
Corrao, Francis L., 145
Cortelyon, Jacques, 16, 235
Cortelyon family, 27
Cosenza, Mario E., 147
Couwenhoven family, 27
Coward, Noel, 6
Cox, Samuel Hanson, 9, 71
Cripplebush, 27
Cullen, Edgar M., 128-30, 240
Cullen, Henry J., 129
Curtis, George William, 67
Cuthbert, Marian, 172
Cuyler Presbyterian Church, 228
Czas, 212
Czechs, 223

Dagher, George, 226
Dagmar, 204
D'Agrosa, Vincent, 145-46
Daily News, Brooklyn, 74
Danckaerts, Jasper, 15, 21, 235
Danes, 12, 203-204
Dania, Inc., 204
Dannevirke, 204
Darrow, Clarence, 184
Daurio, John, 144
Dean, Joseph, 54
De Bevoice family, 35
Dekke, Annanias, 191
DeValera, Eamon, 133, 187
Dewey, Thomas, 167
Dickens, Charles, 200, 238
Dodgers, 6, 14, 172
Dorsey, Charles A., 165
Douglas, Stephen A., 70, 122
Drake, Joseph Rodman, 36, 238
Druses, 225
Duflon, J. F. L., 55, 229
Durant, Will, 185
Dwight, Jr., Theodore, 38
Dwight, Timothy, 52
Dwight's American Magazine, 38
Dutch, 4 f., 11, 15-29, 36, 233-37; in colonial period, 15-25; farm house, 19-21; churches, 21-24; during American Revolution, 25-26; after Revolution, 26-29; community leaders, 27-28, 39-40
Dutchtown, 90

Eames, Theodore, 38, 42
Eames and Putnam's Classical Hall, 42, 135
Eastern Parkway, as Jewish neighborhood, 10, 112, 183
East Flatbush, 8, 11
East New York, 8; Italians in, 138, 143; Poles in, 210
Ebbets, Charles, 131
Ebbets Field, 14, 131
Ebony, 172
Edison, Thomas A., 164
Eggleston, Edward, 84
Einstein, Albert, 185
Eisenlohn, Professor, 107

Equal protection amendment, New York State Constitution, 182
Elzy, Robert, 170
Emancipator, 45
Emerson, Ralph Waldo, 72
Emmet, Robert, 49 f.
Emmet, Thomas Addis, 50 f.
Enigheden, 204
Ericsson, John, 199
Ericsson, Leif, 190
Erie Basin, 13, 76, 78, 194
Erin Fraternal Society, 53, 54 f.
Evening Post, New York, 36

Falcons, Polish, 207, 211
Faour, George J., 226
Farnan, John, 40
Farragut, David G., 130
Federation of Jewish Philanthropies, 180-81, 182 f., 186
Female Academy, 71 f.; Thackeray at, 72
Fibich, Michael, 214
Fight for Freedom Committee, 151
Figuccio, Albert, 145
Filipinos, 226-27
Finney, Charles G., 44
Finns, 12, 204-206; migration of, to U.S., 204-205; to Brooklyn, 205; their co-operatives, 205; social institutions of, 205-206; in arts and journalism, 206
First Presbyterian Church, 9, 71
First (Sands Street) Methodist Church, 159
Fischer, Israel, 106
Flatbush, 5, 8, 11, 13, 25-26, 28-29; evolution of name, 25; Jews in, 112
Flatlands, 8, 11, 25 f.; evolution of name, 25
Ford, Gordon Lester, 63-64, 82 ff.
Ford, Henry, 164
Ford, Malcolm, 84
Ford, Paul Leicester, 83-84
Ford, Worthington, 83 f.
Fort Greene district, 8
Francisco the Negro, 154

Freedom's Journal, 160
Freie Presse, Brooklyn, 91
Fremad, 204
French, 228-29; in Brooklyn village, 228
Fulton, Robert, 35, 78, 120
Furman, Gabriel, 42
Furst, Solomon, 103
Furuseth, Andrew, 196

Gaine, Hugh, 26
Gallo, Ernesto, 145
Garfield, James A., 81
Garrison, John, 158
Garrison, William Lloyd, 44, 160
Gaynor, William J., 122, 127-28, 240
Geiger, Erik Gustaf, 206
Germania Savings Bank, 95
Germans, 86-99, 239-40; migration to America, 86-87; to Brooklyn, 87, 97; social institutions, 87, 98; occupations of, 88; in journalism, 90-91; in business, professions, and arts, 91-94; in politics, 95-96
Gervais, Miss, 229
Giacone, Francis X., 146
Gibson, William Hamilton, 84
Giddings, Joshua R., 67, 80
Giffuni, Vincent, 144
Ginsberg, Moses, 183
Gold Coast, 8, 9-10
Gothic Hall, 74
Gough, John B., 73, 99
Gowanus, 11-12, 15 ff., 27; Puerto Ricans in, 230
Graham, Augustus, 37-38, 43
Graham, John B., 37-38
Grand Army Plaza, 10
Grant, Ulysses S., 82, 129
Gravesend, 4, 11; Italians in, 138
Gray family, John, 63
Greeks, 223-24; cultural organizations of, 224
Greeley, Horace, 72-73
Greenpoint, 5, 8, 77, 199; shipyards at, 65; Jews in, 114; Italians in, 138 f., 144; Poles in, 210;

Russians in, 215 f., Lithuanians in, 218; Puerto Ricans in, 230
Greenwood, John, 38
Grvinge, Waldemar, 196
Guigon, Mr., 229
Gullmes, Otto, 206
Gustavus Adolphus, 199

Hadassah, 187
Hadran, N. G., 226
Haerem, Rasmus O., 191
Hakim, Josef H., 224
Hall, Charles Cuthbert, 183
Hall, George, 41, 65 f., 77
Halleck, Fitz-Greene, 36
Hamilton Club, 82
Hamilton Literary Association, 82
Hanson, Peter B., 203
Hanukkah, 113
Harlem, 167, 169
Harrison, Benjamin, 106
Harrison, Gabriel, 75
Hart, Moss, 185
Hart, Simon de, 16
Havemeyer and Elder, 96
Hebrew Educational Society, 182
Hedström, Jonas, 195
Hedström, Olof Gustav, 195
Heeney, Cornelius, 40, 52, 58-59, 240
Heffernan, John A., 132
Hegeman, Adrian, 23
Heilprin, Michael, 102
Henry, A. J., 172
Henry, Mrs. A. J., 172
Herr, Frederick, 91
Hess, Morris, 104
Hitler, Adolf, 185 f.
Hogan, Timothy, 130
Hogarth, George, 160
Holbrook, Josiah, 41
Holy Trinity Russian Orthodox Church, 216
Honda, 65
Hooper, Lucy, 45-46
Horne, Edward, 165
Horne, Lena, 165, 172

Houqua, 62, 80
Hoving, Johannes, 202
"Hutchinson Family," 73 f.
Hylan, John F., 122, 126

Ibsen, Henrik, 197
Immanuel Methodist Church, Swedish, 195
Indians, American, 12, 227-28; occupations of, 228
Ingersoll, Raymond V., 185
International Ladies' Garment Workers' Union, 170
International Seamen's Union of America, 196
Intime Group, 197
Irish, 48-61, 115-34, 239-40; migration to America, 49-56; typical immigrant in Brooklyn, 50-53; churches, 51-52, 121 f.; social institutions, 53, 55; in business, 58 f., 130-31; in politics, 58 ff., 122-28, 133-34; in professions, 60, 116, 128-30, 133; in journalism, 54, 60, 125, 132-33; complexity of, 115; political bosses, 124 ff.; political reformers, 127-28
Irishtown, 117-18
Isaacson, Elias, 103
Isabella, Louis, 145
Israel Zion Hospital, 179
Italian-American Republican Clubs, Kings County League of, 146
Italian Benevolent Society, 147
Italian Country Club, 146, 148
Italian fraternal lodges, 148
Italians, 11, 135-52, 240; migration of, to U.S., 136-37; to Brooklyn, 137-38; Little Italy described, 138-43; religious festivals, 141-42; in business, 143-45; in politics, 145-46; in science, arts, education, and religion, 147; social organizations, 148; attitudes of, toward Mussolini and Fascism, 149-51; in U.S. war effort, 151
Italian Teachers' Association, 147

Italian Welfare League, Brooklyn
branch of, 148
Italo-American Political Union, 145

Jackson, Andrew, 33, 56
Jackson, Samuel, 33
Januszewski, Frank, 212
Jefferson, Thomas, 34, 156
Jewish Center, Brooklyn, 183-86
Jewish Center Library, 186
Jewish Community Council, 188
Jewish Hospital of Brooklyn, 179 f.,
181 ff.
Jews, 10, 100-114, 174-89, 240,
241-42; migration of, to U.S. in
colonial period, 100 f.; early migration to Brooklyn, 101 f.; first
congregations, 103; migration
from western Europe, 104; from
eastern Europe, 105, 108 f., 188;
in politics, 105; in retail trade,
106 f., 177; movement of Jewish
population within Brooklyn,
109 ff.; in garment trades, 111-
12; festivals and fasts, 112-13;
respect for learning, 175; ideals,
176; in business, 176-81; charities
of, 179 ff.; in politics, 181 ff.;
cultural activities of, 183; in professions, 183; social and religious
institutions, 183-86, 187 f.
Johnson, Barent, 27
Johnson, Emil F., 203
Johnson, Evan, 57
Johnson, Jeremiah, 27-28, 39
John Wesley, see Bethelship
Jonas, Jacob, 177
Jonas, Nathan, 176, 177-81
Jonas, Ralph, 176, 181
Jonas brothers, 242
Jones, Mrs. Laura A., 74
Jones, Verina Morton, 165-66
Joralemon, Tunis, 40
Jurek, Frank A., 212

Kaleva Club, 205
Kallman Orphanage, 202
Katibah, H. I., 226
Kearney family, 58

Kelly, Frank V., 178
Kensington, 11
Kerensky, Alexander, 184
Kieft, William, 17
Kiernan, John J., 130
Kimberley, Gideon, 33
King, Benjamin, tavern, 229
Kings County Medical Society, 147
Kings County Pharmaceutical So-
ciety, 164
Kings County Polish Democratic
Club, 212
Kingman, Dong, 222
Kingsley, William C., 124
Kinsella, Thomas, 125, 132
Kirk, Thomas, 54, 59
Kosciuszko, Thaddeus, 208, 214
Kosicke, Judge, 213
Kossuth, Louis, 102
Kowalski, Vincent J., 213
Krzyzanowski, Wladimir, 208, 215
Kucinski, Henry, 214

Labadie, Jean de, 15
Labadist travelers, 12, 15 ff., 21
LaFayette, Marquis de, 53
LaFollette, Robert M., 196
LaGuardia, Fiorello, 134
Laisve, 218, 221
Lark, Sumner, 165
Latimer, Lewis H., 164 f.
Laura, Michael T., 145
Lawrence, Jacob, 153, 172
Lazansky, Edward, 181
Lazarus, Emma, 108 f.
Leavitt, David, 37, 44, 160
Lefevre, 8, 66
Levinthal, Israel H., 184 f.
Levy, Asser, 101, 234
Levy, Benjamin, 101
Lewis, Harry E., 181-82
Liberator, 44 f., 160
Liepmann, Heinz, 185 f.
Lincoln, Abraham, 45, 70-71, 104,
123
Lind, Jenny, 200
Lindgren, Gustaf, 200
Liota, Gasper, 145

Lithuanian-American Citizens Club, 220
Lithuanian Athletic Club, 220
Lithuanians, 218-21; migration of, 218; in journalism, 218-19, 221; social organizations, 219-20; cultural activities, 220
Lithuanian Workers' Literary Society of America, 220
Little Italy, 137-43, 150 f.
Little Poland, 210
Lof, Eric A., 203
Long Island Anzeiger, 90 f.
Long Island Courier, 28, 54
Long Island Historical Society, 75, 82
Long Island Star, 30 ff., 35 f., 38, 46, 54, 74, 135
Loosely's Tavern, 26
Loughlin, John, 121
Lovell and King, 75
Low, Abiel Abbott, 62-63, 64, 82
Low, Seth, father of Abiel A. Low, 62
Low, Seth, son of Abiel A. Low, 80-82, 99, 178
Lundberg, Oscar, 200
Lutheran churches, Augustana Synod, 201
Lyceum movement, 41-42

McBride family, 58
McCaine, Alexander, 159-60
McCarren, Patrick, 124 ff.
McClellan, George B., 178
McCloskey, Elizabeth, 59
McCloskey, George, 54
McCloskey, Hugh, 125, 132
McCloskey, John, 59
McCloskey, Patrick, 59
McCooey, John H., 126, 178
McCue, Alexander, 124, 129
McDonnell, Charles Edward, 122, 209
McFarlan family, 58
MacGuire family, 58
McKane, John Y., 128
McKee, Joseph V., 134
McKeever, Edward, 131

McKeever, Stephen, 130-31
McLaughlin, Hugh, 122, 124 f., 127
MacMonnies, Frederick, 84
Malinkowski, Anthony, 214
Malone, Sylvester, 121-22
Maniusko Singing Society, 247
Mapleton Park, Syrian Jews in, 225
Marchisio, Juvenal, 146
Marcy, William M., 122
Margoshes, Samuel, 185
Marino, A. W. Martin, 147
Markham, Edwin, 185
Massasoit, 164
Maurillo, Dominick F., 147
May, Mitchell, 181
Mayo, Anthony F., 145
Mazzini Society, 151
Megapolensis, Johannes, 100
Mercein, Andrew, 40
Meyer, Julius, 92
Midwood, 11; Jews in, 112
Midwout, 18, 23, 25, 155
Miller, Herbert, 172
Mitchel, John Purroy, 126
Mitchel, Ormsby McKnight, 71
Molloy, Thomas E., 122
Monitor, 199-200
Moody, Lady Deborah, 4, 34
Moore, Fred R., 165
Moran, William J., 130
Moscowitz, Grover M., 183
Moses families, 101
Moslems, 225
Mumford, Lewis, 3
Murphy, Henry Cruse, 53, 59-60, 122 ff., 240
Murphy, John Garrison, 40, 78
Murphy, Mark, 132
Murphy, Timothy, 59
Music, 73-74
Mussolini, Benito, 149 ff.

Nassau, 35
Nast, Thomas, 84
Nathan, Ernst, 105 f.
National Association for the Advancement of Colored People, **171**

National Homes, Polish, 210 ff.
National Urban League, 170
Nativism, 55-58
Navy Yard, 13, 33, 76 f.
Navy Yard district, 8, 11; Italians in, 138 f., 144
Nazi-Banned Books, Library of, 186
Negroes, 11, 153-73, 240, 243; in colonial period, 4, 153, 154-56; as slaves, 26, 154-57; migration of, during First World War and after, from South, 153, 167-69; mature society of, in Brooklyn, 1880–1914, 153-54, 163-66; in Brooklyn village, 158 ff.; as abolitionists, 160 ff.; in the arts, 153, 165, 172; in industry, science, professions, journalism, public service, 164-66, 170, 172; in politics, 165, 170-71; in sports, 172-73
Negro Society for Historical Research, 166
New Lots, 8; Jews in, 112, 114
Newman, Leopold, 104
New Utrecht, 5, 18 f., 25-26, 155
New Yorkin Uutiset, 206
Nicholas II, 219
Nilsson, Christine, 200
Norden, 206
Nordisk Tidende, 197
Nordstjernan, 203
Northall, Julia, 74
Northall, William Knight, 55, 74
Norwegians, 12, 190-99; migration of, to U.S., 190-95; in maritime activities, 191-96; in industries and arts, 196; in journalism, 197
Norwegian Seamen's Home, 198
Norwegian Turn Society, 197
Nosek, Edward, 214
Nova, Algernon, 183
Novoye Russkoye Slovo, 215
Nowy Swiat, 212

O'Brien, Francis, 58
O'Connell, Daniel, 52, 55, 187
O'Donnell, Jeremiah, 58

O'Dwyer, William, 116, 122, 133-34, 240
O'Hara family, 58
Opportunity, 170
Oriental, 62
Our Lady of Lebanon, Church of, 9, 225
Our Lady of Loreto, Church of, 147
Our Lady of Czenstochowa, Church of, 209 f.
Owen, Robert, 162
Ozone Park, Poles in, 210

Paderewski, Ignace Jan, 207
Paino, Angelo, 144
Parker, Alton B., 129
Park Slope, 8
Passover, 113
Patchen, Jacob, 38 f.
Pellegrino, Carmelo, 144
Pennell, Joseph, 84
Pennington, James, 160
Pershing, John Joseph, 214
Petach Tikvah, Temple, 184
Peterson, Jerome B., 165
Phillips, Wendell, 67 ff., 80, 186
Pierce, Franklin, 122 f.
Pierrepont, Hezekiah, 35, 59
Pilgrims, Church of the, 9, 68, 225
Plattsdeutsch House, 98
Plymouth Church, 9, 66-70, 183, 225; as antislavery forum, 67-69; Lincoln at, 70; Thackeray at, 72; Hutchinson family at, 73
Poles, 207-15; in First World War, 207; in American history, 208; migration of, to U.S., 209; settlement of, in Brooklyn, 209, 210; churches and social organizations of, 209, 210-12; in business, 212 f.; in journalism, 212; in politics, 212 f., 215; in professions, 213; in Second World War, 214
Polhemus, Jacob, 22 f.
Polish-American Co-operative Savings and Loan Association, 213
Polish Business Men's Association of Greenpoint, 212

Polish Day Nursery, 212
Polish Legion of American Veterans, 212
Polish National Alliance, 212
Poole, Ernest, 84
Power, John, 51
Psaki, Nicholas, 223
Puchalski, Boleslaus, 209
Puerto Ricans, 11, 230-32, 243; migration of, 230; occupations of, 230-31; social activities of, 231
Pulaski, Casimir, 208, 214
Purim, 113

Radcliff, Peter W., 38, 42, 60
Ralph, Julian, 96, 106
Rapalje family, 33
Rapalje farm, 33-34
Ravaglia, Signor, 135
Ray, Peter W., 164 f.
Reddick, Lawrence Dunbar, 172
Red Hook, 8, 76; Italians in, 139, 143 f., 147; Puerto Ricans in, 230; *see also* Little Italy
Reformed Dutch Church: in Breukelen, 21-24; in Flatbush, 21; in the city of Brooklyn, 27
Reid, Donald, 172
Remsen family, 27, 35
Restaurationen, 190 f.
Richards, Daniel, 64
Ridgewood, 8; Germans in, 99; Italians in, 138
Riis, Edward Valdemar, 204
Riis, Jacob A., 203 f.
Rivington, James, 26
Robinson, James R. (Jackie), 172
Roebling, John Augustus, 92-94
Roebling, Washington, 93 f.
Roeblings, The, 3
Roehr, Edward Franz, 89 ff.
Roehr, Henry, 89-91
Rolvaag, Ole Edvart, 247
Roosevelt, Eleanor, 184
Roosevelt, Theodore, 96, 129, 203
Rosh Hoshanah, 112
Rothschild, Simon F., 107
Rottenberg, Samuel, 183
Rueger, Julius, 91-92

Rumanians, 223
Russian People's Home, 216-17, 247
Russians, 215-18; migration of, to U.S., 215-16; to Brooklyn, 216; in industry, 216; churches and social organizations of, 216-17
Russwurm, John B., 160, 162
Ryerson family, 27
Rynning, Ole, 193

Sabbatino, Salvatore, 144
Sabbatino, Sylvester, 145
Sack, Eugene, 188
Saengerbund, 98
Sailors' Temperance Home, Scandinavian, 195
St. Casimir's Roman Catholic Church, 209 f.
Saint Charles, 100
St. Constantine's Greek Orthodox Church, 224
St. George's Church (Lithuanian), 220
St. James Roman Catholic Church, 40, 51 f., 55
St. Paul's Lutheran Church, 203
St. Paul's Roman Catholic Church, 227
Saints Peter and Paul, Church of, 121 f.
St. Stanislaus Kostka Church, 209 f.
Salem Church, 201
Samuelson, Arvid, 200
Sands, Comfort, 33-34
Sands, Joshua, 33-34, 74
Sansay, L., 229
Scandinavians, 12, 190-204, 240, 242; *see also* Danes; Norwegians; Swedes
Scavullo, Frank, 144
Schellenberg, Bernhard, 102
Schenck family, 27
Schieran, Charles Adolph, 95 f., 164
Schlichta, Joseph, 212
Schomburg, Arthur Alfonso, 166
Schomburg Collection, 166, 172
Schoonmaker, Martinus, 24

Schroeder, Frederick A., 95-96
Schroeder charter, 95-96
Schwaben Hall, 98
Scots, 229-30
Scott, Winfield, 123
Scottron, Samuel R., 164 f.
Seamen's Act of 1915, 196
Seamen's Church, Norwegian, 195
Second Presbyterian Church, 68
Seitz, Nicholas, 92
Selijns, Henricus, 22-23
Selijns, Machtelt (Specht), 22-23
Selvaggi, Nicholas, 146
Serri, Frank, 151
Sessa, Antonio, 143
Sessa, Joseph, 143
Seward, William H., 70
Sewell, Samuel, 156
Seymour, Horatio, 124
Shabuoth, 113
Sheepshead Bay district, 8
Sibelius, Jean J. C., 247
Siegmeister, Elie, 248
Sikorsky, Igor, 215
Sille, Nicasius de, 19
Silver, Abba Hillel, 184
Singstad, Ole, 196
Slavs, 240, 242
Sluyter, Peter, 15, 21, 235
Smith, Cyrus P., 74
Smith, Samuel, 68
Smolenski, John, 212
Snow, Robert, 51, 54, 59
Soini, William, 206
Sokol (Czech), 223
Sokols, Polish, 211
South Brooklyn, 13, 64; Poles in, 210, 212
Sowden, James, 30
Spongberg, Viola, 200 f., 247
Spooner, Alden, 30-33, 38 f., 41, 44, 46, 52, 54, 56, 162
Spooner, Judah P., 31
Spooner, Rebecca, 31
Sprague, Joseph, 42
Ssu-tu, Amy, 222
Ssu-tu Chiao, 222
Starling, Marian, 172
Steinbach, Alexander Alan, 188

Steinbrink, Meier, 183
Stella, 204
Stephen, Mansour, 225
Stiles, Henry R., 24
Storrs, Richard S., 9, 68
Stowe, Harriet Beecher, 69
Straus, Isidor, 107
Straus, Nathan, 107
Strindberg, Johan August, 197
Stuyvesant, Peter, 23, 100 f., 154
Stuyvesant Heights, 8, 11; Puerto Ricans in, 230
Stuyvesant Heights-Bedford district, 153, 169
Succoth, 113
Suffolk Gazette, 30
Sulzer, William, 129
Sumner, Charles, 67, 80
Sunset Park district, 8, 12; Finns in, 205
Suydam family, 27
Swedes, 12, 190, 192, 194 f., 199-203; in colonial period, 190; migration of, to U.S., 192, 195, 199; in arts, 200 f.; social and cultural institutions of, 201 ff.; in professions, business, politics, 203
Swedish Cultural Society, Brooklyn branch of, 202
Swedish Engineers' Club, 203
Swedish Finlanders, 206
Swedish Glee Club, 200, 246
Swedish Hospital, 202
Swift, Joseph G., 157, 238
Syphax, John, 165
Syrian Eagle, 226
Syrian Presbyterian Church, 225
Syrians, 13, 224-26; migration of, 224; occupations of, 224; religious organizations of, 225; social institutions, 226; in politics, journalism, professions, arts, 226
Syrjaniemi, Onni, 206

Talley, Marion, 147
Tappan, Arthur, 44, 160
Tappan, Lewis, 44
Taylor, S. P., 74
Temperance movement, 39, 40-41

Thackeray, William Makepeace, 72
Thompson, Henry C., 160
Thompson, Jonathan, 33
Thorne, J. Sullivan, 55
Thursby, Emma, 92
Tiebout family, 27
Tilden, Samuel J., 124
Transfiguration, Church of the (Russian Orthodox), 216
Treadwell, Adam, 33
Trollope, Anthony, 200
Trollope, Mrs. Frances, 200
Tucker, Fanning C., 74
Turecamo, Bartholomew, 144
Turner, Peter, 40, 51, 55
Tweed Ring, 84, 95

Ufeish, Bishop, 225
Ughetta, Henry, 146
Ukrainians, 222-23
Uncle Tom's Cabin, 69
Union, Brooklyn, 82
United Italian Societies of Brooklyn, 148
United Polish Society of Brooklyn, 211
Upjohn, Richard, 8, 66
Upsala College, 203

Van Anden, Isaac, 60, 125
Van Brunt family, 27
Van Doren, Isaac, 40
Van Doren, Jacob, 40
Van Driest, Jan Barentsen, 27
Van Sinderen, Adrian, 39, 43, 45
Van Twiller, Wouter, 17
Vasa, 202
Vermont Gazette, or Green Mountain Post-Boy, 31
Villa, Pancho, 214
Virgin Mary Church, 225
Vita, Daniel de, 145
Volk, Lester, 183
Vort Land No. 200, 204

Waal-boght, 25
Walker, James, 166

Wallabout, 27; evolution of name, 25
Ward, Theodore, 172
Waring, Henry, 33
Washington, George, 26
Watkins, Thomas, 172
Watterson, Henry, 130
Webb, Eckford, 65
Webster, Daniel, 67
Webster, D. Macon, 165
Wechsler, Joseph, 106 f.
Weidmann, Paul, 91
Wertenbaker, T. J., 20
Westlin, Tobias, 200
Whipple, Edwin P., 72
Whitman, Walt, 48, 57, 61, 66, 73 f., 79
Whittier, John Greenleaf, 44 ff., 67
Wibecan, George E., 170-71
Williamsburg, 5, 8, 10, 65, 162; Germans in, 87 ff.; Jews in, 102 ff., 109-10, 111 f., 114, 117; Italians in, 138, 144; Poles in, 210; Russians in, 215; Lithuanians in, 218; Puerto Ricans in, 230
Wilson, Clarence, 171
Wilson, Perry, 165
Wilson, Woodrow, 207
Wiren, Alexis, 217
Wischmann, Hermann, 92
Wise, George S., 51
Wise, Stephen S., 185
Woods, George, 160
Woodworth, Samuel, 32
Woolman, John, 156
Worn, Martin, 92
Wright, Elizur, 44, 160

Yankees, 30-47, 62-85, 237-39; in journalism, 30-33, 36, 38-39, 82; in trade, 33-35, 62-64, 80-81; in politics, 35 f., 38, 81; and Brooklyn industries, 37-38, 64-65; in professions, 38; in education and cultural enterprises, 41-43, 63-64, 71-75, 79-80, 81-85; in antislavery movement, 43-47, 67-70; in the arts, 83-84

Yoelles, Peter P., 212 f.
Yom Kippur, 112
Young, Wesley, 165
Young Ladies' Collegiate Institute, 40
Young Men's Christian Association, 75, 195; Carlton Branch of, 171 f.

Young Men's Hebrew Association, 179
Young Women's Christian Association, Ashland Place Branch of, 171

Zionism, 187